W9-BSP-162

For Reference

Not to be taken from this room

CHILDHOOD
SEXUAL ABUSE

A Reference Handbook

CHILDHOOD
SEXUAL ABUSE

A Reference Handbook

Karen L. Kinnear

**CONTEMPORARY
WORLD ISSUES**

ABC-CLIO

Santa Barbara, California
Denver, Colorado
Oxford, England

Library of Congress Cataloging-in-Publication Data

Kinnear, Karen L.
    Childhood sexual abuse : a reference handbook / Karen L. Kinnear.
       p. cm.—(Contemporary world issues)
    Includes bibliographical references and index.
      1. Child sexual abuse. 2. Child sexual abuse—Prevention.
    3. Sexually abused children. I. Title. II. Series.
    HV6570.K55   1995
    362.7'6—dc20   95-40065

ISBN 0-87436-691-7

02 01 00 99 98 97 96 95 10 9 8 7 6 5 4 3 2 1

ABC-CLIO, Inc.
130 Cremona Drive, P.O. Box 1911
Santa Barbara, California 93116-1911

This book is printed on acid-free paper ∞ .

Manufactured in the United States of America

To Mom—
who always wanted to write a book about man's
inhumanity to man, but never had the chance.
This one's for you.

1997

Contents

Preface

The purpose of this book is to provide a survey of the available literature and other resources on the topic of childhood sexual abuse and to direct readers to sources for further research. The literature and resources available provide insight into the causes, treatment, and prevention of childhood sexual abuse. Tremendous growth in knowledge and research has occurred in this field in recent years, and this book provides a resource for students, writers, and researchers as well as professionals in the field.

Thoughts and attitudes toward childhood sexual abuse have changed over the years. Earlier, many people believed that if children were sexually abused, they had brought the abuse on themselves by somehow seducing the adult and that they were not harmed by this contact. Over time, the attitude that children were responsible for any sexual abuse they experienced changed to the realization that the adults involved were responsible, not the children. The extent and seriousness of the effects of sexual abuse have also been recognized and studied, from earlier attitudes that little damage was done to a child who was fondled or otherwise abused to the current understanding that the effects of this abuse can be manifested in many ways and can indeed be serious. This book reviews current knowledge and resources in order to help the reader understand the issues involved in this important and timely topic.

This book, like other books in the Contemporary World Issues series, provides a balanced survey of the resources available and a guide to further research on the topic of childhood sexual abuse. Chapter 1 reviews the literature concerning types of sexual abuse, causes, perpetrators, prevention, false memories, cults and satanic abuse, and other relevant areas. Chapter 2 provides a chronology of the significant events relevant to issues surrounding childhood sexual abuse. Chapter 3 offers biographical sketches of individuals who have played or are currently playing key roles in the area of childhood sexual abuse. Chapter 4 provides statistical information on the prevalence and incidence of child sexual abuse, as well as excerpts from federal laws and U.S. Supreme Court decisions in this area. Chapter 5 provides a directory of private and public organizations, associations, and government agencies involved in treating children who have been sexually abused as well as those that treat offenders. In Chapter 6, books, handbooks, manuals, and periodicals are annotated; the literature varies from popular accounts to primary research and provides a wide perspective on this problem. Chapter 7 includes an annotated list of nonprint resources, including films and videocassettes.

Introduction 1

In 1980 Florence Rush, in the preface to her book about childhood sexual abuse, *The Best-Kept Secret*, said that "[i]t is time we face the fact that the sexual abuse of children is not an occasional deviant act, but a devastating commonplace fact of everyday life" (Rush 1980, xii). She does believe, however, that we can overcome and solve this problem:

> Unlike the lower species, we have the ability to change, to look about, perceive what is going on and to question and challenge. Once we perceive, question and challenge the existence of the sexual abuse of children, we have taken the first crucial step toward the elimination of the degradation, humiliation and corrosion of our most valuable human resource—our young. (Rush 1980, 195)

Today, the problem of childhood sexual abuse is foremost in the minds of many professionals as well as the general public. New charges are levied almost daily against parents, priests, day-care operators, or others to whom we entrust our children. In order to understand the scope of the problem of childhood sexual abuse and the many issues involved in this area, this chapter reviews the research in this field and discusses topics of primary interest to many people concerned about childhood sexual abuse.

What Is Child Sexual Abuse?

Although professionals in the field of childhood sexual abuse as well as the general public have become more interested in and concerned about the sexual abuse of children, few can agree on what constitutes child sexual abuse. Definitions vary considerably and legal definitions found in state laws vary from state to state (see Chapter 4). However, most experts agree on certain elements of the definition: exploitation of the child; use of coercion, gentle though it may be; and some level of gratification gained by the adult.

Fraser defines child sexual abuse as "the exploitation of a child for the sexual gratification of an adult" (Fraser 1981, 58). Baker and Duncan suggest that "[a] child (anyone under 16 years) is sexually abused when another person, who is sexually mature, involves the child in any activity which the other person expects to lead to their sexual arousal" (Baker & Duncan 1985, 458).

Sexual abuse is also defined situationally, that is, by the situation or circumstances in which it occurs. For example, in some families or some cultures, it is acceptable, even expected, that family members kiss on the mouth or have a lot of physical contact. In other families and cultures, this behavior clearly would be considered inappropriate. Definitions of sexual abuse often are broken down further into contact and noncontact abuse. Contact abuse can include any activity from kissing to oral sex to intercourse. Noncontact sexual abuse includes such activities as exhibitionism and sexual talk intended to arouse the adult. Sexually abusive behavior can range from an adult walking around nude in front of children to sexual intercourse. According to Jon Conte, it may include exhibitionism, voyeurism, kissing, fondling, fellatio, cunnilingus, vaginal or anal intercourse, or child pornography (Conte 1986). Suzanne Sgroi writes that abusive behavior can include nudity, the adult disrobing in front of a child, exposing his or her genitals to the child, covertly watching the child undress or bathe, kissing the child in an intimate way, fondling the child inappropriately, masturbating while a child watches, masturbating the child, masturbating each other, fellatio, cunnilingus, penetrating the anus or vagina with a finger or other object, penetrating the anus or vagina with a penis, or actual sexual intercourse (Sgroi 1988).

The definition in federal law is specified in the Child Abuse Prevention and Treatment Act (see Chapter 4, pp. 143–163). Sexual abuse is defined as

> (A) the employment, use, persuasion, inducement, enticement, or coercion of any child to engage in, or assist any other person to engage in, any sexually explicit conduct or simulation of such conduct for the purpose of producing a visual depiction of such conduct; or
>
> (B) the rape, molestation, prostitution, or other form of sexual exploitation of children, or incest with a child . . . (Child Abuse Prevention and Treatment Act, as amended, November 4, 1992)

Legal definitions can be either civil or criminal. Child protection or civil statutes consider sexual abuse a condition from which a child should be protected; these laws "include child sexual abuse as one of the forms of maltreatment that must be reported by designated professionals and investigated by child protection agencies" (Faller 1993, 9). Certain sexual acts are prohibited by criminal statutes; they specify what sexual acts are considered criminal and the penalties for breaking these laws. The penalties differ depending on the age of the child, the level of force used, the relationship between the child and the offender, and the type of sexual act.

Several factors characterize child sexual abuse, helping to determine whether or not an incident is considered sexual abuse. One factor is lack of consent. Children do not consent to sexual abuse because they usually are not able to understand fully what is being proposed to them and they are not in a position to refuse any sexual contact with appropriate power. Children are not capable of consenting to sexual activities with an adult; just because the child participates in this abuse does not mean that the child has consented. Another factor is exploitation. Children are manipulated or coerced into sexual behavior by adults who are stronger, more resourceful, and more knowledgeable. They may buy the child gifts, may persuade the child that all fathers teach their daughters about sex, may threaten the child with punishment or with the death of the other parent ("if your mother ever finds out, she'll probably die of a heart attack"), or may provide attention to the child in other ways.

Ambivalence is also a factor in child sexual abuse. Children often feel ambivalent about what is happening to them; they do not like the sexual part of the experience, but they may enjoy the attention they are receiving as well as any rewards or special privileges they may receive because of the abuse. Some children may be confused because some of the physical sensations they experience are enjoyable; these sensations make them feel good. However, they know that the behavior is wrong and although they want the abuse to stop, they do not want to stop receiving the gifts, privileges, or attention they gain by remaining silent.

Force is another factor or characteristic of child sexual abuse that is always found, even if it is not physical. Usually definitions contain an element of power, of force, that "it is forced, tricked, or coerced sexual behavior between a young person and an older person" (Conte 1986, 2). Many ways exist, both physical and psychological, to force the child into a sexual relationship; these may include threatening to withhold attention or special favors, killing an animal in front of the child and telling her that the same fate awaits her if she does not cooperate, threatening to abuse other siblings in the family, or suggesting that the family will be broken up if the child tells anyone. A related factor is secrecy; the abuser must somehow convince the child that he or she should not tell anyone else about the abuse. Ways to keep the child silent include threats, force, bribery, or intimidation.

Dr. Roland Summit has identified the "sexual abuse accommodation syndrome," a means of characterizing the responses of girls who are sexually abused by adults, often by their father or another close male relative. The syndrome has five characteristics: secrecy; helplessness; entrapment and accommodation; delayed, unconvincing disclosure; and retraction. Summit believes that children feel helpless in abusive situations because the abuser has sworn them to secrecy by threatening them with harm, telling them that no one will believe them, or in some other way coercing them into secrecy. Once the sexual abuse has occurred, the child feels trapped and either continues to maintain the secret or discloses it to the other parent or another trusted adult. If the disclosure is not believed or causes too much stress for the child to handle, then the child may retract the disclosure (Summit 1983).

Susan Forward and Craig Buck do not consider incest a sexual act:

What is "sexy" about a seven-year-old from the perspective of mature sexuality? Secondly, most aggres-
sors are getting plenty of sex. If they are not actively
having sex with their partners, which many are, they
have extensive sexual relationships with other
women. The old stereotype of the sexually deprived
man with a cold, nonsexual wife, who has no one to
turn to to meet his sexual needs but his child or children, simply does not hold up in the majority of cases.
(Forward & Buck 1978, 33)

Children can also be sexually abused in child sex rings (often
organized by pedophiles to provide a constant supply of young
children for the pedophiles' sexual arousal); child pornography,
which is illegal in every state; child prostitution; or in ritual
abuse, which may or may not be connected with satanism.

Myths about Sexual Abuse

There are many commonly held beliefs and misconceptions
about child sexual abuse (Victim Services Agency 1991; Hillman
& Solek-Tefft 1988).

Myth 1: Children often lie about being sexually abused. Many
people believe that children make up stories about someone
abusing them, arguing that children have vivid imaginations
and cannot always tell the difference between fact and fiction. However, several studies have thoroughly dispelled
this myth. For example, in 1979, H. B. Cantwell studied approximately 290 cases of alleged sexual abuse in Denver, Colorado, and discovered that only 26 (9 percent) of the cases
could not be substantiated (Cantwell 1981). Joseph Peters reviewed the cases of 64 children who were examined in an
emergency room complaining of being sexually assaulted.
He found that only in a few cases did the medical staff decide
that no sexual assault had occurred (Peters 1976).

*Myth 2: Children are usually sexually abused by dirty old men
who are strangers to them.* The majority of children are sexually abused by someone they know and trust, either a relative, family friend, or caretaker. Very few children are
abused by strangers (see Chapter 4 for statistics).

*Myth 3: Sexual contact between a child and an adult is not harm-
ful to the child if the child is not physically forced to participate.*

Most authorities agree that sexual contact with a child is always harmful to the child, whether or not physical force is used, primarily because of the power of the adult over the child. Most children feel helpless in these situations. It is the unusual child who refuses to let the adult abuse him or her.

Myth 4: Incest is not really harmful, because the child receives nurturing and attention. Children who have been sexually abused present more psychological problems than children who have not been sexually abused. Sex with a child is not harmless because most children have not freely chosen to participate in the incest. They have been coerced in some way.

Myth 5: Mothers who know that their husbands are sexually abusing their children but do not report it to anyone essentially approve of this behavior. Mothers may often feel helpless, believing that they are unable to stop the abuse. This belief may come from the fact that, according to one study, 75 percent of the mothers studied were themselves victims of sexual abuse when they were children (McCarthy 1981). Many mothers are not aware of the abuse and, if they are aware, usually try to stop their husbands, although in some of these families the father is clearly the dominant personality and controls what happens to the family. Even though mothers may have a difficult time stopping the abuse, their inability to stop it does not mean they condone it.

Myth 6: Most cases of sexual abuse are reported. Ruth and Henry Kempe believe that only between 20 and 50 percent of all cases of sexual abuse are reported to the authorities (Kempe & Kempe 1984). Other studies have shown similar results. Many families will try to take care of the situation by removing the child from the perpetrator, convincing the perpetrator to stop, or other similar means.

Incest Taboo

Most societies believe that sexual relations between members of the same family are wrong. Almost every known society currently honors this taboo, generally known as the "incest taboo," to some extent. Sociologists and anthropologists have studied this concept for many years, fascinated by most cultures' prohibition against sex with close family members. The extent and degree of the taboo varies from culture to culture, but most cultures agree that sexual relations between close family members, especially between fathers and daughters and between mothers and sons, should be forbidden. Cultures vary on their insistence about sexual relations between other family members, such as with aunts, uncles, and cousins.

Most authorities agree that incest was believed to be wrong for several reasons. These include the need to increase family size through the addition of new members to increase family alliances, to increase family wealth, or to limit the number of birth defects and other abnormalities that were created in gene pools that were stagnant. (This latter reason, however, could only have become popular after increased scientific knowledge about genes in the last century.) The taboo may also have been created to help preserve family harmony by helping to prevent feelings of jealousy among family members.

Margaret Mead, when studying the customs of the Arapesh of New Guinea, asked the older males about incest, specifically about a brother marrying his sister. They responded in amazement:

> What, you would like to marry your sister! What is the matter with you anyway? Don't you want a brother-in-law? Don't you realize that if you marry another man's sister and another man marries your sister, you will have at least two brothers-in-law, while if you marry your own sister you will have none? With whom will you hunt, with whom will you garden, whom will you go to visit? (Mead 1935, 84)

The Arapesh saw incest not as an inherently wrong behavior, but rather as a way of limiting the size of the family, of eliminating the friendships and relationships that can occur only when marrying someone outside your own family.

The need in societies to create rules to prevent competition for sexual relations within the family is vividly shown by Mead as she reports on conditions for the Mundugumor in New Guinea:

> The taboo on marriage between different generations broke down, overstrained by a too-complicated marriage system, and this left men free to exchange their daughters for extra additional young wives for themselves. But this put father and son into competition for the daughter-sister both of whom wanted her

to exchange for a wife. Mundugumor society became a jungle, with every man's hand against every man's surviving merely through the memory of earlier social forms that some men still attempted to observe, and so unable to adjust because of those very memories. . . . If the male is to remain a nurturing parent within the family, he must nurture, not compete with, his dependent sons, nephews, and so on. If he is to co-operate with other men in the society, he must form patterns of relationship to men in which direct sexual competition is barred. (Mead 1949, 199–200)

Mead also believed that societies must protect young girls:

Older boys and men find little girls of four and five definitely female and attractive, and that attractiveness must be masked and guarded just as the male eye must be protected from the attractiveness of their older sisters and mothers. It seems that the more completely women's femininity—as a positive point, not a mere negation of maleness—is recognized, the more they are taught to protect it. A small girl, chic and entrancing, is sufficiently a temptation to a grown man so that societies usually have devices to protect her, circumscribe her, teach her not to exhibit her sex, which she herself lacks the wisdom to moderate. A small boy, on the other hand, however much his mother may treat him as a male, is less a temptation to her femininity than an extension of her maternity, while in the boy himself strong protections against his attraction to his mother have already been built. Mother-and-son incest is the rarest form of incest in the world, and it takes fairly elaborate cultural arrangements to make genuinely attractive any affairs between older women and men young enough to be their sons. (Mead 1949, 105–106)

Sigmund Freud believed that many people secretly desire to have sexual relations with their mothers or fathers but are able to control these desires with the help of social taboos. His theory, referred to as the Oedipus complex, is based on the Greek myth of Oedipus, who killed his father and married his mother. Freud believed that between the ages of three and five years, boys harbor a secret desire to take their father's place with their mother; they want to have sexual relations with their mothers. He also believed that the incest taboo was originally created to prohibit the participants from acting on these desires for sexual relations between parent and child.

On the other hand, Edward Westermarck disagreed with Freud, arguing that the reason that boys do not mate with their mothers or sisters is because they are not turned on to family members who have raised or have been reared with them; they do not need any social rules or incest taboos to restrain them because they have no such incestuous desires (Westermarck 1891).

According to Carl Sagan and Ann Druyan,

> Incest avoidance is one of the few invariables common to the spectacular diversity of human cultures. Sometimes, though, exceptions were made for (who else?) the ruling class. Since kings were gods, or near enough, only their sisters were considered of sufficiently exalted status to be their mates. Mayan and Egyptian royal families were inbred for generations, brothers marrying sisters—the process mitigated, it is thought, by unsanctioned and unrecorded couplings with nonrelatives. The surviving offspring were not conspicuously more incompetent that the usual, run-of-the-mill kings and queens, and Cleopatra, Queen of Egypt—officially the product of many consecutive generations of incestuous matings—was gifted by many standards. (Sagan & Druyan 1992, 248)

They go on to say

> . . . inbreeding produces a statistical genetic deficit that takes its toll chiefly in the deaths of infants and juveniles. . . . There is considerable evidence for this in many—but by no means all—groups of animals and plants. Even in sexual microorganisms, incest causes striking increases in the deaths of the young [Bell 1988]. In incestuous unions in zoos, mortality in the offspring increased steeply for forty different species of mammals—although some were much more vulnerable to close inbreeding than others [Harvey & Read 1988]. (Sagan & Druyan 1992, 249)

Sagan and Druyan's theory that exceptions to the incest taboo were made for members of the ruling or privileged class in societies has been supported by the research of many experts in the field. For example, sexual relations between chiefs and their daughters are expected in Zaire by the Azande; a Thonga hunter in Mozambique engages in sexual relations with his daughter before a hunt; and brother-sister marriages were permitted, often encouraged, among the ancient Incas, Egyptians, and Hawaiian upper classes in order to continue and preserve the royal lineage or to preserve family money and property (Broude 1994).

Claude Levi-Strauss, a well-known French anthropologist, believed that society had a definite purpose in mind when accepting and advocating for the incest taboo. He says:

> Just as the principle of the division of labor establishes an interdependence between the sexes, compelling them thereby to work together within the family, so the prohibition of incest establishes an interdependence between biological families and forces them to produce new families; and through these alone will the social group succeed in perpetuating itself. (Levi-Strauss 1985, 53)

He believed that economic forces also may have reinforced the incest taboo. Because families sent their daughters to other families, a new family with additional chances of being successful and economically strong was created.

William Graham Sumner noted that "the instances show that the notion of incest is by no means universal or uniform, or attended by the same intensity of repugnance. It is not by any means traceable to a constant cause" (Sumner 1940, 489).

Sociologist Emile Durkheim examined marriage prohibitions across cultures:

> The same cause cannot explain why, in one place, marriages between maternally related kin are specifically prohibited, while elsewhere the prohibition extends to marriages between all consanguine [blood] relatives; why, in one society, the prohibition reaches out to infinity, while in another it does not go beyond the closest collaterals. Why, among the primitive Hebrews, the ancient Arabs, the Phoenicians, the Greeks, and certain Slavs, did this natural aversion

not prevent a man from marrying his father's sister?
(Durkheim 1963, 68)

Anthropologist A. D. Coult theorized that the prohibition
against incest evolved in order to prevent role confusion among
family members. Role strain could result from a man who must
play the role of both father and husband to the same person—his
daughter. In order to prevent confusion, sex between immediate
members of the same family was proscribed, thus preventing a
daughter from also having to assume a wife's role or a son from
assuming a father's role.

Finally, no matter how or why the incest taboo was initiated,
Forward and Buck believe that

> [i]nstead of concentrating on the psychological dam-
> age of incest our society tends to focus on the violation
> of the taboo—causing both victims and aggressors to
> be too intimidated by the possibility of exposure to
> seek help. . . . A rational approach to the problem of in-
> cest begins with an understanding that despite the
> taboo, the roots of incest are in us all, and they are
> sprouting uncontrollably in our society. (Forward &
> Buck 1978, 17)

The Scope of the Problem

Studies to determine the prevalence of child sexual abuse focus
on estimating the proportion of the population who will be sexually abused as children, while studies to determine the incidence of child sexual abuse focus on determining the number of
new cases arising during a given time period, usually a year.

Experts and researchers often differ in their estimates of the
extent of child sexual abuse for many reasons. Most experts
agree, however, that relying on the reporting of child sexual
abuse incidents probably underestimates the extent of abuse,
based on our assumptions about incest and the incest taboo, on
research conducted on adults who were sexually abused as children but did not report this abuse to anyone, and on societal factors such as differing expectations of male and female sexual
behavior. Most estimates come from three sources: research studies conducted on adults who were sexually abused as children,
annual reports of sexual abuse made to child protection agencies,
and the National Incidence Studies, two federally funded studies

conducted for the National Center on Child Abuse and Neglect (Faller 1993). Many researchers believe that up to one in four girls and one in ten boys will be sexually abused by the time they reach the age of 18 (see Chapter 4 for specific prevalence and incidence studies).

Who Is Most at Risk?

Professionals in the field of child sexual abuse are always looking for ways to identify those children who are at highest risk for being sexually abused. They study research that has already been conducted, annual surveys, statistics from agencies that receive reports of child abuse, including sexual abuse, and other sources of information to determine whether or not certain specific characteristics or environmental circumstances are consistently present when a child is abused. They attempt to determine a set of characteristics that will help predict the type of child and the environment in which he or she lives that is most conducive to abuse. These risk factors help professionals in their attempts to prevent childhood sexual abuse.

Early research indicated that only a small number of children were at risk for sexual abuse, with few cases reported. Most of the children at high risk were thought to be in family environments and circumstances that were atypical of the normal family environment. However, more recent research has shown that sexual abuse of children can be found in all socioeconomic classes and family settings. Several factors can heighten the risk. One of these factors is being a girl; girls are at higher risk for sexual abuse than are boys, although many studies have found that boys are sexually abused more often than reports indicate. Girls have been the subject of research more often than boys, because many people erroneously believed that boys were rarely abused. Current studies are correcting that assumption, although most research still indicates that girls are at higher risk for sexual abuse than are boys.

Another risk factor is the age of the child at the onset of the sexual abuse—many studies indicate that children are at highest risk when they are between the ages of 8 and 12 years (Finkelhor 1984; Russell 1983). Yet in the National Incidence Study of Child Abuse and Neglect, researchers found that 60 percent of the sexually abused children were 12 years of age or older (NCCAN 1981). Many of the discrepancies in these studies can be attributed to the definitions of child sexual abuse used, which vary from study to study. Some studies define sexual abuse as intimate touching (touching genitalia) or actual intercourse while others also include such acts as watching a child undress or giving suggestive back rubs. These different definitions contribute to the wide range of reported incidence and prevalence numbers.

Social class is also a risk factor, although the extent and importance of this factor is being questioned in current research. In the past, researchers reported that child abuse was found more often in lower social and economic classes. However, over time many researchers discovered that while child abuse was reported more often in lower classes, they could not conclude that it was more common there. Many people in middle and upper classes have the opportunity to take their children to private physicians who are often less likely to report abuse to appropriate agencies, while public health doctors and emergency room doctors (more likely to see children from poorer families) are more likely to make such reports. Today, many researchers believe that childhood sexual abuse is found equally across all social classes. Diane Russell found no relationship between the occurrence of sexual abuse and the father's level of education or his occupation (Russell 1986). In a survey conducted in Boston, Massachusetts, David Finkelhor also found that family income level was not a factor in the occurrence of child sexual abuse, although in a student-based study, he did find that female students from families with incomes under $10,000 had a higher rate of sexual abuse than those students from families earning over $10,000 (Finkelhor 1984).

Another factor earlier thought to be reliable in predicting sexual abuse was race. However, many studies examining the differences in child sexual abuse between blacks and whites found no significant differences between the races. For example, an American Humane Association study found that 15 percent of reported cases of child sexual abuse were allegedly committed by members of black families; this proportion is similar to the proportion of blacks in the U.S. population (Trainor 1984). Russell also found similar rates among blacks and whites (Russell 1986).

Other studies of child sexual abuse in different racial groups produced no consistent or conclusive evidence. Christine Adams-Tucker found that black children are less likely to be sexually abused than are white children (Adams-Tucker 1981). Other researchers suggest that blacks may be overrepresented in reports of child sexual abuse cases, primarily because they are more likely to use public health care facilities instead of seeing private practitioners who may be less likely to report cases of child sexual abuse (DeFrancis 1969; Finkelhor 1984). In another study, Gail Wyatt found that the rate of child sexual abuse among white American women was 67 percent compared with 57 percent for African American women (Wyatt 1985).

An earlier study by Finkelhor identified several factors that may increase the risk of sexual abuse of girls. These include living with a stepfather, not living with the mother, having a distant or strained relationship with the mother, having a mother who did not finish high school, having a mother who displays sexually punitive behavior, receiving little physical attention, having a family income of less than $10,000, and having fewer than two friends. These factors may accurately provide an indication of who is most at risk for victimization, but studies show that they may account for recognizing only 32 percent of all cases of child sexual abuse among girls (Finkelhor 1980). Girls with stepfathers are twice as likely as other girls to suffer sexual abuse, and fathers who demand obedience from children and believe that women are subordinate to men also are more likely than other men to be abusers of children (Conte 1986).

In a subsequent study, Finkelhor found that family conditions that place children at higher risk for sexual abuse include absence or unavailability of parents, poor relationships between parents and children, conflicts between the parents, and the presence of a stepfather in a family (Finkelhor 1986). Many studies have shown that girls who spend at least some time living without their natural mother or father are more vulnerable to sexual abuse. Finkelhor found that girls were almost three times as likely to experience sexual abuse if they lived apart from their natural mother (Finkelhor 1984). Russell found that girls who lived with their natural mother but without their natural father were more likely to be sexually abused (Russell 1986). Some studies suggest that if a mother works outside of the home, the children are at higher risk of sexual abuse (Russell 1986; Peters 1984), while Finkelhor found no such relationship between mothers' employment and child sexual abuse (Finkelhor 1984).

Finkelhor did find that girls whose mothers were frequently ill were at higher risk of being sexually abused (Finkelhor 1984). Mothers with many children and mothers who abused alcohol or drugs or were severely depressed were likely to have children who would experience sexual abuse (Herman & Hirschman 1981; Peters 1984). Other researchers, using the same criteria, found no relationship between the mothers' illness and sexual abuse of the children (Fromuth 1983).

Studies on the causes of child sexual abuse or the risk factors within families have found certain similarities among families in which sexual abuse has occurred. Lustig and his colleagues identified five family characteristics that often are found in families in which father-daughter incest has occurred. These include the daughter taking over the mother's role, becoming the central female figure in the family; parental sexual incompatibility; the unwillingness of the father to seek sexual gratification outside the family; the daughter's fear of being abandoned or of family breakup; and an unconscious willingness of the mother to let the daughter participate in the incest (Lustig et al. 1966). Mothers in this situation may see no other way to hold the family together; economic concerns often play a major role.

In another study, P. J. Pecora and M. B. Martin identify the following risk factors for intrafamilial sexual abuse: violence in the family; role reversal; father/stepfather alcohol or other substance abuse; dysfunctional marital relations; presence of a stepfather; absent, ill, or depressed mother; abuse of parents as children; rejection of or negative relationship with the daughter; isolation of the family from other people; low socioeconomic status; mother's lack of a high school diploma; and the presence of a strong, domineering father (Pecora & Martin 1994).

Many researchers have also found that girls who have poor relationships with their mothers are more likely to experience some type of sexual abuse. Mothers who are unemotional with their daughters or unable or unwilling to talk to their daughters about sex, about boys, or about anything else that is important to their daughters may have daughters more likely to be sexually abused. S. D. Peters found that there was an inverse relationship between the closeness of the mother and daughter and the likelihood that the daughter would be sexually abused (Peters 1984). Finkelhor found in his survey of college students that daughters who did not feel close to their mothers were more likely to have experienced sexual abuse than those daughters who had a close relationship with their mothers (Finkelhor 1984). Girls who have close relationships with their mothers may be more likely to reveal the fact they are being abused, which may prevent a perpetrator from abusing them in the first place.

Parental conflicts also were reported by victims of childhood sexual abuse. Many researchers have found poor family relationships among children who have been sexually abused. For example, in Finkelhor's study of college-age women he found that those women who reported that their parents had an unhappy marriage or showed little emotion toward each other were more likely to have experienced sexual abuse as children than women who reported no such unhappiness or lack of emotion (Finkelhor 1984). In troubled marriages, fathers may feel helpless about their marital relationship and turn to their daughters to meet their emotional needs.

Many studies have shown a relationship between having a stepfather in the home and sexual abuse, especially abuse of daughters. The absence of a strong incest taboo for nonblood relatives may make it easier for a stepfather to believe that sexually abusing a stepdaughter is not wrong. The 1981 National Incidence Study found that the incidence of stepfather-stepdaughter abuse often exceeds that of father-daughter abuse (NCCAN 1981). Finkelhor also found that girls with stepfathers were more likely to be sexually abused than girls living with their natural fathers (Finkelhor 1984). Many of these studies were conducted when "blended" families were not as common as they are today; researchers must examine these families today to determine whether or not stepfathers are more likely to abuse their stepchildren than natural fathers.

Many people unfamiliar with sexual abuse are quick to point out certain characteristics of children, especially girls, who have been sexually abused, suggesting that in some way they caused their own abuse. For instance, some might suggest if the girls had not looked so pretty or dressed so provocatively they would not have been abused. Some blame the mothers, suggesting that if the mothers had watched their daughters more closely, they would not have been abused. Finkelhor, among others, has been a strong advocate for not blaming the child. He suggests that

> four preconditions must exist for sexual abuse to occur: (1) There must be an offender with the motivation to sexually abuse, (2) the offender must overcome internal inhibitions against abusing, (3) the offender must overcome external obstacles against abusing, and (4) the offender must overcome resistance by the child. To "explain" sexual abuse fully, one must account for the presence of all four of these preconditions. (Finkelhor 1986, 86–87)

Most experts will agree that children are the innocent partners; the offender is clearly responsible for any sexual abuse that occurs.

When investigating allegations of sexual abuse, investigators must be aware of sociocultural factors that can impact the investigation. Most mental health professionals and others involved in investigating allegations of sexual abuse tend to use, often unconsciously, their own socioeconomic and cultural background as the standard of behavior. Many research studies have demonstrated that some restrictions, for example, the incest taboo, exist to a certain degree in all cultures. However, the degree to which cultures allow or encourage sexual activity varies greatly, as does the definition of what is sexual. For example, Kee MacFarlane and Jill Waterman describe how, in Finland, families often enjoy saunas together; in this case, nudity is not unusual or sexually provocative to the adults or the children (MacFarlane & Waterman 1986).

Perpetrators

We often believe that children's safety is threatened more by strangers than by those people the children know. At home and in school, parents and teachers emphasize to children that they should not talk to strangers or accept candy or rides. We picture dirty old men in trench coats ready to flash or snatch our children. Most people do not realize that children who are sexually abused are most likely to be abused by someone they know and trust. Sexual abusers come from all walks of life, all races, and all socioeconomic levels. Furthermore, adults are not the only abusers. Adolescents and teenagers are also capable of abusing children, including their own brothers and sisters.

Conte reveals that there are no unique characteristics that separate abusers from nonabusers. The ages, psychological characteristics, demographic information, and histories of men who have sexually abused children vary considerably. Studies using the MMPI (Minnesota Multi-Phasic Inventory) to determine the identifying characteristics of abusers have not been able to develop a profile of abusers that is distinct from nonabusers. Most of these studies have been conducted using incarcerated sexual offenders as subjects, rather than using those still out in the community (those who are not stereotyped as dirty old men) (Conte 1986).

Determining identifying characteristics has proven difficult for most researchers; however, Conte has suggested six clinical characteristics that are helpful in providing a framework for understanding abusers: denial, sexual arousal, sexual fantasy, social skills, cognitive distortions, and other psychological and social problems (Conte 1985). Most adults who sexually abuse children are not likely to admit this behavior. Serious consequences, both legal and social, face anyone who is convicted of child sexual abuse and the reasons to deny that abuse occurred are understandable.

With regard to sexual arousal, Gene Abel and his colleagues were able to identify violent child molesters by studying their level of sexual arousal when shown violent scenes involving children compared with these levels when shown nonviolent images (Abel, Becker, Blanchard, & Djenderedjian 1978). Sexual fantasies have been suggested as a behavior characteristic of abusers; although its significance remains unclear, many researchers believe the role of sexual fantasy should be considered. Cognitive distortions help abusers rationalize their behavior and include statements such as, "The child didn't physically resist, therefore she must have wanted it" and "Having sex with my daughter helped teach her about sex in a safe way." Adult abusers believe that these statements are true and are thus able to continue the abusive behavior even though they are hurting the children and risk severe punishment if discovered. Finally, many abusers display other psychological and social problems, including drug and alcohol abuse, depression, poor self-image, and feelings of inadequacy.

Nicholas Groth, a psychologist who has worked with inmates in a state prison system, developed a system for classifying child abusers into one of two broad categories—regressed or fixated. Regressed abusers are adult males who live fairly normal, ordinary lives; they had girlfriends as teenagers and wives and children as adults. At some point in their lives, often in their thirties, they develop a sexual interest in children, primarily young girls. Fixated abusers, on the other hand, develop an interest in children while still young, usually in their teens, and continue to be interested in children; they may never be interested sexually in someone their own age (Groth 1978). John Crewdson developed a third category of abuser: The crossover abuser is usually a father whose primary sexual interest is in children (Crewdson 1988).

Sgroi believes that "individuals who are sexual offenders against children do not seem to be motivated primarily by sexual desires; instead, as well documented by Drs. Ann Burgess and A. Nicholas Groth, they tend to engage in sexual behavior with children in the service of non-sexual needs, especially the need to feel powerful and in control. Thus, the dynamics of child sexual abuse involve a sexual expression or acting out of non-sexual issues" (Sgroi 1982).

Kempe and Kempe believe that the number of incest cases may be rising, in large part

> because of the great changes in family life: rising divorce rates, birth control, abortion, increasing tolerance about sexuality in general, and a more tolerant view of sexual acts between nonrelated household members who come from divorced or previously separated homes. This is particularly true of brother-sister incest between stepchildren who are living as a family but are not related; we believe that cultural attitudes about this group of adolescents are rapidly becoming more casual. In some states, marriages between these unrelated siblings are no longer illegal. (Kempe & Kempe 1984, 48)

In a study of 102 families in which incest occurred, Lenore Walker found that the families had many characteristics in common; 36 percent had four or more children, 66 percent had a high level of discord within the family, 32 percent had alcohol-dependency problems, 31 percent had mental health problems, and 26 percent experienced spousal abuse (Walker 1988). Judith Herman studied 40 families in which incest occurred and determined that 55 percent of mothers in these families were ill, disabled, or absent from the home for significant amounts of time (Herman 1981).

In most cases of child sexual abuse committed by a family member, physical force or violence is rarely used, primarily because the child has a trusting and dependent relationship with the abuser. Because the abuser has control and dominance over the child, he or she is often able to coerce the child into sexual activities without resorting to violence. However, some studies indicate that more violence may be used to persuade the child to participate than most experts originally thought. Ann Burgess and her colleagues studied 44 cases of attempted and completed sexual abuse by a family member and found that 39 percent of the offenders pressured the child to participate in the sexual activity while 61 percent threatened harm or used physical force. In those cases in which force was threatened or used, the offending parent resorted to intimidation to gain power over the child (Burgess, Holmstrom, & McCausland 1977).

Fathers/Mothers

In most cases of incest, fathers are the perpetrators; daughters are usually the victims. Instances of mother-son, father-son, and mother-daughter incest also occur, although father-daughter incest is by far the most commonly reported form. Because of the changing nature of the American family, with more second marriages and blended families, several researchers have started comparing rates of incest committed by biological fathers with that committed by stepfathers. Diane Russell is one researcher who has studied the prevalence and seriousness of incest between biological fathers and children and between stepfathers and children. Interviewing a random sample of over 900 adult women in San Francisco, she discovered that 17 percent, approximately one in six women, were sexually abused by a stepfather while 2 percent, or approximately 1 in 40 women, were sexually abused by their biological fathers. When Russell studied the seriousness of the abuse, she found that 47 percent of the stepfathers, compared with 26 percent of the biological fathers, committed "very serious sexual abuse" activities with their children (Russell 1984). Other studies confirm Russell's findings that children are more often sexually abused by stepfathers than by biological fathers (Herman 1981).

Fathers may sexually abuse one child or all of their children for a variety of reasons. They may be promiscuous, indiscriminate about whom they engage in sexual activities; they may have an intense desire for children (usually known as pedophilia) and their children are the most available children around; or they may choose a daughter for sexual activities because their wives are not satisfying to them and they do not want to "destroy" the family by having sexual relations outside of the family. They use their position of authority to control their daughters and obtain sexual pleasure from them.

Getting help is often hard for many incest victims, although when other siblings are threatened, the victim may decide to reveal the abuse. Linda Gordon finds that

> many incest victims only made their move to get help when their younger sisters were threatened by the father's sexual demands. In this respect, as in others, incest victims behaved like beaten wives, who often tolerated violence until it touched their children. This motherliness was both a strength and a weakness: it

encouraged them to tolerate high levels of abuse "for the sake of the children," yet it helped them to limit what they would tolerate. The limits were hardly stringent ones, but the existence of some area of honor was strengthening and helped preserve sanity. (Gordon 1988, 236)

Finkelhor suggests several reasons why parents are more likely reported as perpetrators of child sexual abuse:

Parents (mostly fathers and stepfathers) make up a large proportion of reported cases for several reasons. For one thing, they are conspicuous, create concern, and are thus likely to be pursued by those who know about them until they become official statistics. For another thing, although many families try to contain knowledge about parent-child incest, the dynamics are so volatile and the potential for conflict so great that they must be harder to hush up permanently than other kinds of children's sexual abuse. Thus even though the motivation for silence may be greater, the actual ability to contain it is less. (Finkelhor 1979, 140)

Most people are more likely to perceive as sexual abuse closeness between father and daughter than a similar relationship between mother and son. If a daughter naps or sleeps in the same bed as her father, many people may see that as wrong, but, as Kempe and Kempe suggest, a "mother who allows her boy to sleep in her bed may be thought to 'infantilize' him but not to be acting on unconscious incestuous impulses" (Kempe & Kempe 1984, 69).

Forward and Buck believe that the incestuous father generally has no compassion for his victim and does not recognize that any consequences exist for his behavior. Many offenders may be horrified at their behavior, but not enough to stop the abuse. These authors believe that many incestuous fathers have a deep, constant need for unconditional love and attention; they also believe that incest, like rape, is an act of power and control (Forward & Buck 1978).

Contrary to the beliefs of some researchers, mothers in the home of an incestuous father-daughter relationship may not always know about the incest. If they are aware of the incest, they may not always be consciously allowing the father to molest the daughter. Many mothers may be giving up their personal power, letting their husbands dominate and control them; the mothers become the silent partners in the incest. Men in these situations are looking for power and control, as well as unconditional love, and they can find it most easily when they can lead the mother into denying that anything is wrong, which allows the father to molest the daughter (Forward & Buck 1978).

Cases of mother-son incest often occur in homes where the father is absent. The mother relies on her son to be "the man of the house," to take care of things the way a man would. The son may love his mother but hate the fact that she is forcing him into his father's role. Forward and Buck believe that "because there is often no element of force involved the boy almost invariably comes away with crushing guilt feelings, for he believes he must accept his share of the blame without the mitigating excuse of having been violated" (Forward & Buck 1978, 74).

Cases of mother-son incest are often difficult to uncover because many boys are not sure whether or not they have been abused. Even though they may feel exploited and used, society claims that they are lucky because they have had the opportunity to have sex with an experienced female. Mothers may be able to get away with more fondling and touching of their sons' genitals and other parts of their bodies because of motherly responsibilities such as bathing and dressing (Crewdson 1988).

Mic Hunter has similar findings:

> Many of my clients were told by friends or family when they talked about a woman being sexual with them when they were boys that they ought to feel happy, because they were lucky to have the opportunity to be sexual at such a young age. In addition to being told that they were fortunate to have had the opportunity to be sexual by the perpetrator(s) of the sexual abuse, friends, or family, these men also got this message from the media. (Hunter 1990, 36)

Other researchers also discuss the impact that mother-son incest has on sons. M. Nasjleti believes that "[b]oys often fear that having sex with the mother is indicative of their having a mental illness. Because mothers are viewed as nonsexual beings in this culture, incapable of sexually abusing their own children, boys molested by their mothers often assume responsibility for their own molestation" (Nasjleti 1980, 273).

Siblings

Most researchers agree that sibling abuse is probably more common than statistics indicate, in part because both offender and victim may be embarrassed and ashamed of their behavior and unwilling or unable to confide in anyone. Sibling abuse has often been ignored in the past because much of the abusive behavior is considered normal (e.g., children fight with each other, play doctor with each other). Parents do not spend all their time with their children, and therefore they cannot always be aware of all the things their children are doing. Siblings have plenty of time to play with each other and they also have time to abuse one another. Currently, professionals are becoming more aware of sibling abuse and the consequences of this abuse for the victims.

In a study conducted by Vernon Wiehe, participants had responded to advertisements in newspapers and newsletters of professional associations or had been in contact with organizations concerned with domestic violence. One hundred fifty respondents provided information on their physical, emotional, and sexual abuse experiences. Wiehe found that 67 percent of the respondents admitted that they had been sexually abused by a sibling when they were growing up. Thirty-seven percent reported that they had been physically and emotionally as well as sexually abused (Wiehe 1990).

Children do not often report sexual abuse to their parents or other trusted adults and this also holds true for cases of sibling abuse, for many of the same reasons. The victims initially may not be aware that the behavior is abusive; if an older sibling is the abuser, he or she may use the power and authority of the "older brother or sister" to keep the younger child quiet; victims may be threatened with retaliation, either physical or emotional, if they tell; victims may feel they are responsible for the abuse or for not resisting the abuse when it first started; or the family environment may not encourage revelation of the abuse.

Holly Smith and Edie Israel studied 25 cases of sibling incest reported to the Sexual Abuse Team in Boulder, Colorado, between 1982 and 1985. Emotional distance was a frequent characteristic of families in which the sibling incest occurred. Twenty-four percent of the fathers were emotionally unavailable and unable to empathize with their children; mothers also reported feeling distant from and not emotionally attached to their children, although not to the same extent as the fathers (Smith & Israel 1987).

While sexual abuse of siblings may stop because the perpetrator loses interest before parents or other authority figures become aware of it, Wiehe found that sibling abuse can continue into adulthood:

> Several respondents continued to be victims of their siblings' sexual abuse throughout their teen years and into adulthood. One person who had been a frequent victim of her older brother's sexual abuse when she was growing up at home assumed that the abuse would stop when he went away to college. But one weekend she visited her brother at the college; in the dormitory he attempted to force her to have sex with him again. Another victim's older brother attempted to rape her after she was married and the parent of several children. The perpetrators in these cases thus continued to view their sisters as sexual objects, even into adulthood. (Wiehe 1990, 53)

When treating victims of sibling incest, professionals must be aware of how these cases can divide parents, who must choose between two children. Who do they support: the victim or the perpetrator? This issue is often difficult for parents. Marianne Celano, in a meeting sponsored in conjunction with the Sixth National Symposium on Child Sexual Abuse, describes this dilemma:

> Parents of victims of sibling incest have to divide their concern between two children, and they sometimes have to make a choice to remove one child. Many parents alternate between sympathy for the victim and sympathy for the offender, whom they may perceive as immature, emotionally unstable or victimized him- or herself. I have had a case in which a child was victimized by her older brother and the entire extended family rallied behind the older brother and protected him by sending him out of state to elude criminal prosecution. The victim was furious and blamed herself for the abuse. (Lloyd 1990b, 5)

Other speakers at this meeting emphasized the importance of involving the justice system and of holding perpetrators accountable for their actions; they believe that this is the best way to prevent the perpetrator from abusing again and becoming part of the adult criminal justice system.

Multidisciplinary teams must be involved in order to help parents and children survive and heal from the experience. Professionals in the field often find working with families in which sibling abuse has occurred a challenge because of the issues involved; for instance, breaking up families is difficult, as is trying to reunite them in a healthy manner.

Other Family Members

Other family members, such as uncles, aunts, and grandparents, also are capable of abusing children in their families. Characteristics of cases of grandfather-granddaughter incest are usually quite similar to those of father-daughter incest. The young girls feel responsible for the incest, and grandfathers molest their granddaughters for many of the same reasons that fathers molest their daughters. While these other family members also abuse children related to them they will not be treated separately in this book because they share many of the same characteristics as other abusers.

Nonfamily Members

In addition to family members who abuse children, there are many instances in which children are abused by nonfamily members. These abusers are commonly people who play a caretaker role, usually taking care of and being responsible for the children during part of the day or during special activities. Nonfamily abusers that are considered in this section include Boy Scout leaders, priests, and day-care operators.

Boy Scout Leaders

The Boy Scouts have had their share of problems with pedophiles and other child molesters. From the beginning, Boy Scout activities were offered to all boys, but especially focused on those boys who came from less advantaged neighborhoods. Single mothers often appreciated the opportunity for their sons to belong to the Scouts and were pleased that Scout leaders could be strong positive male role models for their sons. With the increasing number of broken homes and children being raised by single mothers, Scouting offered a valuable service to these mothers and their sons.

Scouting officials have been aware that certain leaders molest boys and they have moved quickly to remove these men from their ranks. However, for a long time there was no master list of sexual abusers within the organization or policy for checking references and backgrounds of men applying to become Scout leaders; a leader who abused boys could move from one troop to a troop in another area or state and never be discovered unless and until he tried to molest boys in his new troop. While the organization did keep confidential files on a number of child molesters, they never had a central clearinghouse or other means to access this information from any area of the country.

In 1981, a Scout publication acknowledged that some people joined Scouting for the distinct purpose of interacting sexually with the boys. But its focus was on children seeking out other children; no mention was made of adult molesters looking for young boys. In retrospect, the Scouts were just as confused as the general public over the issue of sexual molestation and what to do about it. More notice was being given to sexual abuse of children throughout the country but many people still were under the impression that strangers, dirty old men who were most likely homosexual, were out to molest their children. Society was still not aware that most abuse was perpetrated by adults whom the children knew and trusted, people in positions of authority and trust, and usually by heterosexual males.

Past Scouting policy was to try to encourage the molester to resign from Scouting, which often worked, and the organization never pressed charges against the molester. This made it easy for the offenders to move away, join another Scout troop, and start all over again. Later, the Scouts would decide that this policy was not working and, worried about the national press coverage if they did not somehow do a better job of protecting the young boys in their charge, they started to examine the situation more carefully and take positive action to try to eliminate molesters from the Scouting membership. Videos were developed to help boys know what to do if an adult tried to molest them; new rules were enacted, such as the requirement that two adult leaders must be present on all trips, in order to protect the boys; and in 1989, all Scout handbooks contained a pamphlet for parents on how to protect their children from child abuse, as well as drug abuse. In 1990, many handbooks contained a short discussion of sexual abuse, and included information showing how boys could disobey a Scout leader without disobeying the Scout code that required them always to obey adults (Boyle 1994).

The Boy Scouts still have not implemented mandatory criminal background checks on all prospective leaders and other volunteer adult participants, although their application for leaders currently includes a request for references and questions about prior arrest records. Local troop sponsors are encouraged to check references, which can eliminate many men with previous sexual abuse records, perhaps preventing abuse and subsequent litigation. According to Patrick Boyle, between 1984 and early 1992, the Boy Scouts were "sued at least 60 times by families of children abused by Scout leaders. The settlements and judgments against the corporation totaled more than $16 million" (Boyle 1994, 334).

Priests

While Catholic priests are not the only clergy to have some members who sexually abuse children, they have been the focus of most of the press coverage in recent years, primarily because they are required to be celibate. Some experts in the field of childhood sexual abuse claim that the celibacy requirement may force more men confused about their sexuality or sexual desires into the priesthood, hoping to squelch their desires; thus, sexual abuse committed by priests may not be so surprising. However, Father Andrew Greeley, a priest in the Archdiocese of Chicago and a professor of social science at the University of Chicago, believes otherwise:

> [A]s someone who has been warning the church about the sexual-abuse problem since 1986, I insist that it is intolerable anti-Catholic bigotry to blame the present crisis of sexual abuse of young people by priests on celibacy. A certain proportion of priests (3.27 percent in the Archdiocese of Chicago) abuse children not because they are sexually starved but because their "love maps"—their objects of sexual desire—have been vandalized in childhood experiences of their own. Pedophilia, in whatever form, would be the result of celibacy, if, and only if, it were not also a problem among others working in the professions that have access to children. Most pedophiles are married men. If the priest pedophiles were married they would continue to prey on children, perhaps their own children. Nor can the pedophile problem be blamed on "unhealthy" attitudes toward sex among Roman Catholics that have been created by celibacy. In fact, as research done by the National Opinion Research Center and by

The Gallup Organization demonstrates, Catholics have sex more often, are more playful in their sex lives, and enjoy sex more than Protestants. (Greeley 1993, 45)

In October 1991 Joseph Cardinal Bernardin, the Roman Catholic archbishop of Chicago, appointed a commission to examine issues of sexual misconduct with children by priests and to make recommendations for action. The commission found that children who are sexually abused by priests often suffer a loss of self-esteem; an inability to trust other adults, especially other clergy; and feelings of anger at the church. Any type of sexual misconduct by a priest breaks the sacred trust that must exist between a priest and the people he works with and leads. Parish communities are also harmed by sexual misconduct by priests. The Archdiocese of Chicago is one of the first large groups in the country to face the issue of sexual abuse of children by priests. Because of its openness in confronting this issue, the commission has a unique opportunity to teach clergy, as well as members of the community, about the sexual abuse of children and the role of the church in preventing the abuse of children by church representatives. The commission concludes:

> First, child sexual abuse usually has a deleterious impact on the victim, and it is essential that this individual get the needed help as soon as possible. Otherwise, the personal cost to the individual, and to some extent society and the Church, will be very great.
> Second, child abusers are inflicted with an illness which, to date, is incurable. They also need help, and, as a Christian community, we should offer them the therapeutic assistance they require. While we understand the anger of those who have been victimized by priests in this Archdiocese, we are also called to a humane approach to people who are afflicted with this illness. (Dempsey, Gorman, & Madden 1992, 17)

The commission also recommended new screening procedures for those who work with or have access to children; psychological profiles and other types of screening for all entering the local seminaries; training for seminarians in psychosocial development, and both moral and deviant sexual behavior; ongoing training about the nature and effects of childhood sexual abuse; and passing on of relevant information about a priest to church officials in any new assignment area. Priests who are found guilty of sexual abuse of children should receive initial treatment of at least two years and, if recommended, the priest should enter a four-year supervised aftercare program that will include no access to minors, individual therapy, group therapy, and a one-week annual evaluation. The commission does not recommend that a priest be allowed to return to the ministry:

> [I]f the priest admits his problem, apologizes, cooperates with therapy, is capable of age-appropriate relationships, and receives a hopeful prognosis from the therapeutic team, the Archdiocese may consider some kind of return to ministry as long as it does not provide access to minors. . . .
>
> There are also some cases of sexual misconduct with minors which, we do not think, allow a return to any kind of ministry. If a priest is convicted of sexual abuse, has abused multiple victims, has committed multiple offenses, has abused a single victim over a long period of time, has become a public scandal, or is a poor risk for change, he should not be allowed to return to any kind of ministry. . . .
>
> Priests who fall into this category should be encouraged to resign from the priesthood. If they refuse, the Archdiocese may initiate a canonical procedure to laicize them or send them to a residential facility in which they will be allowed no public ministry. (Dempsey, Gorman, & Madden 1992, 46–47)

Several organizations have been started by people who have been sexually abused by priests and other members of the clergy. Some of them, for example, Linkup and Survivor Connections, are membership organizations. They often publish newsletters that include lists of actions taken against priests throughout the country.

Day-Care Operators

The American Humane Association found that employees of day-care centers account for only between 1.0 and 1.5 percent of all child sexual abuse reports from across the country (AHA 1993). However, beginning in the 1980s, especially following the McMartin day-care sexual abuse case (see pp. 105–106), more attention was focused on day-care centers. Finkelhor and his colleagues conducted a nationwide study on allegations of child sexual abuse in day-care settings. They collected data on all reported cases of child sexual abuse in day-care settings between January 1983 and December 1985; these data were collected from day-care licensing offices and child protection services personnel, 48 specialists in sexual abuse, and a search of newspaper articles. The researchers found 270 day-care facilities with allegations of child sexual abuse; between 500 and 550 substantiated cases of child sexual abuse that involved 2,500 children were discovered during the three-year study period. Finkelhor and his colleagues estimated that approximately 5.5 children per 10,000 day-care enrollees are at risk of sexual abuse (compared with 8.9 children per 10,000 children under the age of six years at risk of sexual abuse in their own homes).

With regard to the perpetrators, Finkelhor and his colleagues found that 38 percent of all perpetrators were not direct child-care providers but rather others in the day-care centers, including janitors, bus drivers, family members of the staff, or outsiders. In 83 percent of the cases, a single offender was involved, and female offenders constituted 40 percent of the perpetrators. Girls constituted 62 percent of the victims. Approximately 67 percent of the cases involved one or two children (Finkelhor, Williams & Burns 1988).

Elizabeth Hollenberg and Cynthia Ragan studied risk in day-care settings and concluded the following:

- High-quality day care was not necessarily associated with a lower risk for child sexual abuse. In fact, the key factor in reducing risk was allowing parents to have ready access to their children in the day care setting.
- Surprisingly, factors associated with less risk of sexual abuse in day care included the facility having numerous day care staff and/or being located in a high crime, inner-city neighborhood. This suggests that children may receive more protection in settings that have a general wariness about suspicious activities and therefore offer more supervision. (Hollenberg & Ragan 1991, 20)

Other Juveniles

Studies have indicated that there is no standard profile of a juvenile sex offender. The majority of these offenders are living at home; approximately one-third are living with their natural parents. Ethnic, religious, or socioeconomic characteristics are not significant predictors of future sexual abuse. Many youth who sexually abuse other children have been sexually abused themselves as children (between 30 and 70 percent) and in most cases the abuse was never reported. They do not have a positive self-image, often believe they lack control over their behavior or their lives, and have often been abandoned as children, either physically or emotionally (Ryan 1988).

Pedophiles

Finkelhor defines pedophilia as

> occurring when an adult has a conscious sexual interest in prepubertal children. We infer that sexual interest from one of two behaviors: (1) the adult has had some sexual contact with a child (meaning that he or she touched the child or had the child touch him or her with the purpose of becoming sexually aroused), or (2) the adult has masturbated to sexual fantasies involving children. Thus we are defining pedophilia to be a little broader than sexual abuse or child molesting. It includes the conscious fantasizing about such behavior, too. (Finkelhor 1986, 90–91)

In attempting to explain how a pedophile thinks or what causes pedophilia, Finkelhor examines various theories on pedophilia:

> [It] appeared that most of the theories could be categorized as trying to explain one of four factors: (1) why a person would find relating sexually to a child to be emotionally gratifying and congruent (in the sense of the child fitting the adult's needs), (2) why a person would be capable of being sexually aroused by a child, (3) why a person would be frustrated or blocked in efforts to obtain sexual and emotional gratification from more normatively approved sources, and (4) why a person would not be deterred by the conventional social restraints and inhibitions against having sexual relations with a child. (Finkelhor 1986, 90–92)

Finkelhor and his colleagues believe that these factors can either work together or separately to explain pedophilia. In cases of emotional congruence, pedophiles are seen as emotionally immature, which makes them more easily attracted to children, to whom they can relate on an equal basis. They may also suffer from low self-esteem and have poor social relationships and are therefore attracted to children because they find it easier to interact with them and because they are able to feel powerful and respected, to have control over the children. Pedophiles may also see themselves in children that they sexually abuse; they may be trying to give these children some of the love and attention that they never received as children.

In cases of sexual arousal, pedophiles may be sexually aroused by children because of high hormone levels, previous experiences of arousal from looking at child pornography or erotic videos of children, or some other unknown reasons. Some studies have indicated that child sexual abusers are more likely to be aroused by children than by adults (Freund, Langevin, Cibiri, & Zajac 1973; Quinsey, Steinman, Bergersen, & Holmes 1975).

Another reason for being sexually aroused by children may be that pedophiles had sexual experiences as children, often with adults, and are therefore aroused by children as a result of this experience. R. Langevin and colleagues found that convicted sexual molesters were more likely to have had sexual experiences with adults as children than non–child molesters (Langevin et al. 1985). Biological explanations for why pedophiles are sexually aroused by children have been examined, but nothing conclusive has been discovered.

In cases of blockage, in which pedophiles are unable to develop healthy emotional and sexual relationships with other adult heterosexuals, theories focus on individual psychological reasons. For example, the pedophile may have had a negative sexual experience with another adult or been abandoned by a lover. This group of theories is often used to explain incest in families, asserting that fathers often turn to their daughters because their wives have become cold, distant, or unavailable. These men believe it is safer to engage in sexual activities with their daughters than with another adult woman.

Finally, in cases in which pedophiles are not deterred by social conventions against having sex with children, many researchers believe that pedophiles generally have poor impulse control, are alcohol or drug abusers, or suffer from some type of psychosis or senility. These conditions may lower their resistance to societal forces telling them that sexual relations with children are wrong. Using these conditions as excuses for sexually abusing children, the pedophile believes that he is right, that somehow the child enticed or encouraged him.

Crewdson found that pedophiles who do not have children of their own enjoy getting together and sharing information, while those who abuse their own children are usually secretive:

> The propensity of pedophiles to organize and proselytize illustrates one of the principal distinctions between those who abuse their own children sexually and those who abuse other people's children. . . . Pedophiles . . . are "groupers" who actually seek one another out, to swap not only half-baked philosophies about having sex with children but pictures of their victims and often the victims themselves. For those who devote their lives to the pursuit of sex with children, it's reassuring to consort with other outlaws. What pedophiles really seek from one another is validation, the knowledge that they're not alone. (Crewdson 1988, 96)

Crewdson believes that pedophiles are narcissists, that they believe that they are leading a cultural and social revolution showing how they are providing children with the love and attention that their parents do not give them. They see themselves as

> a politically oppressed minority of "child lovers" whose vocabulary doesn't include words like sexual abuse. To pedophiles it's "transgenerational sex," and they talk endlessly of their love for children and of children's affection for them. Because their devotion to children is so single-minded, they see themselves as vastly superior to other adults, particularly parents who don't have much time for their own children. (Crewdson 1988, 96)

Causes

Many theories exist that attempt to explain the causes of childhood sexual abuse. Most theories focus either on the family or the offender. Some theories offer an integrated model of the causes of child sexual abuse.

Family-Focused Theories

Theories focusing on the family perspective in causing sexual abuse suggest that the mother may be estranged from her husband and the daughter may replace the mother as her father's sexual partner. Many professionals acknowledge the limitation of these theories, in which family dynamics are blamed for the abuse, because the dynamics of sexual abuse are more complicated than many such theories allow. Fathers often blame the mothers for abandoning them and believe they themselves are not at fault; the family situation caused it.

Offender-Focused Theories

Most professionals who suggest the offender as the primary cause of the abuse work in institutions holding offenders; they rarely talk with family members. Kathleen Faller examines this approach:

> Their focus has been on understanding the etiology of sexual abuse by examining the physiological and psychological functioning of offenders. They typically do not have access to families to understand any role they might have played in the victimization, nor its impact on the families. Moreover, as these clinicians develop and implement treatment strategies, they may have to do so in a vacuum and in an artificial environment. There are frequently both problems translating what is learned in treatment in the institution to the offender's normal environment and failure to continue needed treatment when the offender returns to the community. (Faller 1993, 64)

Integrated Models

Finkelhor suggests that four conditions must be met for sexual abuse to occur. These conditions include factors relating to the offender's motivation to abuse a child sexually, factors leading the offender to overcome internal inhibitions to sexual abuse, factors leading the offender to overcome external inhibitions, and factors leading the offender to believe that the child will provide little resistance to the abuse (Finkelhor 1986).

Faller suggests another model in which some causal factors are prerequisites for the occurrence of sexual abuse. Additional factors also play a contributing role. Prerequisite factors are being sexually aroused by children and a propensity to act on this arousal. Contributing factors can come from the family system, the culture, and the offender's current life situation, his personality, or previous experiences (Faller 1993).

Effects

Children are affected in many ways by sexual abuse. The type and severity of effects often depend on a variety of factors, including the age of the child when the abuse first occurred, how long the experience lasted, the development status of the child, the relationship of the abuser to the child, whether or not force was used to assure the child's participation and the degree of force used, the degree of shame or guilt experienced by the child, and the reaction of the child's parent(s) and other professionals if and when the child reveals the abuse or it is discovered by another person. Children who have been sexually abused may display negative behaviors and attitudes, but studies have not clarified whether these behaviors existed before the sexual abuse occurred, whether they were the effects of the abuse, or effects of the intervention process.

Hollenberg and Ragan believe it is difficult to generalize the effects of sexual abuse on all children:

> Just as no single profile of child sexual abuse exists, there is no definitive description of the impact of sexual abuse on child victims. The effects of child sexual abuse are characterized by great variation and range from short-term effects to those that endure throughout adulthood. Many of the symptoms associated with child sexual abuse victimization—such as low self-esteem, anxiety, hostility, depression, hyperactivity, and psychosomatic disturbances—are common to a range of other problems as well. Much remains to be learned about the mediating variables that influence a child's reaction to sexual abuse. Several mediating factors, such as the use of force as a component of abuse and a lack of support from a nonoffending parent, have been associated with increased maladjustment of the child and warrant further research in the future. (Hollenberg & Ragan 1991, 179)

In considering the effects of child sexual abuse, Faller believes that "it is important for professionals to appreciate both the incomplete state of knowledge about the consequences of sexual abuse and the variability in effects. Such information can be helpful in recognizing the wide variance in symptoms of sexual abuse and can prevent excessive optimism or pessimism in predicting its impact" (Faller 1993, 19).

Finkelhor divides the effects of child sexual abuse into four main categories: traumatic sexualization, stigmatization, betrayal, and powerlessness. Traumatic sexualization results from inappropriate sexual contacts and relationships; the effects that victims may experience include avoidance of sex, disgust of anything sexual, a consuming interest in sex, or problems with sexual identity. Stigmatization results as children realize that sexual abuse is socially and morally unacceptable behavior and believe they are responsible for the abuse or feel guilty because they have been abused. As a result, children may withdraw from friends and family members. Betrayal results when children realize that the adult they trusted has hurt them; children may have a difficult time trusting other adults after they have been abused. Feelings of powerlessness occur when children realize that they cannot stop the abuse or later, if and when they reveal the abuse and the intervention process begins and they are overwhelmed by all that is happening to them (Finkelhor 1984).

Several studies examine the duration of abuse as a factor. In a study of women who were sexually abused as children, Russell found that 73 percent of these women whose abuse lasted for more than five years considered the experience extremely or considerably traumatic compared with 62 percent whose abuse lasted from one week to five years, and 46 percent who were abused only once (Russell 1986). On the other hand, Finkelhor found no relationship between the seriousness of effects and the duration of the abuse (Finkelhor 1979). In other studies, such as one conducted by Christine Courtois, researchers found that those people who had been sexually abused for the longest duration felt the least amount of trauma from the experience (Courtois 1979).

After a child has been sexually abused, over time by a parent or other trusted adult, his or her development will be affected by at least four factors, including self-image or how the child feels about himself or herself, how the child sees himself or herself in relation to other people, how the child perceives his or her own needs and desires, and how the child sees and reacts to his or her own sexual feelings (Breslin 1990).

Often after being sexually abused, a child's self-image develops largely on that abuse experience; many children believe that they are dirty or bad and end up with low self-esteem. Children may learn to numb the feelings associated with the abuse experience, hoping to feel better about life and in the process increase levels of self-esteem. This coping strategy may help the child dim the experience but does nothing to enhance his or her feelings of self.

Second, a sexually abused child, because of this experience, loses trust in adults and other people in authority who are supposed to be nurturing and protective. Many times, abusers, especially family members, use shame or fear to keep the child from reporting the abuse to anyone who might be able to help. "This is our little secret," "Don't tell your mother, it would kill her," "You don't want anyone else to know what you are doing," and other similar comments are frequently made by abusers to ensure silence and obedience from the child. Abused children may feel a great deal of fear within this relationship, with a powerful adult making the rules; the child may be so scared and ashamed about what is happening that he or she may be too embarrassed to reveal the abuse to anyone. Silence is thus ensured. When the abuser offers comfort after the abuse, maybe by providing special privileges or gifts to the child, confusion is normal and the child may feel guilty for what is happening.

Third, sexually abused children may suppress their own needs and wants, believing they are secondary to the needs of the adult or that they do not deserve anything, that their main purpose in life right now is to please the adult and fulfill his or her needs. The basic needs of all children to feel safe, secure, loved, and protected by their parents is not fulfilled for abused children. Therefore, they try to please everyone else, without realizing that they are important and have their own needs and desires that should be fulfilled.

Fourth, children normally become socialized and learn about sex with their peer group. They grow up together. However, sexually abused children learn about sex and their sexuality from an adult; it is defined by the adult, with adult terms and expectations. Confusion about sexuality and relationships occurs because the child sees relationships defined on the basis of sex, that is, the relationship does not exist without sex (Breslin 1990).

The effects of sexual abuse may be long-lasting and devastating to victims even as adults. For example, Dr. Richard Berendzen, former president of the American University in Washington, D.C., was physically and sexually abused by his mother and thought he had controlled the effects of this abuse. He studied hard and worked hard and believed that he had overcome its effects, until he went home for his father's funeral and relived some of the abuse. He started calling day-care centers pretending to have a child needing day care, and asked several questions about sexual abuse; the calls were traced to his office and he was forced to resign as president of the university. He sought treatment at the Sexual Disorders Clinic at Johns Hopkins Hospital in Baltimore and finally was able to understand what had happened to him and to do what he believed he needed to do to become a survivor (Berendzen & Palmer 1993). His experience clearly demonstrates that people who are sexually abused as children may suffer from long-lasting effects, even when they think they are fine and have outgrown the experience.

The effects of childhood sexual abuse can be extensive:

> The parental images that children internalize can be more destructive than their personal parents. Parents are the very light and ground of a child's being. The father and mother principle—metaphorically, the sun and the earth—become the inner parents and can, especially in abused children, be experienced as negative. This results in a terribly destructive pattern that is usually more dangerous than the personal parents ever were. It's as if the molest [sic] continues from within. When the "inner child" hurts and feels no good, the negative father image (now the inner molester, in this example) responds, "You are worthless." The mother image whispers, "You are not loved; you are not safe." (Peterson 1989, 2)

Judith Herman found in her study of father-daughter incest that women often directed their anger at other women:

> Whatever anger these women did feel was most commonly directed at women rather than at men. With the exception of those who had become conscious feminists, most of the incest victims seemed to regard all women, including themselves, with contempt. At times, remembering their privileged position as their fathers' favorites, they exempted themselves from their general condemnation of women. In adult life, their only possible source of self-esteem was to maintain an

identification with their powerful fathers. But more often, on a deeper level, they identified with the mothers they despised, and included themselves among the ranks of fallen and worthless women. (Herman 1981, 103)

Herman describes how this anger toward other women prevents the victims from developing supportive relationships with other women, something that many women longed for but could not achieve because they were unable to conquer their anger enough to understand and overcome it.

The effects of sexual abuse on boys may be different in some ways than on girls. For example, Mike Lew believes

our society's response to the sexual abuse of boys and the aftermath of that abuse reflects how we define maleness. Not only does our perception of men (and of victimization) set a context for abuse, it provides a backdrop for our perception of the male survivor. To understand the context in which abuse, survival, healing, and recovery take place, we must examine a number of our cultural beliefs. (Lew 1988, 33)

He goes on to say

Since men "are not supposed to be victims," abuse (and particularly sexual abuse) becomes a process of demasculinization (or emasculation). If men aren't to be victims (the equation reads), then victims aren't men. The victimized male wonders and worries about what the abuse has turned him into. Believing that he is no longer an adequate man, he may see himself as a child, a woman, gay, or less than human—an irreparably damaged freak. (Lew 1988, 41)

Because of these feelings, a man who has been sexually abused as a child may feel a need to prove to himself that he is a man, searching for wealth, recognition, and power.

Some adults who have been sexually abused as children seek help for some of their problems. Often these problems may be related to the sexual abuse although they are not aware of the connection. They may have entered therapy in order to get help with depression, eating disorders, substance abuse, or other problems, not realizing that their early experiences of sexual abuse could be the source of these problems. Several problem areas for sexual abuse victims are discussed below.

Post-Traumatic Stress Disorder

The *Diagnostic and Statistical Manual of Mental Disorders (III-R)* gives the following definition of post-traumatic stress disorder:

> The essential feature of this disorder is the development of characteristic symptoms following a psychologically distressing event that is outside the range of usual human experience (i.e., outside the range of such common experiences as simple bereavement, chronic illness, business losses, and marital conflict). The stressor producing this syndrome would be markedly distressing to almost anyone, and is usually experienced with intense fear, terror, and helplessness. The characteristic symptoms involve reexperiencing the traumatic event, avoidance of stimuli associated with the event or numbing of general responsiveness, and increased arousal. The diagnosis is not made if the disturbance lasts less than one month. (APA 1987, 247)

People who have been sexually abused as children may push aside the memory of the event; however, at some point they may relive the event, and often experience intense emotional distress as a result. The feelings experienced are similar to those felt by Vietnam veterans; both have complied with what others expected of them and both were informed by others that what they were doing was right.

Sexual Disorders

Adults who have been sexually abused as children may exhibit sexual acting out or promiscuous behavior. They may be trying to overcome feelings of powerlessness they experienced as children or they may be confused over the boundaries of behavior that define affection, sex, and abuse. Jon Briere and Karen Meiselman, in separate studies, examined a control group and a group who had been sexually abused as children, and found that adults sexually abused as children were more likely than the control group to experience sexual problems as adults (Briere 1984; Meiselman 1978).

Eating Disorders

Vernon Wiehe found that several respondents in his study on sibling abuse suffered from eating disorders, including bulimia and anorexia (Wiehe 1990). Many victims of sexual abuse are concerned about their physical appearance. Some may lose weight, while others may gain weight to make sure that no one is attracted to them.

Substance Abuse

Many studies have established a link between sexual abuse and alcohol and/or drug problems in later life. In Wiehe's study of sibling abuse, he found 25 percent of respondents admitted having a substance abuse problem with either alcohol or drugs (Wiehe 1990). In studying female drug abusers at a community treatment center, Jean Benward and Judianne Densen-Gerber interviewed 118 patients and found that 44 percent had been sexually abused as children. Forty-five percent of the abuse experiences occurred when the child was 9 years old or younger; seventy-three percent of the incidents occurred before the child reached her 13th birthday. Based on their results, Benward and Densen-Gerber speculated that those girls who submitted to the sexual encounter without putting up a fight were more likely to exhibit psychological problems, including substance abuse (Benward & Densen-Gerber 1975).

M. Singer, M. Petchers, and D. Hussey found that adolescents who had been sexually abused as children had significantly different patterns of drug use and abuse. These patterns included the regular use of cocaine and stimulants, frequent drinking and drug use, and being high on drugs more often than those who had not been sexually abused. Their findings suggest that people who have been sexually abused as children may use mood-altering substances to help them deal with their emotional difficulties and help in their interpersonal relationships (Singer, Petchers & Hussey 1989).

Depression

Adults who have been sexually abused as children may also exhibit more serious bouts of depression than other people. Briere and Marsha Runtz, in studying a nonclinical sample of 278 university women, found that 15 percent had been sexually abused before the age of 15 and that these women exhibited more depressive symptoms than women who had not been sexually abused (Briere & Runtz 1988).

In Wiehe's study of sibling abuse, he found that 26 percent of his respondents had been hospitalized for depression and 33 percent had attempted suicide (Wiehe 1990). Other studies have also found rates for depression and attempted suicide higher for those people who were sexually abused as children than for those who were not abused. Mary DeYoung found that 68 percent of the women she studied who had been sexually abused as children had attempted suicide and half of those had tried more than once (DeYoung 1982).

Indicators of Childhood Sexual Abuse

Most professionals differentiate between physical indicators and psychosocial indicators of child sexual abuse. Physical indicators usually are determined by a medical professional. In the past several years, medical professionals have gained increased experience in recognizing the signs of child sexual abuse. However, in a discussion of medical indicators, the reader should keep in mind that in most cases of child sexual abuse, no medical evidence of the abuse exists. When physical indicators are present, the ones that most likely indicate sexual abuse include pregnancy and venereal disease. Other indicators include semen in the vagina of a child, a torn hymen, vaginal injury, an injury to the penis or scrotum, labial adhesions, vulvovaginitis, chronic urinary tract infections, anal bruising, or pharyngeal gonorrhea as a result of oral sex.

Sexual-psychosocial indicators include statements from children about sexual matters that a child of that age would not likely know, sexually explicit drawings or comments, sexual aggression when playing with other children, suggestions of sex with adults, and in some cases, masturbation. Children often experiment with masturbation as they are growing, but if children masturbate many times each day, cannot stop, or insert various objects into their vagina or anus, these may be signs that they have been sexually abused. Some nonsexual psychosocial indicators of sexual abuse include sleep disturbances, bedwetting, regressive behavior, fear of certain people, fear of being left alone, cruelty to animals, eating disturbances, depression, or social withdrawal. These symptoms may also be indicators of other problems in the family, so professionals must be extremely careful when diagnosing cases of sexual abuse based solely on any of these nonphysical indicators.

False Allegations of Sexual Abuse

False accusations of child sexual abuse have gained notice in recent years, most often in custody cases following divorces. As Richard Gardner says, "the use of the sex abuse accusation [is] a powerful weapon for wreaking vengeance on a hated spouse as well as obtaining court support for quick exclusion (and even incarceration) of a partner" (Gardner 1991, 1). Gardner is also convinced that most allegations of child sexual abuse in day-care and nursery school settings are false.

A study conducted by the Association of Family and Conciliation Courts (AFCC) reviewed 9,000 disputes over custody and visitation and found 169 allegations of sexual abuse. Of these allegations, investigators determined that sexual abuse had occurred in 50 percent of these cases, did not occur in 27 percent, and the existence of sexual abuse could not be determined in the other 23 percent (AFCC 1988). In another study conducted in Denver, Colorado, researchers evaluated cases of disputed custody that involved allegations of child sexual abuse and found that the accusations were justified in approximately 50 percent of the cases (Kopetsky 1991).

Gordon Blush and Karol Ross suggest that sexual abuse allegations should be examined within the context of the family situation. Allegations of sexual abuse in cases in which the parents are considering divorce or are divorced are less likely to be proven true than allegations in other situations. Red flags that should indicate to evaluators the possibility of false allegations include evidence of a pending separation or divorce, divorce proceedings in process, currently unsuccessful divorce proceedings in process, unresolved visitation or custody issues, unresolved financial issues in a divorce proceeding, and parental involvement in relationships with others (Blush & Ross 1986).

Intervention/Treatment

One of the major concerns in the ways that we intervene in cases of childhood sexual abuse is the damage that may be done to the child in the process of trying to help him or her. Accused parents may try to blame the child or may focus on how this allegation has destroyed the family. Social and legal responses may pull the child from the home, frighten the child with medical examinations, court appearances, and endless interviews with strangers who want to know in detail exactly what happened to the child. Kee MacFarlane believes that

> [a]lthough society reacts with predictable horror at what is done to children by sex offenders, it apparently does not share a similar concern for what subsequently may happen to children in the hands of our intervention system. Whether a child has been sexually assaulted by a stranger, an acquaintance, or a family member, when the incident is disclosed, the family is usually experiencing extreme crisis as it works through feelings of anger, fear, shock, and confusion. During this vulnerable period, the criminal justice, health, and social service systems may descend upon a child and family with such a devastating impact that recipients are left with the feeling that the "cure" is far worse than the original problem. Many authorities agree that the emotional damage resulting from the intervention of "helping agents" in our society may equal, or far exceed, the harm caused by the abusive incident. (MacFarlane 1978, 81)

Many things can happen to a child and his or her family when sexual abuse is believed to have occurred, especially if the offender is a family member. The child may be removed from the home, the perpetrator may be arrested and jailed, the child may be placed in foster care, the family's economic security may be in jeopardy if the father is the offender and he is jailed, the child may feel guilty and responsible for breaking up the family, and the family members may feel embarrassed and ridiculed by former friends and neighbors.

Faller suggests several practices that may reduce the trauma of the initial investigation to the child:

> The interview process can be made less problematic. First, the number of interviews can be minimized, either by videotaping investigative interviews, having professionals who need to hear the child's account behind a one-way mirror, or having more than one

professional in the room, usually with one asking the questions. Second, the use of a skilled and sensitive interviewer can minimize the negative effect of disclosure and even make it a cathartic or empowering experience. Third, allowing a support person to be with the child during part or all of the interview can diminish its traumatic impact. Fourth, conducting the interview in a facility that is private and designed to create comfort can be helpful. The potentially iatrogenic effects of the medical exam can be decreased by obtaining the child's consent to the exam and by using a skilled and sensitive health professional. That person explains that the purpose of the exam is to ensure that the child is "ok," usually does a complete physical, not just a genital exam, and both informs the child, at each step of the exam, what will happen next and allows the child some control over the process. If the child is resistant to the exam, even when properly undertaken, then serious consideration should be given to not doing it. If it is deemed medically necessary, it might be rescheduled, when the child is less upset, or it might be done under anesthesia. (Faller 1993, 7)

In research for the National Center on Child Abuse and Neglect, Lucy Berliner and Jon Conte studied the effects of disclosure and intervention on children who have been sexually abused. They found that these children did not associate the process of intervention with any negative feelings or impacts. The idea that removing a child from the home after sexual abuse has occurred causes more stress than the abuse itself was not supported in their findings. Berliner and Conte did discover, however, that children were less anxious when their parents and the professionals they were interacting with were honest about what was happening and what would happen to them; children who were shielded from this knowledge were more anxious. Children were also capable of understanding the need for intervention, yet the level of the children's anxiety increased as the number of professionals with whom they were required to interact increased. The researchers concluded that professionals working with sexually abused children must consider each child individually, not rely on parents for accurate reports of the child's anxiety levels. They also found that the experience of testifying in court is not necessarily traumatic to the child (Berliner & Conte 1990).

In assessing the sexually abused child and determining the appropriate treatment, Sgroi considers ten important issues that may have an impact on the decision to provide specific services and treatment for the child: the "damaged goods" syndrome, guilt, fear, depression, low self-esteem and poor social skills, repressed anger and hostility, inability to trust, blurred role boundaries and role confusion, pseudomaturity, and self-mastery and control (Sgroi 1988).

Reporting

Reporting child sexual abuse to the authorities can be frightening, threatening the emotional and financial security of the family. Many reasons to report sexual abuse exist, although many parents who reported abusive situations can also provide several reasons for not reporting the abuse. Reasons for reporting include the following:

- The child may feel relieved that someone else knows about the abuse and he or she is reassured by contact with the authorities.
- The abuse will stop.
- The offender will not abuse other children.
- Most cases do not go to trial; they are settled out of court, so the family often does not have to worry about the child having to testify in court.
- Children's sense of justice and right can be affirmed.
- Crime victims' compensation, which is financial assistance provided to victims of crime, is available only to those people who report the crime to law enforcement agencies.

The many reasons that people may have for not reporting sexual abuse include the following:

- Family members think they can confront the abuser themselves and stop the abuse.
- Family members may be afraid that the offender will be sent to jail, threatening the financial security of the family.
- The police cannot be trusted.
- Family members may be afraid that they are accusing the wrong person.

- The family will be embarrassed and possibly threatened by other family members, friends, neighbors, and society.
- The child may have to go through too much trauma.
- Family members do not want to "ruin the lives" or reputation of another family (if the abuse has been committed by a nonfamily member).

Investigation

Child Protective Services (CPS) personnel are the local authorities in the investigation of child sexual abuse. Both federal and state legislation mandate the CPS to protect children and investigate cases of sexual abuse. CPS personnel are involved in cases in which the sexual abuse is perpetrated by a family member. When the offender is not in a caretaking role, then law enforcement personnel often are responsible for investigating the case, although CPS may also be involved in these investigations.

Most states mandate health care, mental health, and education professionals to report all suspected cases of child sexual abuse; others, such as day-care providers or church officials, may be required to report in some states. Once CPS receives a report, they are required to investigate the allegations within a specified period of time, usually between 24 hours and 5 days, depending on the state. Many states require that law enforcement personnel participate in the investigation with CPS personnel when sexual abuse is alleged, primarily in order to gather evidence in the event that offenders are prosecuted.

Treatment

A variety of treatment options exist for children who have been sexually abused and their families, including individual, group, marital, and family therapy, as well as crisis intervention services, day care, homemaker services, and foster care. Typically, child sexual abuse treatment programs offer a variety of services, which may include art and play therapy, marital counseling, psychological testing, individual and group therapy, parenting classes, substance abuse programs, court advocacy, and life skills courses. Multidisciplinary teams are being used in more and more cases to help develop comprehensive case management and treatment plans as well as to review progress in each case. These teams often are used when the child is the subject of a petition in juvenile court, although they are also used when there is a criminal proceeding and even when there are no criminal proceedings.

Faller reports on the importance of communication and multidisciplinary teams in the treatment of sexual abuse:

> The team meets periodically to assess progress and make future plans. Because of the complexity of case management decisions and the fact that a decision in one realm can have an impact on other aspects of the case, especially on treatment progress and outcome, multidisciplinary decision making is crucial. In the absence of a multidisciplinary team, such decisions should be made in consultation with other relevant professionals. (Faller 1993, 59)

Treatment goals in cases of child sexual abuse usually include reducing the crisis atmosphere that the family is experiencing; helping the family cope with the situation; helping family members control rage, hurt, and other emotions they are experiencing; helping family members accept the existence of the abuse so that they can enter and profit from treatment; and reducing the family's isolation from society.

One of the first model treatment programs, now known as the Child Sexual Abuse Treatment Program, was established in 1971 by Henry Giarretto in Santa Clara County, California. The Juvenile Probation Department (JPD) in Santa Clara was the reporting agency for all cases of child sexual abuse. The help that JPD provided to families was often fragmented, contributing to further trauma to the child and the family. Members of the JPD asked Giarretto, a marriage and family counselor, to help establish a pilot project to provide counseling to the children and their families. At the end of the eight-week pilot project period, all of the people involved recognized the benefits of this program and expanded it to include the coordination of services required by the family, such as financial advice and legal assistance, and to help facilitate the reunification of the family. This reunification of the family could take place only after individual counseling sessions were held to help each individual family member cope with and address the abuse and other dysfunctional aspects that may have contributed to the abuse. The program's focus is on healing and resocializing the family through the use of humanistic psychology.

In studying current treatment approaches and programs, Hollenberg and Ragan found that

[c]urrent research indicates that significant gaps exist in available treatment services in cases of child sexual abuse. Perhaps because child sexual abuse has been regarded primarily as the child's problem, most of the available treatment programs limit their focus to the child victim following an incident of sexual abuse. It is increasingly apparent, however, that sexual abuse is part of a cluster of serious intergenerational family problems that need to be addressed through family-oriented treatment. This is most apparent in regard to the importance of maternal support, which several studies have found to be a vital resource for the sexually abused child's recovery. Thus, mental health services that target a range of familial problems and help nonoffending parents support their sexually abused children may contribute positively to the children's recovery. (Hollenberg & Ragan 1991, 184–185)

Interviewing the Child

Several issues exist when interviewing the child who allegedly has been sexually abused, including where the interview should occur, when it should occur, who should be present, how information will be recorded and how many interviews may be required. Experts generally agree that the interview should take place in a location that the child believes is safe. In most states, the CPS worker conducts the interview; in some states law enforcement personnel are also present, while in other states law enforcement personnel spend their time interviewing the alleged offender. Interviews may be videotaped, audiotaped, or the interviewer may just take notes of what is said. Child Advocacy Centers (CACs), child-oriented facilities specifically organized to centralize the investigation of child sexual abuse, are located in many cities. Usually housed in old homes or other nonbusiness-like buildings to encourage the child to feel safe, the CACs attempt to provide a comfortable, safe environment in which CPS personnel and other professionals can interview the child and provide a variety of services to the child and his or her family.

Medical Examinations

Medical examination of a child may be performed for a number of reasons. The exam can reassure the child and his or her parents that the child is healthy and will not be permanently harmed physically by the abuse. As physicians see more cases of child sexual abuse they are able to recognize readily the physical signs, if any exist, and are therefore becoming more reliable in their diagnoses of sexual abuse. Also, children who have been forced to have sexual intercourse with an adult may be at high risk for any number of sexually transmitted diseases, including AIDS (acquired immunodeficiency syndrome), and the sooner these conditions are diagnosed, the sooner treatment can be started.

Social and Law Enforcement Services

Social services agencies play an important role in treating the child and the family in sexual abuse cases. Often children are not the only ones in need of support during this period. If the abuse has been perpetrated by another family member, either the child or the family member is generally removed from the home. If one parent is charged with sexual abuse, that parent may be jailed if the rest of the family decides to prosecute, or he or she may have left the home; in any case, the family may now be without his or her financial support and in need of some type of help until the situation is resolved. Emergency housing may be needed to remove the child and other family members from the home and they may also need food, medical, or other types of support during the crisis. Social service agencies can help families find needed shelter, financial support, and other types of help.

Law enforcement agencies are required to ensure that the victim is safe from further abuse and the offender is prevented from harming others. They are also involved if family members decide to press charges against the offender. Law enforcement personnel may also participate in multidisciplinary teams to help in case management.

The Use of Anatomically Correct Dolls

Anatomically correct dolls are usually cloth dolls with certain body features (fingers, mouths, penises, vaginal openings, anal openings, and pubic hair) that allow children to demonstrate any sexual activities in which they were involved. They were introduced in the late 1970s and have become more popular in recent years.

The use of anatomically correct dolls is one means of assessing the extent and nature of the alleged sexual abuse. Some professionals are adamant about the reliability and validity of using these dolls, while other experts believe that their use does not yield reliable results. Proponents believe that the dolls help the children recall details of the sexual abuse and provide a means of expressing what happened to them by allowing them to show the abuse rather than trying to verbalize the experience. On the other hand, some professionals argue that the dolls may suggest possibilities to children that lead to false allegations of sexual abuse, may encourage sexual exploration without actually validating previous abuse, may encourage children to fantasize about events, and may be too suggestive for young children to understand.

In a study comparing abused and nonabused children and their actions in playing with anatomically correct dolls, L. Jampole and M. K. Weber found that those children who were sexually abused were more likely than the nonabused children to involve the dolls in sexual activities; only 2 nonabused children out of 10 engaged the dolls in sexual play (Jampole & Weber 1987). In another study, D. Glaser and C. Collins found that children used the dolls in 78 percent of their play activities and only 2 out of the 86 nonabused children incorporated sexual activities in their play with the dolls (Glaser & Collins 1989). Other studies have shown similar results; some report that none of their nonabused children involved the dolls in any type of sexual activity (Sivan et al. 1988; August & Foreman 1988). While these studies indicate that only children who have been sexually abused are likely to have the dolls engage in sexual activities, some studies do indicate that nonabused children will sometimes engage in sexual doll play.

Even if the dolls themselves are not suggestive, some researchers argue that therapists and other professionals can use them in suggestive ways, depending on how they are introduced to the child and what types of questions are asked. Cathy Mann suggests that training should be provided to all professionals involved in using these dolls to treat children who have been sexually abused (Maan 1994). Maan reports that the American Professional Society on the Abuse of Children has developed preliminary guidelines on ways to use these dolls in investigating cases of sexual abuse of children. She cites five uses that the organization views as acceptable:

1. As an icebreaker to help initiate discussions with children about sexual matters.
2. As anatomical models (for example, to assess children's knowledge of bodily functions).

3. To help children demonstrate rather than describe their experiences. This is especially important if the children's verbal skills are limited or if they are too embarrassed to describe their experiences.
4. As a stimulus for children's memories. (For example, features of the dolls such as pubic hair or genitalia may help sexually abused children remember the details of the abuse.)
5. As a screen. Exposure to the dolls represents an opportunity for children to spontaneously disclose aspects of their sexual abuse. (Maan 1994, 3)

Some sexual abuse investigators find the use of dollhouses beneficial, especially with preschoolers. Faller describes the best dollhouses:

Larger dollhouses, with sturdy furniture and people 3 to 6 inches tall, are optimal. The bigger the people, the easier it will be for the child to show activities and for the interviewer to see them. Most dollhouse people do not have removable clothing, which makes it difficult for the child to demonstrate some sexual abuse. However, the dollhouse provides a better opportunity to address the issue of the context of the sexual abuse than most other media.

Like drawings, dollhouse play can have goals other than data gathering about possible sexual abuse. For example, dollhouse play can be used to get to know the child and to understand something about how the child generally perceives families and family activity. And again like drawings, the dollhouse can be used indirectly and directly to gather information about possible sexual abuse. (Faller 1993, 52)

Interviewing the Mother

If the child has been sexually abused by the father or stepfather, interviewing the mother is critically important in determining her ability to support the child. As Faller states:

A major purpose of the initial interview with the mother is to assess her ability to provide support for the child. Mothers whose children have been sexually victimized by someone who is close to them, such as a spouse, are placed in a very difficult position. Often they have no inkling of the abuse until confronted by a professional. Mothers who are consciously aware of the victimization and condone or accept it are extremely rare. However, some mothers ignore signs of sexual abuse, for a variety of reasons, or are preoccupied with matters other than their children's well-being.

. . . initial denial is common. . . . Mothers should not be disparaged because they require time and sometimes treatment to believe their children have been sexually abused. Only when denial persists for months in the face of compelling evidence, and the victim is blamed, should the mother be considered unworkable. (Faller 1993, 34)

Kempe and Kempe also believe that the mother should be helped to recognize and understand her own emotions and feelings. They observe that "the mother often feels criticized and pressured by both professionals and friends to divorce her husband in order to appear to be a good mother" (Kempe & Kempe 1984, 148). Mothers should be encouraged to take their time, to try to sort out and understand everything that is happening to them, and to determine what is in their own best interest as well as the child's best interest.

Information to be gathered from the mother includes past history of abuse or neglect, past history of sexual abuse, current living situation, education level, employment history, parenting skills, style of discipline, relationship with spouse or partner, sexual history, history of substance abuse or mental illness, criminal history, and beliefs about the allegations of sexual abuse of the child. This same information should be gathered from the offender.

Recidivism

Arguments have been made for incarcerating the perpetrator for the remainder of his or her life, believing that there is no successful means of treating people who sexually abuse children. Other experts believe that at least some perpetrators can be saved, that is, they can be successfully treated.

The primary issue in treating sexual offenders is whether or not they can be treated and safely released back into society. Little research has been conducted on this topic; many of these focus on offenders being caught and convicted a second or third time. Because the focus is on being convicted again, many experts believe that the studies do not adequately measure the reoccurrence of sexual abuse; most sexual abuse of children is not reported and does not come to the attention of the proper authorities. Also, many offenders, especially family members, are never convicted and sent to prison, which makes studying them extremely difficult.

Finkelhor also questions the generalizability of results obtained from criminal justice system subjects:

> A major problem with research on sexual abusers has to do with the fact that almost all such research is based on subjects recruited from the criminal justice system, either incarcerated offenders or probationers in treatment. This fact certainly casts doubt on the generalizability of almost all known findings about sexual abusers. Incarcerated offenders or probationers in treatment constitute at most a very tiny and unrepresentative fraction of all sexual abusers. . . . Thus those sex abusers who are convicted or even seen within the criminal justice system are a small fraction of all offenders, and probably those who were most flagrant and repetitive in their offending, most socially disadvantaged, and least able to persuade criminal justice authorities to let them off. It seems virtually certain that such a group cannot be deemed representative of offenders. (Finkelhor 1986, 138)

Several studies found that men who sexually abused boys or were exhibitionists were more likely to repeat their offenses than those who sexually abused girls (Frisbee & Dondis 1965). Other researchers also have found that those who sexually abuse boys often start the abuse earlier and are more committed to their pedophilia as a lifestyle (Quinsey 1985; Groth 1979). In 1980, Meyer and Romero discovered that only two factors predicted recidivism: a prior arrest for a sex offense and a history of indecent exposure (Meyer & Romero 1980).

Brian Abbott studied the reoffense rates of incest offenders eight years after treatment. He studied 72 offenders who were accepted into the Child Sexual Abuse Treatment Program (CSATP) in San Jose, California; these offenders had a parent-child type relationship with the abused children (father, stepfather, adoptive father, uncle, grandfather, etc.), a bond of trust had existed between the child and the offender, and the offender did not show any evidence of a primary sexual attraction to children. The offenders were treated in the CSATP; twenty-six completed the program, 20 were discharged due to lack of progress, and 26 left the program prematurely. Recidivism rates were studied over an eight-year period. The reoffense rate for the overall sample was 5.5 percent. All reoffenders came from the group who were discharged from the program for lack of progress. Abbott concludes:

> These findings indicate that treating the incest offender in the community in conjunction with a county jail sentence and probation supervision does not significantly jeopardize community safety and, in fact, the offender is less likely to re-offend than if committed to state prison, with or without treatment. This finding is of importance in light of the fact that it is much more cost-effective to treat the offender in the community rather than committing him to state prison either with or without treatment. (Abbott 1991, 27–28)

In another study, researchers found that 19 percent of those abusers who sexually abused their own children, compared with 29 percent of abusers who abused other children, were recidivists—they continued to abuse children after they were initially caught (Smith et al. 1985).

Confronting the Abuser

For people who admit, as adults, that they were abused as children, and for people who recover repressed memories of abuse as children, some therapists believe that healing from these experiences can occur only if they confront the abuser. However, confrontation is often a serious undertaking, to be considered very carefully and thoughtfully. Mike Lew suggests that for some people it could be a "logical next step in recovery; for others it could be a dangerous and self-destructive act" (Lew 1988, 228). He believes that confrontation means facing the abuse and standing up to it, not necessarily having a direct encounter with the abuser. "Confrontation is not the goal of recovery, it is a tool for recovery. Its value lies in how it is used. You deserve to take enough time to make the best decision for yourself. You can change your mind about the confrontation at any time during this process" (Lew 1988, 231).

Elizabeth Loftus discusses the fact that many people who have retrieved repressed memories of abuse with the help of therapists are then asked whether or not they want to confront the abuser with these memories:

> She can either continue with therapy, working to resolve her grief and rage in a private, noncombative way, or she can choose to stand up to the abuse (and stand up for herself) by confronting her abusers. The decision to confront is never promoted as easy or risk-free. Most incest-survival authors warn that confrontations should be considered only if and when the survivor is fully prepared and well along the road to recovery. (Loftus & Ketcham 1994, 171)

Most people who consider confronting their abusers are told to build up their support systems (of friends and relatives), to rehearse the meeting, and to analyze their reasons for wanting to confront the abuser. Once they face their abuser, they are often met with denial and outrage on the part of the accused. Lew suggests that the accuser remember that he or she is not required to provide proof or to convince the abuser and the rest of the family that the abuse actually did happen; the only purpose should be to free the person abused, in essence, to "take back your power, to prove to yourself that you will not be frightened or controlled any longer, and thus to guarantee that you will never be a victim again" (Lew 1988, 231).

The Legal System

The use of the legal system to protect children and prosecute offenders presents several complex issues. Many experts believe that children are often more traumatized by the court proceedings than by the initial sexual abuse. Court proceedings can be long and drawn out and quite frightening for a young child to experience. Being on the witness stand and enduring questions of a very personal nature are hard for anyone, especially a child. Some experts believe that children are better off not being involved in criminal proceedings, that is, not pressing charges, while other experts believe that in the long run the child benefits by the experience.

David Lloyd finds when children become victims of sexual abuse or other violence, they are forced into an adult criminal justice system that does not differentiate between children and adults. "Child victims of crime are specially handicapped. First, the criminal justice system distrusts them and puts special barriers in the path of prosecuting their claims to justice. Second, the criminal justice system seems indifferent to the legitimate special needs that arise from their participation" (Lloyd 1982, 51).

State statutes have improved over the years, with most now specifically defining prohibited acts involving sexual abuse of children. In the past, many laws prohibiting incest required evidence of sexual intercourse in order to obtain a conviction. Today, many of the laws define incest broadly and do not always require evidence of sexual intercourse.

State juvenile or family courts often specify the procedures necessary to place a child in emergency custody, to remove an alleged abuser from the home, to authorize the placement of the child in protective services or with other substitute caretakers, and to terminate parental rights. All states have reporting laws, and approximately one-half of them require that reports be made directly to a child protective services office, while the other half specify that either a child protective services office or law enforcement agency must receive the reports.

Laws concerning the sexual exploitation of children have been passed in all states, and in 1977 the U.S. Congress passed the Federal Protection of Children Against Sexual Exploitation Act, which has been amended several times since it first became law (see Chapter 4, pp. 178–187, for excerpts of this law).

In 1984 the U.S. Attorney General's Task Force on Family Violence issued its recommendations that would minimize the trauma to the victim of violence while still protecting the rights of the accused. The recommendations included using the same prosecutor throughout the court process, allowing hearsay evidence at preliminary hearings to minimize the number of times the victim was required to testify, allowing the child's testimony to be presented on videotape, using anatomically detailed dolls to describe abuse, appointing a special volunteer advocate for the child, legally presuming that children are competent witnesses, allowing flexible courtroom settings, controlling press coverage, and limiting court continuances of each case (U.S. Attorney General's Task Force on Family Violence 1984).

Many judges will not allow expert witnesses to testify in court in child sexual abuse hearings because the field of expertise in child sexual abuse is not clearly defined. As Crewdson says, "Where, they ask, does it [expertise] reside? With the police officer? The social worker? The psychologist? The family counselor? The sociologist? The professionals, who argue the same question among themselves, have yet to come up with an answer" (Crewdson 1988, 165).

Many communities recognize the importance of minimizing the trauma that a child encounters when he or she becomes involved in the legal process of dealing with being sexually abused. These communities have looked for innovative ways to minimize this trauma by coordinating multidisciplinary teams and services to minimize repeated interviews and other traumatic activities, coordinating civil and criminal court proceedings, and initiating policies, procedures, and projects to set up pretrial diversion programs for first-time offenders who show remorse and desire treatment.

Children as Witnesses

When children are required to testify in court, prosecutors must play an active role in preparing these children for the trial. Even though some jurisdictions have created special units to prosecute sex crimes and crimes against children, most prosecutors are not comfortable with children who are witnesses, they are not familiar with children's needs, and they are not trained in ways to deal with children (NCCAN 1991). In most instances, child sexual abuse cases do not come to trial; they are resolved by plea bargains often because prosecutors do not want to risk losing a case based on the testimony of a child and would rather attempt a plea bargain.

Over half of the states presume that children are competent to testify in court proceedings. Based on the 1990 Federal Victims of Child Abuse Act, competency hearings in federal courts can be held only after a written motion and demonstration of compelling need. Young children are generally capable of testifying in court, depending on their own developmental status, stress level, language ability, and socioeconomic factors. While some attorneys and other experts believe that children are highly suggestible, most research indicates that this is not the case when they are asked to remember something of critical importance in their lives. Some defense attorneys may suggest that children have been coached or brainwashed into suggesting that they have been abused; other defense attorneys may suggest that the children must be mentally ill for allowing someone to abuse them or that they suffer from hallucinations and believe the abuse really happened when in fact it did not.

Another concern for those in the legal profession is recantation of allegations by child witnesses. Some children may become so scared at the intensity and length of the entire legal process or may be under such great pressure from family members that they may recant their charges in order to relieve the stress they feel.

In criminal cases of sexual abuse of children, basic conflicts exist between the rights of the accused offender and the rights and needs of the child who was allegedly abused. For example, in adult criminal cases, the accused has the right to face the accuser, to confront and cross-examine witnesses, and to receive a public trial. When children are involved, the issue of face-to-face confrontation is especially critical. Many experts believe that requiring a child to face the adult who has sexually abused him or her in court is too traumatic for many children to handle. This adult, a person of authority, may intimidate the child enough to make the child unwilling or unable to testify against him. Therefore, many courts have allowed children to have their testimony videotaped so that he does not have to face his abuser. In 1990, the U.S. Supreme Court ruled in *Maryland* v. *Craig* (1990) that a Maryland law allowing children to testify via a closed-circuit television outside of the courtroom with only the prosecutor and defense attorney present did not violate the defendant's right of confronting the accuser.

The reliability of children as witnesses is also questioned. Can they accurately remember what happened to them? Do they remember details? Often the child's testimony may provide the only evidence of sexual abuse—most abusers do not abuse children in front of witnesses, and often there is no physical evidence of the abuse. Some experts believe that children often have a difficult time distinguishing fact from reality, while others believe that children are unlikely to disclose facts about sexual abuse if they have not been sexually abused, that they rarely lie about abuse.

Several studies have also shown that children are highly resistant to accepting misinformation about events that concern their personal safety and well-being. Gail Goodman and colleagues found that children as young as four years old were able to provide accurate accounts of events as long as these events had some significance to them. The children rarely recalled wrong information and resisted accepting misinformation as fact. Children were more likely to leave out information than to provide incorrect information (Goodman et al. 1990). In another study, Goodman and colleagues examined children's memories of stressful events. They hypothesized that while, over time, children would retain less information about an event, those children who were highly stressed would retain more information than the less-stressed children and would resist attempts at misinformation. They found that children who were most stressed were the most resistant to misinformation and recalled more details than less-stressed children. While the amount of information the children recalled decreased after one year, the amount of incorrect information did not increase during this same period (Goodman et al. 1991).

Because of the increasing number of child sexual abuse reports, more and more children are being required to testify in court proceedings against their abusers. The ability of jurors to assess the reliability of children's allegations of child sexual abuse is critical in determining the guilt or innocence of the alleged abuser. Hollenberg and Ragan found that age is sometimes a factor:

> Past research on children's testimony suggests that jurors may judge a child's credibility based on the child's age rather than on the actual accuracy of the child's testimony. Bottoms and colleagues hypothesized that such age-related judgments may be reversed in cases of child sexual abuse, such that increases in child witness' age become a liability rather than an asset. This hypothesis rests on the idea that when sexual abuse allegations are made, the less sexual knowledge the witness has, the more credible the witness will appear. Therefore, a young child witness, who is assumed to have limited sexual knowledge, would be judged as more credible than an older witness. (Hollenberg & Ragan 1991, 127)

After reviewing three studies on the effects on children of testifying in cases of sexual abuse Debra Whitcomb and her colleagues found inconclusive evidence of harm or benefit:

> Based on the results of these studies, it cannot be stated conclusively that testifying is either harmful or beneficial to sexually abused children. . . . Virtually all

of the children improved emotionally, regardless of their experiences in court. At worst, testifying may impede the improvement process for some children . . . at best, it may enhance their recovery. . . . Only a small number of children appeared to suffer long-term trauma from the experience of testifying. (Whitcomb et al. 1994, 5)

Use of Expert Witnesses

In recent years, both the prosecution and defense have been increasing the use of expert witnesses in court proceedings. Many researchers believe this trend is disturbing, including Debra Whitcomb:

This trend is disturbing for several reasons:

- Child sexual abuse is a relatively new and inexact field of study. Much remains unknown, and there are many areas of controversy.
- The majority of behavioral scientists who testify as experts in these cases are not certified as forensic specialists in their respective disciplines (which include psychiatry, psychology, social work, counseling, and to a lesser extent, pediatrics). They may have little knowledge of the very circumscribed role expert testimony should play in most criminal cases.
- A small number of behavioral scientists have become, in effect, professional experts who "ride circuit" around the country to testify in well-financed cases. This practice is detrimental both to the legal professional and to the mental health professions.
- The absence of consensus among behavioral scientists about many of the issues surrounding child sexual abuse and children's testimony . . . paves the way for "battles of the experts" which tend to obscure, rather than clarify, the fact-finding process. (Whitcomb 1992, 111)

The presence of expert witnesses can have a serious impact on the level of stress the child experiences. For example, opposing experts may be called upon to conduct a psychological or physical examination of the child, adding to the child's confusion and stress. The majority of courts do agree on one subject—that prosecution witnesses almost universally are not allowed to express any direct opinions about the credibility of specific children as witnesses. However, many defense attorneys will suggest that children's testimony is not reliable because of improper questioning techniques, that children are unable to distinguish between fantasy and reality, and that they are unable to distinguish between truth and lies.

Child Advocate Programs

Community-based victim assistance and advocacy programs can be found throughout the United States. These programs offer a variety of services, such as referrals for counseling services; notification of court dates, investigation status, and case dispositions; provision of relevant information; accompaniment of child and family to court proceedings; assistance with transportation and family support; and emotional support.

In juvenile court hearings, child victims of abuse have a guardian ad litem (GAL) appointed by the court to represent their best interests. The Child Abuse Prevention and Treatment Act of 1974 requires that a GAL be appointed in states that want to receive federal funds. Guardians ad litem usually play a larger role than child victim advocates. States vary in what they allow the GALs to do: their roles may include attending all depositions, hearings, and trial proceedings; recommending to the court measures to ensure the child's welfare; possessing all reports, evaluations, and records to advocate effectively for the child; and coordinating resource delivery and special services the child may require.

Prevention

While many professionals believe that prevention is an important part of reducing the incidence of child sexual abuse, effective means of prevention are still being sought. Teaching children that they have a right to control access to their bodies, how to distinguish "good" from "bad" touches, not to keep secrets about bad touches, how to say no to someone, and that it is important to tell someone about the abuse are important in protecting children, but the effectiveness of this approach is still undetermined. Children who are sexually abused are often placed in situations in which they are afraid of the abuser, are threatened with harm, fear breaking up the family, have no one to trust, or may indeed tell the other parent but find him or her unconvinced. Many children are embarrassed and therefore unable to tell anyone. Although teaching children to tell someone about the abuse may not be the most effective way of preventing sexual abuse, until professionals are able to determine what makes a person sexually abuse a child and how to find and help that person before abuse occurs, it may be the most effective means of at least lowering the number of children sexually abused.

Prevention efforts have grown in popularity since the late 1970s. Activities can be grouped into four main categories: public awareness activities, provision of materials to parents to teach their children about sexual abuse, education for professionals, and prevention education programs for all children. Several national organizations, such as the National Center on Child Abuse and Neglect, the American Medical Association, the National Education Association, the National Committee to Prevent Child Abuse, and the Committee for Children, have all developed sexual abuse prevention resources for parents to help in talking with their children about sexual abuse. The U.S. Congress appropriated $25 million for the states to use for sexual abuse prevention training for parents, state child-care licensing personnel, and providers of day care. The U.S. Department of Health and Human Services developed the Model Child Care Standards Act—Guidance to States to Prevent Child Abuse in Day Care Facilities in 1985 to help develop ways of screening day-care workers. The National Committee for the Prevention of Child Abuse encourages the development of quality sexual abuse prevention programs by publishing guidelines for local projects to use in developing such programs.

Parental Education Programs

Many people believe that providing prevention education for parents is the most effective means of reaching the children. Parents can reinforce information contained in education materials better than any other group. However, many parents have a difficult time talking with their children about sex and may also have trouble talking about sexual abuse. Finkelhor studied 521 parents of children between the ages of 6 and 14 in the Boston metropolitan area. He found that only 29 percent of the parents discussed sexual abuse with their children; and when these discussions did occur, only 22 percent mentioned the possibility of abuse by a family member and only 65 percent discussed the possibility of someone asking the child to take off his or her clothes. Most parental discussions with children occurred when the child was approximately nine years old; many studies have shown that at least one-third of all child sexual abuse occurs before the child reaches age nine and therefore these parental discussions may have occurred too late to prevent abuse (Finkelhor 1982). Also, if either parent is the one abusing the child, then he or she is not likely to agree to teach the child about sexual abuse.

Prevention Programs for Professionals

Teachers, pediatricians, day-care workers, clergy, police, and other professionals who come in frequent contact with children also must be trained in ways to identify the sexually abused child as well as in ways to prevent this abuse. Finkelhor and Araji have recommended several objectives for setting up professional training programs:

1. Professionals must be able to communicate, in ways children can understand, any information about the nature and dynamics of sexual abuse.
2. They must be taught to identify children who have been or are being sexually abused or who are at high risk for being abused.
3. They must be able to question a child about the possibility of abuse with sensitivity and understanding.
4. They must know how to react when a child divulges that he or she has been sexually abused without showing alarm, panic, or blaming the child.
5. They must be able to refer children and their families to proper resources for treatment and support.
6. They must be able to talk with the child about basic concepts of preventing child sexual abuse. (Finkelhor & Araji 1983)

Prevention Programs for Children

Most prevention programs are focused on teaching children about sexual abuse and what to do if someone attempts to abuse them sexually or currently is abusing them sexually. Most of these programs take into account the age and cultural background of the child and the economic status of the child's family when designing and presenting programs.

In evaluating programs, several studies have shown that programs geared at elementary-school-age children have shown some positive gains; one review of 25 studies reported that children exposed to these programs have shown significant gains in knowledge about child sexual abuse and what to do if someone abuses them (Finkelhor and Strapko 1992). The National Committee for the Prevention of Child Abuse summarized the successes of prevention programs:

> With respect to the children, participants who have received these instructions demonstrate an increase in knowledge about safety rules and are more aware of what to do and who to turn to if they have been or are being abused. However, children have greater difficulty in accepting the idea that abuse may occur at the hands of someone they know. Also relatively little is known about whether any of the concepts presented in the classroom settings translate into behavioral changes that would prevent sexual assault. Parents and teachers who have attended the informational meetings which generally precede the classroom presentations report greater understanding of the problem of sexual abuse and greater confidence in how to respond to a child's disclosure. Further, while not preventing initial maltreatment, the programs do create an environment in which children can more easily disclose prior or ongoing maltreatment. As with all prevention programs, these gains are not universal across all participants; some children, parents, and teachers remain uninformed following the presentations. (National Committee for the Prevention of Child Abuse 1986, 1–2)

Generally, research suggests that children younger than five years old are not able to retain information presented to them about sexual abuse and make a connection between the information and anything that might ever happen to them. Some children are just too young or immature to understand many of the concepts about sexual abuse that are presented to them. Many instructions are difficult for young children to understand. The National Committee for the Prevention of Child Abuse agrees:

Many child development specialists and concerned advocates feel these instructions place an inappropriate burden on young children to be self-protective. They argue that most preschoolers cannot distinguish between appropriate and inappropriate touch, nor can they take the actions necessary to protect themselves from harm. Rather than targeting the child for intervention, proponents of this position suggest that parents need to be reached and made more aware of their responsibility to protect their children. On the other hand, other experts stress that it is important to integrate safety concepts into a child's educational process beginning at the earliest possible age. (National Committee for the Prevention of Child Abuse 1986, 2)

Many programs, even those for older children, have found that when they retested children on the information about sexual abuse they were given earlier, many had retained little information over time, especially after a period of eight months to a year had passed.

Conte suggests that until researchers better understand the process by which children are coerced into being sexually abused, prevention programs will have limited success:

There has not yet been a systematic study of the victimization process toward the end of identifying new concepts or skills that might be useful in preventing child sexual abuse. The more that is learned about the coercive process that sexual abuse is, the more questions are raised about whether current prevention activities are likely to be all that useful to children exposed to this coercion. Nothing that current prevention efforts teach, for example, is likely to be helpful in overcoming the fear instilled in children by the violent dismemberment of a living animal before them, with the threat that they or ones they love will be similarly treated if they tell about their abuse. (Conte 1986, 34)

Conte believes that all prevention programs aimed at children should include the following ideas:

• Children own their bodies and nobody has the right to share them.

- There is a difference between good touches and bad touches.
- Secrets about touching or other forms of abuse should never be kept.
- Children should trust their own feelings about something being right or wrong.
- Children should be taught how to say "no."
- Children should be encouraged to tell someone if they are being abused. (Conte 1986)

Gillham takes a slightly different perspective in looking at prevention programs. He categorizes prevention activities into three groups: primary, secondary, and tertiary. Primary prevention activities include increasing the awareness among all groups having contact with children of child molesters and their characteristics, recognizing that boys are at risk almost as much as girls, teaching children how to deal with strangers, teaching children about the privacy of their bodies, establishing legal policies that catch serious molesters and repeat offenders and keep them behind bars, and teaching children about all types of abuse. Secondary prevention activities include creating an atmosphere in which children feel safe to report abuse; encouraging parents, teachers, and other caretakers to act when they suspect a child has been sexually abused; encouraging and training teachers to be aware of the signs of sexual abuse; recognizing that children rarely lie about something as serious as sexual abuse; being particularly aware of children at high risk for sexual abuse; and, if the offender lives in the same home with the child, removing the offender from the home. Tertiary prevention requires the provision of supportive responses to the disclosure that a child has been sexually abused, minimizing the impact of the interview and treatment process, convincing children that they are not to blame for the abuse, and offering counseling services to adults who were abused as children (Gillham 1991).

Repression/False Memories

The subject of repressed memories is controversial. In the past several years, many articles and books have been written about adults who recall, often with the help of a therapist, one or more incidents of sexual abuse that they experienced as a child but have just recently remembered. Therapists working with these adults and many other experts truly believe the memories are real; how could someone recall these experiences, often quite vividly and in great detail, if they did not really happen? Yet other experts, as well as the families of these "victims," truly believe that the accounts are fabricated. They question how anyone could forget that something as serious as this had happened; many believe that therapists, using a checklist of symptoms of child sexual abuse victims, incorrectly identify the client's current problems as child sexual abuse.

Therapists who believe in repressed memories are looking for something that happened in a person's childhood to explain why the person currently suffers from depression, obesity, anxiety, anorexia, or an assortment of other problems. They use a checklist that includes such symptoms as difficulty falling or staying asleep, nightmares, feeling different from other people, fear of the dark, fear of trying new experiences, and eating disorders; the therapists discover their clients have a number of these characteristics, and they suggest sexual abuse as a possible cause of the clients' problems. Many clients will at first deny that they were sexually abused as children, but desperate to find a cause for their problems and open to therapists' suggestions, they may start thinking about the possibility of abuse. With their therapist's help and over time, many clients start to believe that they were indeed sexually abused as children and begin to remember specific instances of abuse.

The mental health profession has been bitterly divided over the concept of repressed memories. Some researchers and clinicians believe that childhood sexual abuse can be determined by a set profile, a group of characteristics that can be checked off a list, and that repressed memories are valid indicators of this abuse. Victims of sexual abuse can be treated only by confronting these memories, believing them, and working with the clients to overcome other problems in life. Other clinicians and researchers are less ready to acknowledge the validity of repressed memories in identifying abuse victims. They believe that therapists may inadvertently help a person believe that he or she was sexually abused as a child based on minimal evidence, especially if a checklist of various characteristics is used.

The American Psychiatric Association (APA) has issued a statement on memories of sexual abuse (see pp. 134–138 for the complete statement). The APA suggests that psychiatrists "maintain an empathic, non-judgmental, neutral stance towards reported memories of sexual abuse" in order to help their patients (APA 1993, 4). Until more is known about memory and repressed memory, the APA believes that psychiatrists must focus on helping their clients resolve their problems without letting their own personal beliefs influence the patient.

People who believe that repressed memories of early childhood sexual abuse are true believe that many traumatic memories are hidden away in our unconscious minds, although some of the emotions associated with them work their way into our conscious lives and can have a major impact on how we see life and cope with its many problems. They believe that the mind buries these terrible memories and when we are better able to cope with them, usually with the help of therapists, we are able to pull these memories from the hidden recesses of our brains and recall these experiences in great detail. Only by bringing these memories into our conscious minds are we able to work them out, and help resolve many of our current problems that have been created by these experiences.

Sigmund Freud was convinced that emotions can be powerful enough to block memory, that traumatic memories can be repressed and may never become conscious. He compared the recovery of repressed memories to excavating an ancient buried city one layer at a time. Using the case of Lucy R., Freud demonstrated his theory that "an idea must be intentionally repressed from consciousness" in order for hysterical symptoms to develop in a person (Freud and Breuer 1895). Even though Freud changed his mind about his theory about hysteria (that women became hysterical because of something that happened to them sexually in early life), Judith Herman believes that the "legacy of Freud's inquiry into the subject of incest was a tenacious prejudice, still shared by professionals and laymen alike, that children lie about sexual abuse" (Herman 1981, 11).

Ellen Bass and Laura Davis believe that repressed memories are often found in victims of childhood sexual abuse. Regarding repressed memories, they claim that "[i]f you are unable to remember any specific instances [of abuse] . . . but still have a feeling that something abusive happened to you, it probably did" (Bass & Davis 1988, 21–22). In a later edition of their book *The Courage to Heal*, they soften this statement by declaring that "[i]f you genuinely think you were abused and your life shows the symptoms, there's a strong likelihood that you were" (Bass & Davis 1994, 26).

E. Sue Blume also believes that repression is a common characteristic of all survivors of childhood sexual abuse:

> The incest survivor develops a repertoire of behaviors designed to preserve the secret . . . these behaviors are not calculated or even conscious. They become automatic and, over the years, almost part of her personality. She denies that she was abused by repressing the memory of her trauma. This is the primary manifestation of "the secret": incest becomes the secret she keeps even from herself. Repression in some form is virtually universal among survivors. (Blume 1990, 67)

For many researchers and other professionals in the field of child sexual abuse, it is easy to understand why children may repress these memories, especially if the abuse is committed by the child's father. Fathers are supposed to be the protectors of the family—they are not supposed to hurt their own children. Many people believe that there can be nothing worse for a child to bear than to have been sexually abused by the person that he or she trusts most to protect and help, not hurt.

Dr. Elizabeth Loftus, a psychologist and a leading expert in memory, believes that despite decades of research on various aspects of memory, no scientific evidence currently exists to support the idea that memories of trauma are routinely repressed and reliably recovered years later. Her research has "helped to create a new paradigm of memory, shifting our view from the video-recorder model, in which memories are interpreted as the literal truth, to a reconstructionist model, in which memories are understood as creative blendings of fact and fiction" (Loftus & Ketcham 1994, 5). Loftus also has investigated memory distortion:

> [M]emory fades with time, losing detail and accuracy; as time goes by, the weakened memories are increasingly vulnerable to "post-event information"—facts, ideas, inferences, and opinions that become available to a witness after an event is completely over. I told the story about a series of experiments I conducted featuring a shocking film simulation of a robbery. At the end of the short film, a child is shot in the face. Subjects who watched the film with the shocking ending were able to recall details with significantly less accuracy than subjects who watched a similar film without the violent ending.
>
> This study . . . tells us about the distortions that can occur in the acquisition stage of memory, when an

event occurs and information is laid down in the memory system. Other studies tell us about the retention and retrieval stages of memory, after a period of time goes by and we are asked to recall a particular event or experience. Hundreds of experiments involving tens of thousands of individuals have shown that post-event information can become incorporated into memory and contaminate, supplement, or distort the original memory (Loftus & Ketcham 1994, 62)

Many experts, including Loftus, understand the importance of memory and our belief that we can trust our memories, that they are reliable and can help us make sense of our lives. Most people do not want to believe that their minds, their memories, can play tricks on them, that they can distort their reality and provide a false sense of history, of what has happened to them in their lives. Loftus says,

But perhaps the most compelling reason to believe these stories of recovered memories is that not believing is edged with painful complexities and ambiguities. Not believing shakes up our sense of our own self. . . . In a chaotic world, where so much is out of control, we need to believe that our minds, at least, are under our command. We need to believe that our memories, inherently trustworthy and reliable, can reach back into the past and make sense of our lives. (Loftus & Ketcham 1994, 67–68)

Michael Yapko also questions the validity of repressed memories. He believes that culture and current social conditions play a role in the growth of popularity in repressed memories:

[T]he epidemic of allegations of child sexual abuse does not exist independently of the culture in which the allegations are made. In the past, when therapists were convinced that abuse reports were sheer fantasy, there wasn't much of an abuse problem. Now that the media and the mental health profession have announced that it is widespread, we are beginning to see the phenomenon in more and more instances . . . in ever-increasing numbers, therapists all across the country are actively or passively encouraging clients

> to identify themselves as victims of abuse—or to be
> "politically correct," as "abuse survivors." (Yapko
> 1994, 19–20)

Yapko gathered information from over 860 therapists
throughout the United States to determine their ideas and practices regarding the roles that suggestion and memory play in
therapy, focusing on repressed memories of sexual abuse. His
findings were reported in his book *Suggestions of Abuse*. He was
dismayed to find that many therapists appear to believe in and
practice on the basis of "sheer myth"; they encourage their
clients, either covertly or overtly, to believe they have been sexually abused based on unreliable and unbelievable use of repressed memories. Clients who came in with a variety of
symptoms were led to believe that they had been sexually
abused even though they had no conscious memory of such
abuse. Therapists, using suggestibility, hypnosis, and other techniques, convinced many clients that they were indeed sexually
abused as children. Many of these clients were highly suggestible; looking for answers to their questions, they found their
therapists, whom they often looked up to and wanted to believe
in, as either an authority figure or as someone who has more
knowledge in this area than they have and therefore must be believed. For many clients looking for a solution to their problems,
while sexual abuse did not seem right, they were happy to have
an "answer" to their problem, and believed that now they could
get on with the "cure." Yapko is "concerned that therapy clients
will be led to believe destructive things that are untrue, to recall
memories of terrible things that never actually happened, to
jump to conclusions that are not warranted, and to destroy the
lives of innocent people—including their own—in the process"
(Yapko 1994, 22).

Yapko also discusses another aspect of therapy and the appeal of "discovering" that a client has been sexually abused as a
child:

> The answers to the question of why someone would
> make a false allegation of abuse lies not much deeper
> than the therapist's explanation to the client: "From
> your symptoms, it is clear that you were abused." It
> provides a clear and specific scapegoat—someone else
> to blame for one's own failures. It provides a specific
> identity—that of an "abuse survivor." It provides an

instant support network of empathetic and sympa-
thetic people in this cold, impersonal world, namely
all the others who show up at recovery meetings. It
provides an apparently safe outlet for exploring and
communicating one's feelings. (Yapko 1994, 132)

Yapko and others are concerned with the innocent people
whose lives are changed forever when repressed memories of
childhood sexual abuse occur. So-called victims who accuse family members of horrendous acts of abuse destroy families and
themselves. Confronting and accusing a family member of sexual
abuse based solely on the basis of repressed memories has devastating effects on both the accuser and the family member being
accused. If the allegation of abuse is not true, the family members
usually are devastated by these allegations and by the inevitable
destruction of the family. Many family members do not understand the concept of repressed memories; "either you remember
something or you don't" is the feeling of many people when confronted with this issue.

Therapist Renee Fredrickson believes that

[w]hen you have retrieved enough memories, you
will reach critical mass, which is a sense of the overall
reality of your repressed memories. . . . After enough
memories, debriefed enough times, you will suddenly
know your repressed memories are real. It is the opposite of the maxim that if you tell a lie long enough,
you will believe it is real. . . . if you talk about your repressed memories long enough, you will intuitively
know they are real. (Fredrickson 1992, in Loftus 1994,
148)

Fredrickson advocates the use of seven basic techniques for
retrieving repressed memories: imagistic work, dream work,
journal writing, body work, hypnosis, art therapy, and feelings
work. Imagistic work involves taking a basic image that a person
has (e.g., being held down on a bed by someone) and describing
in detail every sensation and, when necessary, adding subjective
impressions. Fredrickson believes these images come from the
unconscious and represent real memories. Dream work relies on
believing that dreams may help retrieve memories of abuse;
dreams may symbolically represent memories and one only has
to interpret these dreams to understand what has happened in

real life. Journal writing, like imagistic work, can help retrieve memories by starting with a feeling or image and writing down everything that a person can think of that relates to that image or feeling. The theory is that this information must come from the unconscious—how else could it be created? Through body work, including massage and body-manipulation techniques, Fredrickson and others believe that a person can access body memories; that a physical body never forgets what happens to it and in therapy it is just a matter of accessing these memories in order to discover what has happened that the conscious mind has repressed. Hypnosis, according to some experts, can retrieve repressed memories, usually through age regression. Art therapy, according to Fredrickson, can access certain types of unconscious memories—acting out through art forgotten memories that spontaneously appear as well as imagistic memories that appear as images drawn by the subject. Drawing can help generate memories of childhood sexual abuse. Finally, feelings work can help a client tap into an emotional response to a specific memory; feelings work can include grief therapy (Loftus & Ketcham 1994).

Psychologist Carol Tavris, in an article on incest in the *New York Times Book Review*, takes on Ellen Bass and Laura Davis, who wrote *The Courage to Heal*, and others who believe in repressed memories and repressed memory therapy. She finds fault with the incest-survivor recovery movement:

> The problem is not with the advice they offer to victims, but with their effort to create victims—to expand the market that can then be treated with therapy and self-help books. To do this, survival books all hew to a formula based on an uncritical acceptance of certain premises about the nature of memory and trauma. They offer simple answers at a time when research psychologists are posing hard questions. . . . Uniformly these books persuade their readers to focus exclusively on past abuse as the reason for their present unhappiness. Forget fighting with Harold and the kids, having a bad job or no job, worrying about money. Healing is defined as your realization that you were a victim of sexual abuse and that it explains everything wrong in your life. (Tavris 1993, 1)

Based on current research on repressed memory, no definitive conclusions can be drawn about the validity of such memories.

Researchers will continue to study them to determine whether these memories are real or only a result of suggestion by therapists and other trusted adults.

Child Exploitation and Prostitution

Child exploitation has been and still is rampant in many countries. For example, in the Philippines, when Ferdinand and Imelda Marcos fled the country, Corazon Aquino became president and was left with a group of children (beggars, prostitutes, thieves) who had been frequently exploited in the streets as well as in the factories. During several wars, when Subic Bay was an active military site, thousands of children were under the control of pimps and performed any service for anyone who could pay. Pedophiles came to Pagsanjan, south from Manila. According to Cameron Forbes,

> the guidebook does not mention . . . that other great attraction of Pagsanjan: the children—young boys and girls who are for sale. The youngest, recorded on a hospital treatment sheet, was five years old. Some of these are the children of the *Ibanqueros,* others from the poor coastal villages of Bicol and the Visayas. Buyers should be warned, however, that Pagsanjan is not what it was. For a time it was the pedophile capital of the world. (Forbes 1990, 236)

He goes on to describe Pagsanjan:

> But it was even better in the old days when there were about two thousand child prostitutes here and it was a buyer's market. Pedophiles flocked to the lodges along the river and took their pick of the boys in the swimming pools, some for "short-time," some to set up house and have relatively long-lasting relationships. And they all fed on the poverty of Pagsanjan, whether by paying three hundred pesos for "short-time" or by regular wages to the boys or by giving gifts to the families of the children or by buying them taxis or even houses. (Forbes 1990, 238)

According to John Crewdson,

[i]n 1835, the Society for the Prevention of Juvenile Prostitution [in England] reckoned that four hundred Londoners depended for their livelihoods on the earnings of child prostitutes. London hospitals, it was said, had recorded twenty-seven hundred cases of venereal disease among children during the preceding eight years. One of the major accomplishments of England's Victorian-era child welfare brigades was to raise the legal age for prostitution from nine to thirteen. (Crewdson 1988, 36)

Child prostitution exists in most countries, from Southeast Asia to the United States. It may be more open and accepted in some developing countries, but wherever children are seen as desirable sexual objects, sexual exploitation of children can be found. In Western countries, runaways are the majority of child prostitutes; in Latin America, they are street children. The need for children to earn a living is often cited as the most popular reason why children become prostitutes—either the children themselves decide to become prostitutes or their families sell them into prostitution (Moorehead 1990).

In the United States in 1988, the National Incidence Studies estimated 450,000 children left home and stayed away from home for at least one night, and another 127,000 children were thrown out of their homes. Many of these children end up on the streets, trying to survive the best way they can, often through activities such as pornography, sexual exploitation, and drugs. According to the National Center for Missing and Exploited Children,

[s]exual victimization of these homeless children occurs in every state. Outreach workers in New York City estimate that children as young as 8 years old are forced to prostitute themselves for money, affection, and drugs. Some children are held in virtual bondage. They have multiple sex partners on a daily basis and are bought and sold by exploiters. Many contract diseases such as tuberculosis (TB), hepatitis-B, gonorrhea, syphilis, chlamydia, and HIV/acquired immune deficiency syndrome. They often are malnourished and practice poor hygiene, leaving them vulnerable to disease. (National Center for Missing and Exploited Children 1992, v)

Some organizations, such as the Rene Guyon Society and the North American Man/Boy Love Association (NAMBLA), believe that most child exploitation and sexual abuse laws should be removed from the statutes. Members advocate sex with children, arguing that children are fully capable of entering into loving relationships with adults, and that it is only our Victorian upbringing that prohibits us from realizing that there is nothing wrong with sex between a child and an adult.

Some professionals believe that the American obsession with male sexually aggressive behavior and touching in general is responsible for the increase in reporting of cases of incest. Sociologist Warren Farrell, in an interview by Philip Nobile in *Penthouse*, says that "[m]illions of people who are now refraining from touching, holding, and genitally caressing their children, when that is really part of a caring, loving expression, are repressing the sexuality of a lot of children and themselves. Maybe this needs repressing and maybe it doesn't" (Nobile 1977, 126). In an article in *Hustler,* Dr. Edwin J. Haeberle argues that children are being denied their "right to sexual satisfaction." Haeberle argues for the abolition of all incest laws: "It would be a crime to force our children and adolescents into blind acceptance of a morality long overdue for reform" (Haeberle 1978, 124).

Cults and Ritual Abuse

Allegations of children being sexually abused in cults and ritual abuse have grown in recent years. Ritual abuse may include malicious acts of physical, sexual, and psychological abuse; group acts of religious worship involving abuse; and terrorizing people psychologically in order to force them to participate in certain activities. It may include animal and/or human sacrifice. Satanism is not always involved.

Lloyd believes that no clear, consistent definition of ritual abuse exists. The media and professionals in the field of child sexual abuse may apply the term to situations that include any bizarre acts of either physical, sexual, or psychological abuse of children; abusive acts involving children during religious worship or displays of demonic powers; and psychological intimidation of children to force them to believe in demonic powers. Lloyd defines ritual child abuse as "the intentional physical abuse, sexual abuse or psychological abuse of a child by a person responsible for the child's welfare, when such abuse is repeated and/or stylized and is typified by such other acts as cruelty to animals, or threats of harm to the child, other persons, and animals" (Lloyd 1990a, 2).

Lloyd further defines cult ritual child abuse as

> the intentional physical abuse, sexual abuse or psychological abuse of a child by persons who are in a religious cult and are responsible for the child's welfare, when such abuse is repeated and/or stylized and is typified by such other acts as cruelty to animals, or threats of harm to the child, other persons, and animals, and is performed to reinforce the cult's religious cohesion. (Lloyd 1990a, 4)

Lloyd defines group ritual child abuse as

> the intentional physical abuse, sexual abuse or psychological abuse of a child by a group of persons responsible for the child's welfare, when such abuse is repeated and/or stylized and is typified by such other acts as cruelty to animals, or threats of harm to the child, other persons, and animals, and is performed to reinforce the group's cohesion. (Lloyd 1990a, 4)

Ritual abuse is defined by Susan Kelley as "repetitive and systematic sexual, physical, and psychological abuse of children by adults as part of cult or satanic worship" (Kelley 1988, 228). In a 1989 paper on ritual abuse, the Los Angeles County Commission for Women defined ritual abuse as

> [a] brutal form of abuse of children, adolescents, and adults, consisting of physical, sexual, and psychological abuse, and involving the use of rituals. Ritual does not necessarily mean satanic. However, most survivors state that they were ritually abused as part of satanic worship for the purpose of indoctrinating them into satanic beliefs and practices. Ritual abuse rarely consists of a single episode. It usually involves repeated abuse over an extended period of time. (Los Angeles County Commission for Women 1989, in Sakheim & Devine 1992, xii)

The study of satanism is fairly new; few studies have been conducted and most professionals in the field have limited knowledge about satanic cults and ritual abuse. Satanic cults theoretically program their followers using techniques that are only known to the high priests and priestesses. To most professionals in the field of cults and mind control, no one has yet found a practicing satanic cult that murders babies and animals. Martin Katchen and David Sakheim found that "[m]any satanists believe therefore that a relationship exists between incest, magic, idolatry, sacrifice, and the consumption of blood. . . . It is thereby assumed that forbidden incestuous relationships, the consumption of blood, the human sacrifice all provide the power to do magic" (Katchen & Sakheim 1992, 25).

Kenneth Lanning, the FBI's expert on ritual abuse, found that

> [f]or at least eight years, American law enforcement has been aggressively investigating the allegations of victims of ritual abuse. There is little or no evidence for the portion of their allegations that deals with large-scale baby breeding, human sacrifice and organized satanic conspiracies. Now it is up to mental health professionals, not law enforcement, to explain why victims are alleging things that don't seem to be true. Mental health professionals must begin to accept the possibility that some of what these victims are alleging just didn't happen and that this area desperately needs study and research by rational, objective social scientists. (Lanning 1991, 172)

In differentiating between ritual sexual abuse and satanism, Lanning believes that

> [n]ot all spiritually motivated ritualistic activity is satanic. Santeria, witchcraft, voodoo, and most religious cults are not satanism. In fact, most spiritually or religiously based abuse of children has nothing to do with satanism. Most child abuse that could be termed "ritualistic" by various definitions is more likely to be physical and psychological rather than sexual in nature. If a distinction needs to be made between satanic and nonsatanic child abuse, the indicators for that distinction must be related to specific satanic symbols, artifacts, or doctrine rather than the mere presence of any ritualistic element. (Lanning 1992, 21)

Crewdson examined satanic child abuse and found that in most cases, real physical evidence has rarely been found, although some investigations have turned up suggestions of some type of ritual abuse:

> In Richmond, Virginia, one person was convicted in a sexual abuse case where police recovered candles and other ritualistic paraphernalia. In El Paso, Texas, across the Rio Grande from Mexico, a young prosecutor named Deborah Kanof won a conviction of a thirty-five-year-old mother who had been charged with abusing eight children at the East Valley YWCA. Some of the victims in that case said they had been taken from the "Y" to a nearby house, where they were made to have sex with the teacher while men dressed in masks and werewolf costumes looked on. The woman got life in prison plus 311 years, the longest sentence of child sexual abuse in Texas history. (Crewdson 1988, 125)

Finkelhor and his colleagues, in their study of children sexually abused in day-care settings, found that children who were ritually abused appeared to suffer the most serious psychological impairments (Finkelhor et al. 1988).

Lanning suggests several possible explanations for why people think that they have been victims of ritual, or satanic, abuse. One explanation is pathological distortion:

> The allegations in question may be errors in processing reality influenced by underlying mental disorders such as dissociative disorders, borderline or histrionic personality disorders, or psychosis. These distortions may be manifested in false accounts of victimization in order to gain psychological benefits such as attention and sympathy. . . . Although not always pathological, many "victims" may develop pseudomemories of their victimization and eventually come to believe the events actually occurred. (Lanning 1992, 24)

Another possible explanation is traumatic memory, that is, events may become confused or distorted as a result of severe trauma. Victims may dissociate from the events by forcing their minds to go somewhere else, in order to avoid the experience and the memory of the abusive experience. Lanning considers re-pressed memory:

> It may be that we should anticipate that individuals severely abused as very young children by multiple offenders with fear as the primary controlling tactic will repress the memory. This repressed memory of their victimization may be distorted and embellished when later recalled. Perhaps a horror-filled yet inac-curate account of victimization is not only not a coun-terindication of abuse, but is in fact a corroborative indicator of extreme physical, psychological, and/or sexual abuse. (Lanning 1992, 25)

Lanning includes normal childhood fears and fantasy; misper-ceptions, confusion, and trickery; overzealous intervenors; urban legends; or a combination of many factors as other possi-ble explanations.

Multiple Personality Disorder

At the annual APA convention in 1991, George Ganaway spoke about the connection between multiple personality disorder (MPD) and memories of satanic ritual abuse. While many of his colleagues believed that traumatic experiences in childhood, including experi-ences of satanic ritual abuse, can lead to MPD, Ganaway believed that MPD was not as common as it appeared, that "the brutal sce-narios of bloody rituals and satanic tortures reflect 'psychic reality' rather than historical, fact-based reality" (Loftus & Ketcham 1994, 85). Ganaway believes that therapists can unknowingly influence patients and plant suggestions that can lead to incorrect memories of childhood sexual abuse as well as satanic ritual abuse.

Dr. Paul McHugh, writing about MPD, says:

> Close the dissociation services and disperse the pa-tients to general psychiatric units. Ignore the alters [the alter personalities]. Stop talking to them [the alter personalities], taking notes on them, and discussing them in staff conferences. Pay attention to real present problems and conflicts rather than fantasy. If these simple, familiar rules are followed, multiple personal-ities will soon wither away and psychotherapy can begin. (McHugh 1993, 6)

Dr. Robert S. Mayer, a nationally recognized authority on MPD, believes that people with MPD have a hard time trusting people, including their therapists, for several reasons:

> But multiples do not trust easily. They almost always test their therapists for a long time before they allow themselves to show any symptoms. This stems from the cause of the illness: severe trauma in childhood, usually physical or sexual abuse that is most often inflicted before the age of five and sometimes continues for years. Typically, the victimizer is a family member, often a mother or father or both. . . . the child is forced to rely on his own scant resources. Some dissociate, which means they essentially banish the painful experiences from conscious awareness. One way to do this is to create an additional personality to absorb the pain. (Mayer 1991, 28)

Richard Ofshe, an expert on cults and mind control, doubts if MPD exists as a separate diagnostic category. He believes that highly suggestible people often begin to display the personality characteristics and symptoms that their therapists are unconsciously or indirectly suggesting to them.

Child Pornography and Sex Rings

Child pornography and sex rings are another form of child sexual abuse. Many pedophiles enjoy looking at photographs of nude children and use these photographs to encourage and excite their own sexual desires. Child sex rings are also used by pedophiles to share and exchange children for the explicit purpose of having sex with these children.

One effective way of catching pedophiles is through the sale and exchange of child pornography. Many pedophiles enjoy taking pictures of their young victims. John Crewdson finds

> [h]omemade pornography not only feeds the pedophile's fantasies, it becomes a permanent record of the children he has known. The victims themselves may not stay young forever, but in the pedophile's album the eight-year-old remains forever eight. Not only do pictures of smiling children validate his behavior; such photographs also have a more practical

application. In attempting to break down the resistance of a prospective victim, the pedophile can produce documentary evidence that children have sex with adults. (Crewdson 1988, 101)

Child pornography may also be used to seduce potential children for sex. Offenders may leave pictures of children in various erotic poses where other children can see them, in the hope that these other children may think that this behavior is okay and be encouraged to try similar activities. A father may show child pornography to his own child in order to "prove" to the child that there is nothing wrong with what he wants to do with the child.

Some pedophiles who have trouble finding young children to molest will search for or create their own child sex rings. Lanning defines child sex rings as "one or more offenders simultaneously involved sexually with several child victims" (Lanning 1992, 9). Child sex rings are not necessarily commercial and do not always imply group sex. Offenders usually sexually interact with one child at a time. Characteristics of child sex rings include multiple victims and multiple offenders, and the children involved are usually adolescent boys, rather than girls, who are more likely to be sexually abused within the family.

Burgess divides child sex rings into three categories: solo, transition, and syndicated. Offenders keep their activities and any photographs they have secret in the solo rings, which always involve one offender and multiple victims. Offenders share their children, experiences, and photographs with other offenders in transition rings. Syndicated rings operate under a well-defined structure that recruits children, offers sexual services, produces pornography, and has an extensive list of customers (Burgess 1984).

Lanning divides child sex rings into two types: historical child sex rings and multidimensional child sex rings. Historical child sex rings have the following characteristics in common: offenders are male, most offenders are true pedophiles, at least two-thirds of the children involved are boys, sexual motivation is the only reason the offenders participate, offenders collect child pornography and child erotica, and offenders usually control the children through the use of seduction. Initially, offenders usually control boys through the "use of bonding, competition, and peer pressure" (Lanning 1992, 14). In order to bond boys together, the offenders can either use an existing organization, such as the

Scouts or a sports team, or can create their own organization, such as a computer club or a cult. Later, when attempting to keep a boy in the ring when he wants to leave or when trying to get rid of a boy, the offenders may resort to blackmail, threats of violence, or actual violence. The boys rarely think of themselves as victims and therefore do not reveal the sexual abuse to anyone outside the ring. Many of the boys involved are the more vulnerable boys in society; they are searching for attention and love and they believe that belonging to a sex ring is one way of receiving this attention (Lanning 1992).

Multidimensional child sex rings have the following characteristics in common: multiple offenders and multiple victims, the use of fear to control the victims, and involvement of some type of bizarre or ritualistic activity. In these rings, approximately half of the victims are girls; the offenders may not be true pedophiles because they may not have sex as their primary motive; authorities investigating these groups have not found photographs of the victims, child pornography, or sexual paraphernalia; and the offenders control the children by frightening them, creating traumatic memories. Types of bizarre or ritualistic activities include "ceremonies, chanting, robes and costumes, drugs, use of urine and feces, animal sacrifice, torture, abduction, mutilation, murder, and even cannibalism and vampirism" (Lanning 1992, 18).

In investigating cases of child sexual abuse and child exploitation, Lanning believes,

> [l]aw enforcement officers must stop looking at child sexual abuse and exploitation through a keyhole—focusing on one act, by one offender, against one victim, on one day. Law enforcement must "kick the door open" and take the big picture—focusing on proactive techniques, offender typologies, patterns of behavior, multiple acts, multiple victims, and child pornography. This is absolutely essential in the investigation of child sex rings. (Lanning 1992, 31)

In general, investigators must document any indicators of sexual abuse that they find, document both victim and offender patterns of behavior, identify adult witnesses and suspects, collect any medical evidence, search for other victims, obtain search warrants early in the process so evidence is not destroyed, collect all physical evidence, search for all corroborative evidence including child pornography and child erotica, monitor events with body tape recorders or video recorders if possible without involving or endangering the child, use surveillance techniques in monitoring the suspects, and be creative in prosecuting offenders. It is important that the investigators understand the seduction process when looking into sex rings; young boys may be hesitant to admit to being involved in sex rings because of the fear of being thought homosexual and the embarrassment of being caught in such activities (Lanning 1992).

Computerized bulletin boards are another tool currently available for pedophiles to find others with similar interests and often to find young people, mostly boys, to meet.

References

Abbott, Brian R. 1991. *Sexual Re-offense Rates among Incest Offenders Eight Years after Leaving Treatment.* San Jose, CA: Giarretto Institute.

Abel, Gene, J. V. Becker, E. B. Blanchard, and A. Djenderedjian. 1978. "Differentiating Sexual Aggressives with Penile Measures." *Criminal Justice and Behavior* 5: 315–322.

Adams-Tucker, Christine. 1981. "A Socioclinical Overview of 28 Sex-abused Children." *Child Abuse and Neglect* 5: 361–367.

AFCC (Association of Family and Conciliation Courts). 1988. *The Sexual Abuse Allegation Project: Final Report.* Denver, CO: AFCC.

AHA (American Humane Association). 1993. *Highlights of Official Child Neglect and Abuse Reporting.* Denver, CO: American Humane Association.

APA (American Psychiatric Association). 1987. *Diagnostic and Statistical Manual of Mental Disorders.* 3d ed. Washington, DC: American Psychiatric Association.

———. 1993. *Statement on Memories of Sexual Abuse.* Washington, DC: American Psychiatric Association.

August, R., and B. Foreman. 1988. "A Comparison of Sexually and Non-Sexually Abused Children's Behavioral Responses to Anatomically Correct Dolls." *Child Psychiatry and Human Development* 20(1): 39–47.

Baker, Anthony W., and Sylvia P. Duncan. 1985. "Child Sexual Abuse: A Study of Prevalence in Great Britain." *Child Abuse and Neglect* 9(4): 457–467.

Bass, Ellen, and Laura Davis. 1988. *The Courage to Heal: A Guide for Survivors of Child Sexual Abuse.* New York: HarperPerennial.

———. 1994. *The Courage to Heal: A Guide for Survivors of Child Sexual Abuse.* 3d ed. New York: HarperPerennial.

Bell, Graham. 1988. *Sex and Death in Protozoa: The History of an Obsession.* Cambridge: Cambridge University Press.

Benward, Jean, and Judianne Densen-Gerber. 1975. "Incest as a Causative Factor in Antisocial Behavior: An Explanatory Study." *Contemporary Drug Problems* 4: 323–340.

Berendzen, Richard, and Laura Palmer. 1993. *Come Here: A Man Overcomes the Tragic Aftermath of Childhood Sexual Abuse.* New York: Villard Books.

Berliner, Lucy, and Jon R. Conte. 1990. "Effects of Disclosure and Intervention on Sexually Abused Children." Final report to NCCAN of grant #90CA1181. Seattle, WA: University of Washington Sexual Assault Center.

Blume, E. Sue. 1990. *Secret Survivors: Uncovering Incest and Its Aftereffects in Women.* New York: Ballantine.

Blush, Gordon, and Karol Ross. 1986. *The SAID Syndrome.* Sterling Heights, MI.

Boyle, Patrick. 1994. *Scout's Honor: Sexual Abuse in America's Most Trusted Institution.* Rocklin, CA: Prima Publishing.

Breslin, Eleanor E. 1990. "Introduction." In *Therapy for Sexually Abused Children and Their Siblings: Group Therapists' Guide*, ed. Joanne Szybalski and Susan Setziol. San Jose, CA: Giarretto Institute.

Briere, Jon. 1984. "The Effects of Childhood Sexual Abuse on Later Psychological Functioning: Defining a Post-Sexual Abuse Syndrome." Paper presented at the Third National Conference on Sexual Victimization of Children, Children's Hospital National Medical Center, Washington, DC (April).

Briere, Jon, and Marsha Runtz. 1988. "Symptomatology Associated with Prior Sexual Abuse in a Non-Clinical Sample." *Child Abuse and Neglect* 12: 51–59.

Broude, Gwen J. 1994. *Marriage, Family, and Relationships: A Cross-Cultural Encyclopedia.* Santa Barbara, CA: ABC-CLIO.

Burgess, Ann W. 1984. *Child Pornography and Sex Rings.* Lexington, MA: Lexington Books.

Burgess, Ann W., Lynda Lytle Holmstrom, and Maureen P. McCausland. 1977. "Child Sexual Abuse by a Family Member: Decisions Following Disclosure." *Victimology: An International Journal* 2(2): 236–250.

Cantwell, H. B. 1981. "Sexual Abuse of Children in Denver, 1979." *Child Abuse and Neglect* 5: 75–85.

Child Abuse Prevention and Treatment Act, as Amended. November 4, 1992. Washington, DC: U.S. Department of Health and Human Services.

Conte, Jon R. 1985. "Clinical Dimensions of Adult Sexual Abuse of Children." *Behavioral Sciences and the Law* 3: 341–354.

———. 1986. *A Look at Child Sexual Abuse.* Chicago: National Committee for Prevention of Child Abuse.

Courtois, Christine. 1979. "The Incest Experience and Its Aftermath." *Victimology: An International Journal* 4: 337–347.

Crewdson, John. 1988. *By Silence Betrayed: Sexual Abuse of Children in America.* Boston: Little, Brown & Company.

DeFrancis, Vincent. 1969. *Protecting the Child Victim of Sex Crimes Committed by Adults.* Denver, CO: American Humane Association.

Dempsey, Julia Quinn, John R. Gorman, and John P. Madden. 1992. "The Cardinal's Commission on Clerical Sexual Misconduct with Minors: Report to Joseph Cardinal Bernardin." Chicago: Archdiocese of Chicago.

DeYoung, Mary. 1982. *The Sexual Victimization of Children.* Jefferson, NC: McFarland.

Durkheim, Emile. 1963. "The Nature and Origin of the Taboo." In *Incest,* ed. Edward Sagarin. New York: Lyle Stuart.

Faller, Kathleen Coulborn. 1993. *Child Sexual Abuse: Intervention and Treatment Issues.* Washington, DC: National Center on Child Abuse and Neglect.

Finkelhor, David. 1979. *Sexually Victimized Children.* New York: Free Press.

———. 1980. "Risk Factors in the Sexual Victimization of Children." *Child Abuse and Neglect* 52: 265–273.

———. 1982. "Child Sexual Abuse in a Sample of Boston Families." Unpublished paper. Durham, NH: University of New Hampshire Family Violence Research Program.

———. 1984. *Child Sexual Abuse: New Theory and Research.* New York: Free Press.

———. 1986. *A Sourcebook on Child Sexual Abuse.* Newbury Park, CA: Sage Publications.

Finkelhor, David, and Sharon Araji. 1983. "The Prevention of Child Sexual Abuse: A Review of Current Approaches." Unpublished paper prepared for the National Center on Prevention and Control of Rape.

Finkelhor, David, Linda Williams, and Nanci Burns. 1988. *Sexual Abuse in Day Care: A National Study.* Durham, NH: University of New Hampshire Family Laboratory.

Finkelhor, David, and Nancy Strapko. 1992. "Sexual Abuse Prevention Education: A Review of Evaluation Studies." In *Child Abuse Prevention,* ed. D. Willis, E. Holder, and M. Rosenberg. New York: John Wiley.

Forbes, Cameron. 1990. "Child Exploitation in the Philippines." In *Betrayal: A Report on Violence Toward Children in Today's World*, ed. Caroline Moorehead. New York: Doubleday.

Forward, Susan, and Craig Buck. 1978. *Betrayal of Innocence: Incest and Its Devastation*. New York: Penguin Books.

Fraser, B. G. 1981. "Sexual Child Abuse: The Legislation and the Law in the United States." In *Sexually Abused Children and Their Families*, ed. Patricia Beezley Mrazek and C. Henry Kempe. New York: Pergamon.

Fredrickson, Renee. 1992. *Repressed Memories: A Journey to Recovery from Sexual Abuse*. New York: Simon and Schuster.

Freund, Kurt, Ron Langevin, Stephen Cibiri, and Yaroslaw Zajac. 1973. "Heterosexual Aversion in Homosexual Males." *British Journal of Psychiatry* 122: 163–169.

Frisbee, L. V., and E. H. Dondis. 1965. *Recidivism among Treated Sex Offenders*. Sacramento: California Department of Mental Hygiene.

Fromuth, Mary Ellen. 1983. "The Long-Term Psychological Impact of Childhood Sexual Abuse." Ph.D. diss., Auburn University.

Gardner, Richard. 1991. *Sex Abuse Hysteria: Salem Witch Trials Revisited*. Cresskill, NJ: Creative Therapeutics.

Gillham, Bill. 1991. *The Facts about Child Sexual Abuse*. London: Cassell Educational Limited.

Glaser, D., and C. Collins. 1989. "The Response of Young, Non-Sexually Abused Children to Anatomically Correct Dolls." *Journal of Child Psychology and Psychiatry* 30: 547–560.

Goodman, Gail S., J. E. Hirschman, D. Hepps, and L. Rudy. 1991. "Children's Memory for Stressful Events." *Merrill-Palmer Quarterly* 37: 109–158.

Goodman, Gail S., L. Rudy, B. L. Bottoms, and C. Aman. 1990. "Children's Concerns and Memory: Issues of Ecological Validity in the Study of Children's Eyewitness Testimony." In *Knowing and Remembering in Young Children*, ed. R. Fivush and J. Hudson. New York: Cambridge University Press.

Gordon, Linda. 1988. *Heroes of Their Own Lives: The Politics and History of Family Violence, Boston 1880–1960*. New York: Viking.

Gorer, Geoffrey. 1938. *Himalayan Village*. London: Michael Joseph.

Greeley, Andrew. 1993. "A View from the Priesthood: It's Bigotry To Blame Celibacy for Church Problems." *Newsweek* (August 16): 45.

Groth, Nicholas A. 1978. "Guidelines for Assessment and Management of the Offender." In *Sexual Assault of Children and Adolescents*, ed. Ann

Burgess, Nicholas Groth, Lynda Holmstrom, and Suzanne Sgroi. Lexington, MA: Lexington Books.

———. 1979. *Men Who Rape.* New York: Plenum.

Haeberle, Edwin J. 1978. "Children, Sex, and Society." *Hustler* (December): 124.

Harvey, P. H., and A. F. Read. 1988. "Copulation Genetics: When Incest Is Not Best." *Nature* 336: 514–515.

Herman, Judith L. 1981. *Father-Daughter Incest.* Cambridge, MA: Harvard University Press.

Herman, Judith L., and Lisa Hirschman. 1981. "Families at Risk for Father-Daughter Incest." *American Journal of Psychiatry* 38(7): 967–970.

Hillman, Donald, and Janice Solek-Tefft. 1988. *Spiders and Flies: Help for Parents and Teachers of Sexually Abused Children.* Lexington, MA: Lexington Books.

Hollenberg, Elizabeth, and Cynthia Ragan. 1991. *Child Sexual Abuse: Selected Projects.* Washington, DC: National Center on Child Abuse and Neglect.

Hunter, Mic. 1990. *Abused Boys: The Neglected Victims of Sexual Abuse.* New York: Columbine.

Jampole, L., and M. K. Weber. 1987. "An Assessment of the Behavior of Sexually Abused and Non-Sexually Abused Children with Anatomically Correct Dolls." *Child Abuse and Neglect* 11: 187–192.

Katchen, Martin H., and David K. Sakheim. 1992. "Satanic Beliefs and Practices." In *Out of Darkness: Exploring Satanism and Ritual Abuse*, ed. David K. Sakheim and Susan E. Devine. New York: Lexington Books.

Kelley, Susan J. 1988. "Ritualistic Abuse of Children: Dynamics and Impact." *Cultic Studies Journal* 5: 228–236.

Kempe, C. Henry, F. N. Silverman, B. F. Steele, W. Droegemueller, and H. K. Silver. 1962. "The Battered Child Syndrome." *Journal of the American Medical Association* 181: 17–24.

Kempe, Ruth S., and C. Henry Kempe. 1984. *The Common Secret: Sexual Abuse of Children and Adolescents.* New York: W. H. Freeman and Company.

Kopetsky, Leona. 1991. "Parental Alienation Syndrome: Recent Research." Paper presented at the Fifteenth Annual Child Custody Conference, Keystone, Colorado.

Langevin, R., L. Handy, H. Hook, D. Day, and A. Russon. 1985. "Are Incestuous Fathers Pedophilic and Aggressive?" In *Erotic Preference Gender Identity and Aggression*, ed. R. Langevin. New York: Erlbaum.

Lanning, Kenneth V. 1991. "Ritual Abuse: A Law Enforcement View or Perspective." *Child Abuse and Neglect* 15: 171–173.

———. 1992. *Child Sex Rings: A Behavioral Analysis.* Arlington, VA: National Center for Missing and Exploited Children.

Levi-Strauss, Claude. 1985. *The View from Afar.* Trans. Joachim Neugroschel and Phoebe Hoss. New York: Basic Books.

Lew, Mike. 1988. *Victims No Longer: Men Recovering from Incest and Other Sexual Child Abuse.* New York: Harper & Row.

Lloyd, David. 1982. "Testimony before the President's Task Force on Victims of Crime." Final Report. (December).

———. 1990a. *Ritual Child Abuse: Understanding the Controversies.* Huntsville, AL: National Resource Center on Child Sexual Abuse.

———, ed. 1990b. *Sibling Incest: Proceedings of a Think Tank.* Huntsville, AL: National Children's Advocacy Center.

Loftus, Elizabeth, and Katherine Ketcham. 1994. *The Myth of Repressed Memory: False Memories and Allegations of Sexual Abuse.* New York: St. Martin's Press.

Lustig, N., J. W. Dresser, S. W. Spellman, and T. B. Murray. 1966. "Incest: A Family Group Survival Pattern." *Archives of General Psychology* 14: 31–40.

Maan, Cathy. 1994. "Current Issues in Using Anatomical Dolls." *Violence Update* 4: 1–4.

McCarthy, Loretta. 1981. "Investigation of Incest: Opportunity to Motivate Families To Seek Help." *Child Welfare* 15: 679–689.

MacFarlane, Kee. 1978. "Sexual Abuse of Children." In *The Victimization of Women,* ed. J. Chapman and M. Gates. Beverly Hills, CA: Sage Publications.

MacFarlane, Kee, and Jill Waterman. 1986. *Sexual Abuse of Young Children.* New York: Guilford Press.

McHugh, Paul R. 1993. "Multiple Personality Disorder." *Harvard Mental Health Letter* 10: 4–7.

Maryland v. Craig, 110 S.Ct. 3157, 111 L.Ed.2d. 666 (1990).

Mayer, Robert S. 1991. *Satan's Children: Case Studies in Multiple Personalities.* New York: G. P. Putnam's Sons.

Mead, Margaret. 1935. *Sex and Temperament in Three Primitive Societies.* New York: William Morrow and Company.

———. 1949. *Male and Female: A Study of the Sexes in a Changing World.* New York: Morrow Quill Paperbacks.

Meiselman, Karin. 1978. *Incest: A Psychological Study of Causes and Effects with Treatment Recommendations.* San Francisco: Jossey-Bass.

Meyer, L., and J. Romero. 1980. *Ten-Year Follow-up of Sex Offender Recidivism.* Philadelphia: Joseph Peters Institute.

Moorehead, Caroline, ed. 1990. *Betrayal: A Report on Violence toward Children in Today's World.* New York: Doubleday.

NCCAN (National Center on Child Abuse and Neglect). 1981. *Study Findings: National Study of the Incidence and Severity of Child Abuse and Neglect.* Washington, DC: U.S. Department of Health and Human Services.

———. 1991. *Symposium on Judicial Needs Relating to Child Sexual Abuse.* Washington, DC: U.S. Department of Health and Human Services.

Nasjleti, M. 1980. "Suffering in Silence: The Male Incest Victim." *Child Welfare* 49: 269–275.

National Center for Missing and Exploited Children. 1992. *Female Juvenile Prostitution: Problem and Response.* Arlington, VA: National Center for Missing and Exploited Children.

National Committee for the Prevention of Child Abuse. 1986. *Child Assault Prevention With Preschoolers: What Do We Know?* Chicago: National Committee for the Prevention of Child Abuse.

Nobile, Philip. 1977. "Incest: The Last Taboo." *Penthouse* (December): 117–118.

Pecora, P. J., and M. B. Martin. 1994. *Risk Factors Associated with Child Sexual Abuse: A Selected Summary of Empirical Research.* Denver, CO: American Humane Association.

Peters, Joseph J. 1976. "Children Who Are Victims of Sexual Assault and the Psychology of Offenders." *American Journal of Psychotherapy* 30: 398–421.

Peters, S. D. 1984. *The Relationship between Childhood Sexual Victimization and Adult Depression among Afro-American and White Women.* Ph.D. diss., University of California at Los Angeles: University Microfilms No. 84-28, 555.

Peterson, Judith. 1989. *Adults Molested as Children: Group Therapists' Guide.* San Jose: Giarretto Institute.

Quinsey, Vern L. 1985. "Men Who Have Sex with Children." In *Law and Mental Health: International Perspectives,* ed. D. Weisstub. New York: Pergamon.

Quinsey, Vern L., C. M. Steinman, S. G. Bergersen, and T. F. Holmes. 1975. "Penile Circumference, Skin Conduction, and Ranking Responses of Child Molesters and 'Normals' to Sexual and Nonsexual Visual Stimuli." *Behavior Therapy* 6: 213–219.

Rush, Florence. 1980. *The Best-Kept Secret: Sexual Abuse of Children.* New York: McGraw-Hill.

Russell, Diana E. 1983. "The Incidence and Prevalence of Intrafamilial and Extrafamilial Sexual Abuse of Female Children." *Child Abuse and Neglect* 7: 133–146.

———. 1984. "The Prevalence and Seriousness of Incestuous Abuse: Stepfathers vs. Biological Fathers." *Child Abuse and Neglect* 8: 15–22.

———. 1986. *The Secret Trauma: Incest in the Lives of Girls and Women.* New York: Basic Books.

Ryan, Gail. 1988. "The Juvenile Sexual Offender: A Question of Diagnosis." Data presented at the National Symposium on Child Victimization. Anaheim, CA.

Sakheim, David K., and Susan E. Devine, eds. 1992. *Out of Darkness: Exploring Satanism and Ritual Abuse.* New York: Lexington Books.

Sagan, Carl, and Ann Druyan. 1992. *Shadows of Forgotten Ancestors: A Search for Who We Are.* New York: Random House.

Sgroi, Suzanne. 1982. *Handbook of Clinical Interventions in Child Sexual Abuse.* Lexington, MA: Lexington Books.

———. 1988. *Vulnerable Populations: Evaluation and Treatment of Sexually Abused Children and Adult Survivors.* Lexington, MA: Lexington Books.

Singer, M., M. Petchers, and D. Hussey. 1989. "The Relationship between Sexual Abuse and Substance Abuse among Psychiatrically Hospitalized Adolescents." *Child Abuse and Neglect* 13: 319–325.

Sivan, Abigail B., D. P. Schor, G. K. Koeppl, and L. D. Noble. 1988. "Interaction of Normal Children With Anatomical Dolls." *Child Abuse and Neglect* 12: 295–304.

Smith, Holly, and Edie Israel. 1987. "Sibling Incest: A Study of the Dynamics of 25 Cases." *Child Abuse and Neglect* 11: 101–108.

Smith, Peggy, Marvin Bohnstedt, Elizabeth Lennon, and Kathleen Grove. 1985. *Long-Term Correlates of Child Victimization: Consequences of Intervention and Non-Intervention.* Washington, DC: National Center on Child Abuse and Neglect.

Summit, Roland. 1983. "Child Sexual Abuse Accommodation Syndrome." *Child Abuse and Neglect* 7: 177–193.

Sumner, William Graham. 1940. *Folkways: A Study of the Sociological Importance of Usages.* Boston: Citadel Press.

Tavris, Carol. 1993. "Beware the Incest-survivor Machine." *New York Times Book Review* (January 3) 78: 1.

Trainor, C. 1984. "Sexual Maltreatment in the United States: A Five-year Perspective." Paper presented at the International Congress on Child Abuse and Neglect, Montreal.

U.S. Attorney General's Task Force on Family Violence. 1984. *Final Report of the U.S. Attorney General's Task Force on Family Violence.* Washington, DC: Government Printing Office.

Victim Services Agency. 1991. *Incest Treatment: A Curriculum for Training Mental Health Professionals.* New York: Victim Services Agency.

Walker, Lenore E. A., ed. 1988. *Handbook on Sexual Abuse of Children: Assessment and Treatment Issues.* New York: Springer Publishing Company.

Westermarck, Edward. 1891. *The History of Human Marriage.* New York: Macmillan.

Whitcomb, Debra. 1992. *When the Victim Is a Child.* 2d ed. Washington, DC: National Institute of Justice.

Whitcomb, Debra, Gail S. Goodman, Desmond K. Runyan, and Shirley Hoak. 1994. "The Emotional Effects of Testifying on Sexually Abused Children." *National Institute of Justice Research in Brief* (U.S. Department of Justice) (April).

Wiehe, Vernon N. 1990. *Sibling Abuse: Hidden Physical, Emotional, and Sexual Trauma.* Lexington, MA: Lexington Books.

Wyatt, Gail Elizabeth. 1985. "The Sexual Abuse of Afro-American and White American Women in Childhood." *Child Abuse and Neglect* 9: 507–519.

Yapko, Michael D. 1994. *Suggestions of Abuse: True and False Memories of Childhood Sexual Trauma.* New York: Simon & Schuster.

Chronology 2

S exual relations between adults and children have a long history. In early Christian history, women were considered the property of first the father and then the husband; female children were also considered property and had no rights. The early church considered 12 the age at which a young girl could be married; future husbands would examine these young girls much as they would measure the value of a horse.

Both the Bible and the Talmud encouraged men to have sexual relations with young girls; they were allowed to do this through socially sanctioned marriage, concubinage, and slavery. As Florence Rush says, "The Talmud held that a female child of `three years and one day' could be betrothed by sexual intercourse with her father's permission. Intercourse with one younger was not a crime but invalid" (Rush 1980, 17). In the Bible, the female was considered property, along with a man's house and ox. Marriage was a business deal, a financial transaction, according to Rush, who observes that "[m]arriage was the purchase of a daughter from her father, prostitution was a selling and reselling of a female by her master for sexual service, and rape was the theft of a girl's virginity which could be compensated for by payment to her father" (Rush 1980, 19).

She goes on to say that "[w]hen a father disposed of his daughter's sexual favors in a legal monetary transaction, sex between a man and an unmarried, unbetrothed daughter was both legitimate and respectable, and the girl was not a harlot nor the man a rapist. . . . True, a father was advised not to prostitute his daughter, but if he did so he broke no laws and was not subject to punishment" (Rush 1980, 23).

Rush describes sexual relations between men and girls as defined by Christian law as follows:

> Christian law did not focus upon whether a man did copulate with a child but rather when he copulated with her. Sex between men and children was debated not out of concern for a child but out of regard for the technical violation of the impediment of affinity [that once a man had sex with a woman, he was in a condition of "affinity" with her family and marriage or sex between other members of her family was not allowed]. And since canonists defined sex with a child under seven as invalid rather than illegal, some subsequent jurists took this distinction to mean that rape of one so young was not possible. When the delineation between childhood and adulthood was raised from age seven to ten, jurists who were presented with a case of rape of a seven-year-old "doubted whether rape could be committed upon a child under ten years old." (Rush 1980, 35)

In Hindu law and tradition, a girl must be married before puberty; if she is not married before she starts menstruating, she and her family are doomed to a tragic afterlife. A female child is born without a soul and her only salvation is to be married before her first menstrual period; this, along with being a faithful and obedient wife, will often guarantee that she will have a peaceful afterlife.

In ancient Greece, pubescent girls were forced to marry men usually between 15 and 20 years older than they were, and boys from noble families, at age 10, were required to have adult male lovers, who also would act as the boys' teachers and counselors. An adult male would court a young boy and, once the boy's father approved of and selected one lover for his son, the lover was allowed by law to "possess the boy by rape" (Rush 1980, 50).

Approximately four thousand years ago, the Code of Hammurabi declared that a man who "knew" his own daughter was banished from the city of Babylon.

Early American history also provides stories of the sexual abuse of children. Florence Rush describes the times:

> During the colonial period, young indentured servants were used for sexual gratification; Southern slave owners exploited eleven-, twelve-, and thirteen-year-olds for breeding by having them indiscriminately impregnated by other slaves, overseers and their masters. Others were more carefully selected for personal use or to be hired out to brothels. America also had "street arabs" who at ages ten and eleven became featured attractions in bordellos. West Coast trades did a lucrative business in purchasing little Chinese girls and then selling them at a profit. A young healthy American child could bring sixty or seventy dollars for one evening, but a Chinese girl purchased at $1,500 to $3,500 could yield the owner who hired her out a 25 to 35 percent net return. (Rush 1980, 63)

The remainder of this chapter presents chronologically many of the major events in the more recent history of childhood sexual abuse.

900   Lady Murasaki writes *Tales of Gengi,* the story of her experiences with royal Japanese court manners. She was adopted by Prince Gengi of Japan at the age of ten. She was obviously more than a daughter to him, and in describing the situation, she says that if she were truly his daughter, "convention would not have allowed him to go on living with her on terms of such complete intimacy" (Lady Murasaki 1955, 146).

1576   Jurists in England rule that a female child can consent to sex at age 10 and can be married at age 12. Thus, having sexual relations with a female child under the age of 10 is a felony and having sexual relations with a female child between the ages of 10 and 12 is a misdemeanor. It is still common for men to make exceptions to this rule, and female children generally are given little or no protection. Prior to this ruling, sex with a child under the age of three according to Hebrew practice and sex

1576
cont.
with a child under the age of seven according to canon law, was considered invalid, meaning that it was not believed to have occurred and was therefore ignored.

1828
In India, Ram Mohan Ray tries to eliminate child marriage but is not able to gather enough followers or persuade the legislature to enact such a law. Child marriage has a long Hindu tradition.

1870s
In London, over 20,000 children live on the streets, many of them dying of illness and starvation. Boys usually survive by stealing and girls survive by becoming prostitutes.

1877
The American Humane Association is founded and is the only national organization working to protect both children and animals from abuse, neglect, cruelty, and exploitation. Their Children's Division works to break the cycle of abuse through training, risk assessment, research, and policy development programs initiated to provide effective child protective systems. They begin their efforts by working to protect animals and add children to their repertoire when they realize that no other organization exists to help and protect children.

1897
Sigmund Freud begins to doubt the validity of his theories on hysteria, in which he first believed that many of his female clients had been sexually abused by their fathers, resulting in hysteria. He theorized that these women were seduced by their fathers and then as adults experienced a variety of symptoms, including loss of appetite, vomiting, sneezing, and temporary blindness. He now believes that many of his patients were not sexually abused by their parents; they were merely attracted to the opposite-sex parent when they were very young. He will later develop his theory of the Oedipus complex, in which he theorizes that children are sexually attracted to their opposite-sex parent.

1910
Reginald Wright Kaufman writes *The House of Bondage*, in which he describes the current social attitudes that lead children into prostitution, how they are seduced into it and often cannot escape from it.

About this time, child protection agencies start a campaign against sexual attacks on young girls. The focus is on attacks by strangers, and the girls are often blamed as sex delinquents rather than being seen as victims. Many people believe that the young girls are the seducers; most men cannot help but be lured by them.

1920s   Sociologists start studying delinquent girls and discover that many have been victims of sexual abuse within their families. Up until now, many experts believed that strangers were the primary abusers of young girls.

1927   Many sources indicate that over 80 percent of the people in India participate in child marriages. Katherine Mayo writes *Mother India,* a book about the lower status of women and the abuse that young girls are subjected to in child marriages. Because she is an outsider (she is American), many Indians attack her, claiming she does not understand the reasons for child marriage and that she manipulated the facts; she is accused of racism. Nevertheless, her descriptions of what happens to child brides, based on a review of hospital records and interviews with medical personnel, are horrifying to most people outside of India. She describes the ruptured vaginas, lacerated bodies, peritonitis, venereal disease, and death of young women who are the victims of what most people consider sexual abuse. Many Indians, including poet Rabindranath Tagore, respond to her criticisms by condoning child marriage and denying that it is abusive to the young girls.

1937   Dr. Lauretta Bender and Dr. Abram Blau, after studying children who were sexually assaulted, conclude that children are not necessarily innocent in cases of sexual abuse. These children may not be irreparably harmed by the sexual relations with an adult. Bender and Blau believe that in some cases the children were the actual seducers rather than the adults, that these young girls either looked seductively at the men or dressed provocatively and that the men were the victims (Bender & Blau 1937).

1950   In order to protect young girls, Israel forbids a father or groom to set up a marriage with a girl who has not yet reached her sixteenth birthday. The Israelis later realize that this is not against the law according to the Talmud and in 1960 will strengthen this law by declaring that any person contracting a marriage for a young woman under the age of 17, no matter what the ancient law stipulated, would be subject to imprisonment or fines or both.

1953   Dr. Alfred Kinsey and his colleagues publish their landmark study of sexual behavior, *Sexual Behavior in the Human Female.* The researchers seem surprised to find that one in four women they interviewed reported some sort of undesired sexual contact or experience initiated by an adult male. In cases of what we would today call sexual abuse, Kinsey also believes that men are in danger of being persecuted by females intent on protecting children and themselves. By punishing the offender, the law often damages everyone involved more than any pain the sexual abuse causes. For example, Kinsey and his colleagues cite cases in which men are thrown in jail for exposing themselves; their families are left destitute, their wives divorce them, and the children often become wards of the court. They believe that this is much more damaging than the physical and emotional pain inflicted on the child by the sexual abuse (Kinsey et al. 1953).

1954   Olympia Press publishes *Lolita* by Vladimir Nabokov. It is banned in many public libraries and denounced by many critics. The story revolves around an aging European pedophile, Humbert Humbert, and Lolita, a 12-year-old American who is kidnapped by Humbert, drugged, and finally sexually abused by him. He basically imprisons her, watching her every move, thwarting her attempts at escape, until she finally escapes from him.

1962   Seven couples who advocate legalizing sex with children start the Rene Guyon Society. They work toward getting this policy enacted into law but do not allow anyone who claims to have had sex with children to join their organization because this behavior is still illegal. They advocate to allow children to have sex with other children as well as to allow sex between children and adults. Their motto is "Sex by year eight or else it's too late."

C. Henry Kempe, a pediatrician from Denver, Colorado, in an article in the *Journal of the American Medical Association*, describes the battered child syndrome, characteristics of physically abused children that all physicians should be able to determine, helping them more easily identify abused children. This is the first formal recognition of child abuse in the medical community. This article results in a surge of research on abuse—physical, sexual, and psychological—and brings national attention to the seriousness and extent of child abuse (Kempe et al. 1962).

1964   The Sex Information and Educational Council of the United States (SIECUS) is founded and is the first organization to provide honest and straightforward information about sex to parents, children, and teachers. Among other activities, it denounces all acts of sexual exploitation and sexual abuse. However, the organization also believes that children often are unable to report events accurately, may willingly participate in the sexual activity, may actually precipitate the sexual relations, and for the most part, are not significantly harmed by exposure to fondling and exhibitionism.

1969   The Children's Division of the American Humane Association, under the direction of Vincent DeFrancis, publishes the results of its study of sex crimes perpetrated against children in Brooklyn and the Bronx, New York. They studied a sample group of 250 cases reported to police and child protection agencies. This is one of the early studies to estimate the prevalence and incidence of sexual abuse of children and to take into consideration the emotional trauma done to the child by such abuse.

1970   Parents Anonymous, a national self-help group for parents to help prevent child abuse, is founded. The national

1970
cont.

organization offers a variety of services to local chapters, including parent support groups, parent education workshops, advocacy, and public awareness activities. The organization will offer over 2,100 groups for children and their parents at no charge to the families.

The National Commission on Obscenity and Pornography publishes a report concluding that pornography is not necessarily harmful to children or adults. Pornography may actually encourage open discussions between parents and children about sex. It is "not a factor in the causation of crime" and as a result "is not a matter of public concern" (The Report of the Commission on Obscenity and Pornography 1970, xi). This report does not discuss the exploitation of children who appear in all types of child pornography and denies that children are victimized by pornography.

1971

Henry Giarretto establishes one of the first model treatment programs, now known as the Child Sexual Abuse Treatment Program, in Santa Clara County, California. The Juvenile Probation Department (JPD) in Santa Clara, the designated reporting agency for all cases of child sexual abuse, has difficulty providing coordinated services to sexually abused children and their families. Members of the JPD ask Giarretto, a marriage and family counselor, to help establish a pilot project to provide counseling to the children and their families. At the end of the eight-week pilot project period, everyone who is involved in the project recognizes the benefits of this program and it is expanded to include the coordination of services required by the family, such as financial advice and legal assistance, and to help facilitate the reunification of the family.

1972

The C. Henry Kempe National Center for the Prevention and Treatment of Child Abuse and Neglect opens to provide a clinically based resource for training, consultation, program development and education, and research in all forms of child abuse and neglect. The Center is committed to multidisciplinary approaches to improve the recognition, treatment, and prevention of all forms of abuse and neglect, including sexual abuse.

1973   The Runaway Youth Act is passed by the U.S. Congress. It authorizes the spending of $8 million to develop shelters for children who have run away from home. Many people hope that this will help protect the estimated one million children living on the streets from becoming prostitutes, getting involved in drugs and alcohol, or becoming involved in pornography.

1974   The National Center on Child Abuse and Neglect (NCCAN) is established by the Child Abuse Prevention and Treatment Act (Public Law 93-247) as the primary federal agency charged with helping states and communities address the problems of child maltreatment. NCCAN oversees all federal child abuse and neglect efforts and allocates child maltreatment funds appropriated by Congress. They are responsible for conducting research on the causes, prevention, and treatment of child abuse and neglect; collecting, analyzing, and disseminating information to professionals concerned with child abuse and neglect; increasing public awareness of the problems of child maltreatment; and assisting states and communities in developing programs related to the prevention, identification, and treatment of child abuse and neglect.

         Marian Wright Edelman organizes the Children's Defense Fund (CDF) to protect America's youth. She wants to provide a strong and effective voice for all children, to educate the nation about the needs of children, and to encourage the support of children before they get sick, are abused, drop out of school, or get into trouble.

1976   Alfred M. Freedman and his colleagues write *Modern Synopsis of Comprehensive Textbook of Psychiatry II*, a psychiatric text used in many medical schools. It proclaims that "the occurrence of mother-son incest bespeaks more severe pathology than does father-daughter incest" (Freedman, Kaplan, and Sadock 1976, 772).

         NCCAN supports the first comprehensive incidence study of child abuse and neglect. Known as the National Incidence Study, in its written report published later in 1981, it estimates that 44,700 cases of child sexual abuse,

1976 or 0.7 per 1,000 children, were known to professionals
cont. during the period from April 1979 to March 1980
(NCCAN 1981).

1977 The Federal Protection of Children against Sexual Exploitation Act is passed by the U.S. Congress. This law
prohibits the production of any sexually explicit material that uses a child under the age of 16 if the material
will cross interstate lines. Penalties include 10 years in
prison and $10,000 fines. The focus of this law is on the
transporting, shipping, or mailing of child pornography, and little can be done to prevent someone from
giving this type of material away or in other ways ex-
changing it for something else; the law only prevents
the sale of this type of material. Many experts realize
that this law does very little to stop the growing market
for child pornography.

1978 The North American Man/Boy Love Association
(NAMBLA) is formed. Members advocate for sex between men and boys, arguing that children should be
sexually liberated because children are fully capable of
entering into sexual relations with appropriate knowledge and understanding of what is happening. They
also believe that the age of consent laws in all states
should be abolished.

1979 The Illusion Theater in Minneapolis, Minnesota, produces the first live-theater program focusing on the prevention of sexual abuse. Children are the primary
audience for this program, which focuses on letting
children know that it is not okay if someone sexually
abuses them, that it is not their fault, and if they have
any questions or if they have been sexually abused, that
it is okay to talk to another adult about it.

Sociologist Diana Russell conducts the first truly random study to estimate the extent of sexual abuse of
children. She interviews over 900 women from the San
Francisco area about their sexual experiences as children. Her findings indicate that 38 percent of these
women had been sexually abused as children.

1980   *Michele Remembers* is published, the story of Michele Smith and her escape from a satanic cult. The publication of this book triggers many reports from other people of satanic cults and ritual abuse and begins to generate a great deal of interest in satanic cults.

         Florence Rush publishes *The Best Kept Secret: Sexual Abuse of Children,* one of the first comprehensive studies on child sexual abuse. Rush, with detailed research and analysis, shows that child sexual abuse is not the occasional deviant act of some stranger, but a common occurrence in many families. With a historical overview of the sexual abuse of children, she shows how sexual abuse is still condoned in today's society.

         Five sexual abuse treatment and training institutes are funded by the National Center on Child Abuse and Neglect (NCCAN). These include: (1) the Joseph J. Peters Institute in Philadelphia, Pennsylvania, (2) the Knoxville Institute for Sexual Abuse Treatment in Knoxville, Tennessee, (3) the Child Abuse Unit for Studies, Education, and Services (CAUSES) in Chicago, Illinois, (4) the Sexual Assault Center at the Harborview Medical Center in Seattle, Washington, and (5) the Institute for the Community as Extended Family (ICEF) in San Jose, California. Each of these institutes is set up to add to the knowledge of child sexual abuse and to demonstrate ways to disseminate this information nationally to professionals in the field.

1981   The Boy Scouts publish the *Scoutmaster Handbook,* their first publication to include information about sexual abuse. The discussion focuses on males infiltrating troops for the sole purpose of sex, but the emphasis of the document is on young boys who are searching for sex, not adults who molest children.

1983   A two-and-a-half-year-old child alleges that his teacher at the McMartin Preschool in southern California has hurt his bottom. Subsequent investigations at this preschool and others in the same area find at least 350 children who claim to have been sexually abused while attending preschool. Children say that they have

1983
cont.

watched other children being sexually abused as well as being sexually abused themselves. Allegations include fondling, exposure to vaginal, oral, and anal sex, and ritualistic and satanic acts of abuse. After seven years of legal proceedings and much media attention, no one is convicted.

On September 26, two young girls and their mothers go to the police department in Jordan, Minnesota, and tell the officers that James John Rud, a 27-year-old trash collector, has sexually abused the two young girls. Within six months the case will attract national attention. Two dozen men and women, many of them well respected in the community, will be charged in a conspiracy of sex, torture, and murder. The victims are their own children. The children will eventually allege acts of not only sexual abuse but murder as well. The stories seem incredible, many lawyers insist the children made everything up, what appear as strong cases against some parents end up as bizarre stories no one believes, the prosecutor's behavior in all cases is soundly criticized, and all charges are eventually dropped. This is a classic case of charges of sexual abuse being made only to have the children's imagination and the public's fear take over. In the end, people believe that some children were indeed sexually abused, but everyone involved in the case got carried away and overreacted. Many families were hurt financially and emotionally, but nothing was resolved.

An organization named VOCAL (Victims of Child Abuse Laws) is started in Minnesota by people who claim to have been falsely accused of sexually abusing children. It is started as a result of the many people charged with sexually abusing children in Jordan, Minnesota, who believe they have been railroaded by the legal system and want to offer support to others who have been falsely accused.

1984

The Attorney General's Task Force on Family Violence presents its final report. They find that many children endure up to 12 or more separate interviews through the course of court hearings in cases of child sexual abuse. The Task Force makes several recommendations to minimize the trauma to the victim of violence while still protecting the rights of the accused. They recommend using the same prosecutor throughout the court process, allowing hearsay evidence at preliminary hearings to minimize the number of times the victim is required to testify, allowing the child's testimony to be presented on videotape, using anatomically detailed dolls to describe abuse, appointing a special volunteer advocate for the child, legally presuming that children are competent witnesses, allowing flexible courtroom settings, controlling press coverage, and limiting court continuances of each case.

1986   The Children's Justice Act is passed by the U.S. Congress and becomes law. It provides funds to the states to train law enforcement personnel in ways to manage child abuse. In order to receive funding, each state must establish an interdisciplinary task force that includes medical and mental health professionals, child advocates, judges, and attorneys. The purpose is to improve the chances of prosecution while reducing the trauma to the victims.

1988   The Boy Scouts introduce "Youth Protection Guidelines," a course on sexual abuse for professional and volunteer leaders. The course, presented on videotape, describes what sexual abuse of children is and how troops can work to prevent the sexual abuse of Scouts. Presenters include David Finkelhor and Kenneth Lanning, both sex abuse experts. Information is provided on new rules developed by the organization to combat the sexual molestation of Scouts, such as requiring more than one adult leader on all trips, limiting conversations between an adult and a Scout to areas where they can be observed by other people, and prohibiting an adult from sharing a tent with a young Scout.

Kelly Michaels is found guilty and sentenced to 47 years in prison in one of the most bizarre and disturbing day-care cases in the country. Children attending the Wee Care preschool in Maplewood, New Jersey, allege that Michaels, their teacher, would gather them

1988
cont.

together at nap time and lead them through the church that housed Wee Care into a choir room. In this room, she made them remove their clothes and often removed her own clothing as well. The children report they were forced to engage in sexual acts, to eat feces and urine, and to lick peanut butter off her genitals. Many of the children also accuse Michaels of putting kitchen utensils and Lego toys into their vaginas and rectums. None of the staff members say they saw, heard, smelled, or suspected any of these activities.

The National Network of Children's Advocacy Centers is formed in response to the need for a coordinated effort to provide services for children who are sexually abused. The National Network consists of member and affiliate programs that provide technical assistance, training, and networking for communities that want to establish a Children's Advocacy Center. These advocacy centers offer coordinated, multidisciplinary services to children who have been abused, particularly those who have been sexually abused, and their families. Each center offers a variety of services, usually coordinated by a case management team. The National Network establishes minimum standards that each member program must meet in order to be part of the network.

1990

The U.S. Supreme Court rules in *Maryland v. Craig* that a Maryland law that allows children to provide testimony in a sexual abuse case using closed-circuit television outside of the courtroom with only the prosecutor and defense attorney present does not violate the defendant's right to confront his accuser.

The Victims of Child Abuse Act is passed by the U.S. Congress. It allows children testifying in court to use anatomically correct dolls to demonstrate what happened to them, presumes children are competent witnesses, protects children's privacy, allows children to testify via closed-circuit television or by using videotaped testimony, authorizes the appointment of a guardian ad litem to protect the best interests of the child and provides for victim impact statements from the children. Speedy trials are encouraged as are the use of multidisciplinary teams to treat and help the sexually abused child. The statute of limitations for starting prosecution of child sexual abuse allegations is also extended until the child reaches the age of 25.

1993   President Bill Clinton signs into law the National Child Care Protection Act, sponsored by Representative Patricia Schroeder (D.-CO), to create a national database of convicted child molesters. Youth organizations will be able to submit the names of their employees and volunteers to a state agency that is designated to run these names through the database of molesters as well as through the FBI's database of convicted criminals, which includes murderers and kidnappers.

The New Jersey Court of Appeals rules that Kelly Michaels from the Wee Care preschool in Maplewood did not receive a fair trial, in part because the judge's questioning of the children was not impartial: He questioned the children in his chambers, and while the jury watched on closed-circuit TV, he played ball with them, sometimes held them on his lap and knee, whispered in their ears and had them whisper in his ear, and encouraged and complimented them, stated the ruling. The state appeals the decision.

References

Bender, Lauretta, and Abram Blau. 1937. "The Reaction of Children to Sexual Relations with Adults." *American Journal of Orthopsychiatry* 7: 500–518.

Freedman, Alfred M., Harold I. Kaplan, and Benjamin J. Sadock. 1976. *Modern Synopsis of Comprehensive Textbook of Psychiatry II.* Baltimore: Williams and Wilkins Company.

Kempe, C. Henry, F. N. Silverman, B. F. Steele, W. Droegemueller, and H. K. Silver. 1962. "The Battered Child Syndrome." In *Journal of the American Medical Association* 181: 17–24.

Kinsey, Alfred C., Wardell B. Pomeroy, Clyde E. Martin, and Paul H. Gebhard. 1953. *Sexual Behavior in the Human Female.* Philadelphia: W. B. Saunders.

Mayo, Katherine. 1927. *Mother India.* New York: Harcourt, Brace, & Co.

Lady Murasaki. 1955. *The Tales of Gengi.* New York: Doubleday Anchor.

National Center on Child Abuse and Neglect (NCCAN). 1981. *Study Findings: National Study of the Incidence and Severity of Child Abuse and Neglect.* Washington, D.C.: U.S. Department of Health and Human Services.

The Report of the Commission on Obscenity and Pornography. 1970. New York: Bantam.

Rush, Florence. 1980. *The Best Kept Secret: Sexual Abuse of Children.* New York: McGraw-Hill.

Biographical Sketches 3

Gene Abel

Dr. Abel is the director of the Behavioral Medicine Institute of Atlanta, the largest treatment program in the Southeast for sex offenders. Approximately 250 people are in treatment at any given time, and 90 percent of them are child molesters. Abel is also professor of psychiatry at Emory University School of Medicine and Morehouse University School of Medicine. He is internationally known for his research work with sexually aggressive people, primarily adults who sexually abuse children. He has headed six federal research projects for NIMH and has published approximately 100 medical articles in numerous scientific journals. Dr. Abel also maintains a database containing the results of his research with 400 known sex offenders and over 100 normal people; this database can provide information on a variety of topics.

One of his best-known accomplishments is the Abel Screen, which he developed as a method of screening people to determine those who may have a sexual interest in children or may already be sexually abusing children. It has proven to be a reliable, cost-effective technique. The screen consists of a series of four easily administered tests; the combined scores reveal 20 separate types of sexual interest. The first test consists of computer-generated slides of children, adolescents, adults, and couples; the individual rates his interest in each slide. The second test is a physiologic measure of the subject as he views the slides and is taken without the subject's knowledge. The final two tests are question-and-answer tests.

The Abel Screen can be used as the first step in evaluating someone who might be at high risk to be a sex offender and who perhaps should not be placed in environments in which children are present. If a person fails the screen, the next step in assessment is usually the administration of more intrusive procedures.

Marilyn Van Derbur Atler

Marilyn Van Derbur, Miss America of 1958, in 1991 stood before a small audience at the University of Colorado Health Sciences campus (who came to hear about plans for a new program at the Kempe National Center, which is dedicated to preventing and treating child abuse and neglect) and revealed that she was an incest survivor. She had been sexually abused as a young girl by her father from the time she was five years old until she left home for college at age 18. Her father, Francis S. Van Derbur, was a well-known philanthropist, socialite, and Denver businessman. He died in 1984, years before his daughter revealed her secret to the world. Marilyn was one of four sisters, growing up in a family that had everything. The girls had everything they needed and wanted in life; they went skiing in the winter and rode their horses in the summer, and they attended the proper schools, took music lessons, and played games. The girls also had something else, a father who sexually abused at least two of them.

In her four-page disclosure of childhood sexual abuse, Van Derbur wrote: "People ask me why I didn't tell what was happening to me. . . . In order to survive, I split into a day child, who giggled and smiled, and a night child, who lay awake in a fetal position, only to be pried apart by my father. Until I was 24, the day child had no conscious knowledge of the night child" (Loftus, 1994, 79). She pushed herself hard to win her father's approval, but the day child never received much attention from her father. She graduated Phi Beta Kappa; won the Miss America pageant, sometimes making over 20 appearances in one day; and was a member of the University of Colorado ski team. Her father never gave her the kind of love and attention she was looking for.

When she was 24 years old, the memories of sexual abuse became conscious. She currently travels around the country talking to a variety of groups about incest. She has developed, with others, several videos to help educate the public about child sexual abuse and to help the victims recover from their experiences.

Fred Berlin

Fred Berlin received his B.A. in psychology from the University of Pittsburgh in 1964, his M.A. in psychology from Fordham University in 1966, and both his Ph.D. in psychology (1970) and his M.D. (1974) from Dalhousie University in Canada. His completed his residency in the Department of Psychiatry and Behavioral Science at the Johns Hopkins Hospital in Baltimore, Maryland. In 1980, he founded and currently is the director of the Sexual Disorders Clinic and an associate professor in the Department of Psychiatry and Behavioral Sciences of the Johns Hopkins University School of Medicine. The Sexual Disorders Clinic is currently known as the National Institute for the Study, Prevention and Treatment of Sexual Trauma.

Working with inpatients who manifest some type of sexual disorder as well as with victims of sexual trauma, Berlin and his associates are dedicated to the prevention of sexual trauma by learning more about the abusers and their disorders as well as about the victims of sexual abuse. Over the years, Berlin and his colleagues have determined that mandatory reporting of child sexual abuse usually kept undetected adult abusers from entering treatment; mandatory reporting also deterred patients' disclosures about child sexual abuse that occurred during treatment; and it did not help in identifying the number of abused children. The rate of self-referrals when reporting became mandatory in Maryland (in 1989) dropped from about 7 per year (73 over a 10-year period) to zero. The researchers' conclusion was that the law, which was intended to protect children, deters abusers from coming forward and entering treatment. Berlin believes that mandatory reporting requirements should not be applied to psychiatrists.

Berlin has numerous publications; he has been an invited participant to the White House Conference on Child Sexual Abuse; he has spoken to a variety of groups and meetings, including the Colleges of Judges in several states, the National Symposium on the Child Victim of Sexual Abuse, and the National Conference of Catholic Bishops, where he delivered the keynote address on sexual problems in the clergy.

Lucy Berliner

Lucy Berliner, the director of the Sexual Assault Center at Harborview Hospital in Seattle, Washington, is internationally recognized for her pioneering work in assessing and treating children who have been sexually abused. Known for training other clinicians around the world in specialized intervention methods, she has written and lectured throughout the country on sexual assault. Berliner has testified in court in cases of child sexual abuse, often being asked to testify as to whether or not she believes a child has been sexually abused. She has mixed feelings about providing this type of testimony. Because no standards exist among mental health workers for evaluating these cases, judges can look at several evaluations from different professionals and believe that one is better than other. This can lead to inconsistency in the outcome of these cases. She also worries about therapists who believe that they have special insights in these cases as well as about other professionals including those in the legal field who believe that therapists do indeed have special insights. "Any individual mental health professional has to be darn careful about settings themselves up to say, `I have some special ability and insight into the truth that no one else has.' I mean all you are doing is forming an opinion that will be a piece of the mosaic" (Hechler 1988, 162). Berliner has a master's degree in social work.

Douglas Besharov

Douglas Besharov is currently a research scholar at the American Enterprise Institute for Public Policy Research and an adjunct professor of law at Georgetown University and American University in Washington, D.C. He was the first director of the National Center on Child Abuse and Neglect in the U.S. Department of Health and Human Services from 1975 to 1979 (then the Department of Health, Education and Welfare). Well known for his thoughts on inappropriate investigations in child sexual abuse cases and on removal of children from their homes, he was a keynote speaker at the first VOCAL (Victims of Child Abuse Laws) conference. He has written extensively on the problems with mandatory reporting laws, which have led to an increase in the number of child sexual abuse reports made to authorities. He believes that by convincing the public that children are being sexually abused and that any suspicion that abuse has occurred must be reported, children have been made more vulnerable than ever before. According to Besharov, the rate of unfounded reports of sexual abuse has risen by over 65 percent, which means that more time is spent investigating reports, many of these reports may not be investigated in a timely manner, and therefore those children who really are being abused may be in greater danger of additional abuse before investigators can help them.

Jon R. Conte

A clinical social worker and researcher, Jon Conte is currently an associate professor and the associate dean of academic affairs at the School of Social Service Administration at the University of Chicago. He has taught in the School of Social Work at the University of Washington. He frequently lectures at both national and international meetings and conferences and has written numerous publications. Conte was the principal investigator on a study examining the effects of childhood sexual experiences on both child and adult survivors. For a project funded by the National Institute of Mental Health, he studied ways of educating children in the prevention of sexual abuse. Other areas of interest include the etiology of sexual violence and the effects of prevention education. He is the founding editor of the *Journal of Interpersonal Violence* and is president of the American Professional Society on the Abuse of Children. He has also appeared on many local and national radio and television programs, including *Good Morning America, Donahue,* and a PBS special "What Your Child Should Know about Sexual Abuse."

David Finkelhor

David Finkelhor, a leading expert on child sexual abuse, received his B.A. in social relations in 1968 from Harvard University, his Ed.M. in sociology from the Harvard Graduate School of Education in 1971, and his Ph.D. in sociology from the University of New Hampshire in 1978. He specializes in the areas of mental health, social psychology, sexual behavior, family violence, victimology, and criminology. He is currently the codirector of the Family Research Laboratory at the University of New Hampshire and a professor of sociology.

He has written extensively on child sexual abuse and family violence. With his associates from the Family Research Laboratory, he conducted a national study of sexual abuse in day care.

They found that day-care centers did not place children at a significantly higher risk of sexual abuse than other settings, but they did suggest to parents that one way of reducing the risk of sexual abuse to their children was to get more involved in the day-care center's activities. In 1986, Finkelhor and several of his colleagues reviewed ten years of research on child sexual abuse and published *A Sourcebook on Child Sexual Abuse,* which helps others working in the field of sexual abuse as well as the general public understand many of the current statistics and information on child sexual abuse.

Finkelhor has received many research grants from the National Institute of Mental Health, the National Center for Child Abuse and Neglect, the Office of Juvenile Justice and Delinquency Prevention, the Boy Scouts of America, and the National Institute on Aging. He has conducted research on incest and family sexual abuse, parental attitudes and reactions to sexual abuse, family violence, the development and dissemination of knowledge of child sexual abuse, sexual abuse in day care, characteristics of incest offenders, incidence of missing children, paternal characteristics and risk of sexual abuse in U.S. Navy families, and youth victimization prevention. He has made professional presentations on incest and sexually abused children to the Conference on Sexually Abused Children, the Vermont Planned Parenthood Association, the New Hampshire Nurses Association, the Sixth Annual Workshop on Child Abuse and Neglect, the National Center for the Prevention and Control of Rape, and Harvard Medical School. He is on the editorial boards of the *International Journal of Child Abuse and Neglect* and the *Journal of Interpersonal Violence* and is an associate editor for the journal *Violence and Victims.*

Henry Giarretto

Henry Giarretto founded the Child Sexual Abuse Treatment Program (CSATP) in Santa Clara, California, in 1971, and organized several self-help groups associated with the program, including Parents United, Daughters and Sons United, and Adults Molested as Children United. Giarretto holds a B.A., an M.A., and a Ph.D. in psychology. He has published articles in several professional journals and in 15 anthologies on child abuse, and he has written a book on the treatment of child sexual abuse. He has presented papers at major national and international conferences on child abuse.

Giarretto formed CSATP in response to the need for coordinated services for sexually abused children and their families. The Santa Clara Juvenile Probation Department (JPD) was the reporting agency for all cases of child sexual abuse; the help they provided to families was often fragmented, contributing to further trauma to the child and the family. Members of the JPD asked Giarretto, then a marriage and family counselor, to help establish a pilot project to provide counseling to the children and their families. At the end of the eight-week project, everyone who participated in the program recognized its benefits and decided to expand it to include the coordination of services required by the family, such as financial advice and legal assistance, and to help facilitate the reunification of the family. This reunification of the family could take place only after individual counseling sessions were held to help each family member cope with the abuse and other dysfunctional aspects that may have contributed to it. The program's focus is on healing and resocializing the family through the use of humanistic psychology.

Giarretto believes that compassion and caring are two critical qualities that influence the ability to treat families successfully. He sees his role as a family advocate, listening to the problems within the family with compassion and helping family members work out their problems. All families, indeed all individuals, are doing the best job they can under the circumstances in which they find themselves. The role of the counselors at CSATP is to give these families, first as individuals, the help, support, and the tools they need to help them understand why they do what they do and to understand their feelings and emotions about themselves and each other. Once they can help the individuals grow, they can help the families reunite.

Gail Goodman

As an associate professor and director of the Dual Degree Program in Psychology and Law in the psychology department at the University of Denver, Gail Goodman is prominent in the field of child sexual abuse. She has published many articles about children's testimony in cases of child sexual abuse, children's memory, and children's perceived credibility. Studies she has conducted include one on the relationship between questions asked during hearings to determine whether children are competent witnesses and children's accuracy in testifying and another on the susceptibility of children to leading questions asked by prosecutors or defense attorneys. She has received many awards for her work. She received her academic degrees (B.A., M.A., Ph.D.) from the University of California at Los Angeles.

C. Henry Kempe

Charles Henry Kempe received his M.D. from the University of California in 1945 and interned in pediatrics in 1945 and 1946. At the University of Colorado Medical Center in Denver, he was a professor of pediatrics and microbiology and chairman of the Department of Pediatrics from 1956 through 1973. During this time, he also headed the battered children's team. He was founder and director of the C. Henry Kempe National Center for the Prevention and Treatment of Child Abuse and Neglect. He was a consultant to the U.S. attorney general, the U.S. Department of Defense, and the World Health Organization and was a member of the American Pediatric Society, the American Society for Pediatric Research, the American Public Health Association, and the American Association of Immunology. In 1984 he was nominated for the Nobel Peace Prize. Kempe played a key role in defining the "battered child syndrome," a means of helping doctors identify children who have been abused. His wife, Ruth Kempe, was also well known in the field of child abuse and was instrumental in much of the initial work done to draw widespread attention to the problem of child abuse in the 1960s.

Ruth S. Kempe

Ruth Svibergson Kempe received her B.A. in 1943 from Radcliffe College and her M.D. from Yale School of Medicine in 1946. She completed her internship and residency in pediatrics at New Haven Hospital and completed a residency in child psychiatry at the University of Colorado School of Medicine in 1961. From 1961 to 1973 she was an assistant clinical professor of pediatrics at the University of Colorado School of Medicine and from 1973 through 1978 was an assistant professor of psychiatry and pediatrics there. She became a staff psychiatrist at the C. Henry Kempe National Center for the Prevention and Treatment of Child Abuse and Neglect, a position which she still holds today. With her husband, C. Henry Kempe, she wrote *Healthy Babies, Happy Parents* in 1958, *Child Abuse* in 1978, and *The Common Secret: Sexual Abuse of Children and Adolescents* in 1984. Ruth Kempe has written and lectured widely on child abuse, and she and her husband played an important role in bringing the problem of child abuse to national attention and in promoting prevention and treatment.

Kenneth V. Lanning

Kenneth Lanning is the supervisory special agent assigned to the Behavioral Science Unit at the FBI Academy in Quantico, Virginia, which helps law enforcement agencies and prosecutors throughout the United States by developing practical applications of the behavioral sciences to the field of law enforcement and criminal justice. He is a well-known expert in the area of child sex rings and child sexual abuse in satanic cults. He has identified two major types of sex rings: historical child sex rings and multidimensional child sex rings. He has spent years researching, publishing, lecturing, and consulting on the sexual victimization of children as well as the characteristics of those who sexually abuse children. He has written about child sex rings and the behavior of child molesters; he provides a law enforcement perspective on these issues.

Elizabeth Loftus

Elizabeth Loftus is one of the country's foremost experts on memory. She received her B.A. in mathematics and psychology from UCLA in 1966, her M.A. in psychology from Stanford University in 1967, and her Ph.D. in psychology from Stanford in 1970. She is currently professor of psychology at the University of Washington in Seattle.

Loftus has spent 25 years conducting laboratory studies on memory, supervising graduate students, and writing 18 books and over 250 scientific articles. Her books include *Eyewitness Testimony: Psychological Perspective* and *The Myth of Repressed Memory*. Along with Katherine Ketcham, she has written *Witness for the Defense: The Accused, the Eyewitness, and the Expert Who Puts Memory on Trial*. Much of her work concerns the malleability of memory, the ways in which our memories of events can be distorted, confused, and incorrect. When testifying in court as an expert on memory, she tries to clarify for the judge and the jury the process of memory: "Think of your mind as a bowl filled with clear water. Now imagine each memory as a teaspoon of milk stirred into the water. Every adult mind holds thousands of these murky memories. . . . Who among us would dare to disentangle the water from the milk?" (Loftus and Ketcham 1994, 3). She believes that memories have a spiritual quality more than a physical reality.

Recently, Loftus has found herself in the center of a major controversy on the validity of recovered memories (see Chapter 1, pp. 70–74). As a result of her research, she believes that for the most part repressed memories do not exist. However, she is quick to point out that she is concerned that if we do not believe these memories, then we may be returning "to those days, not so very long ago, when a victim's cries for help went unheard and accusations of sexual abuse were automatically dismissed as fantasy or wish-fulfillment" (Loftus & Ketcham 1994, 32). She has seen both sides, the families destroyed by allegations of sexual abuse that could not be substantiated at all except for the recovered memories and the pain of the alleged victim of the abuse. She acknowledges that memory is not a black and white entity; it is difficult to understand and no one knows for certain whether or not repressed memories are true.

Virginia McMartin

Virginia McMartin operated the McMartin Preschool in Manhattan Beach, California, when in 1983 she and her grandson, Raymond Buckey, along with five other child-care staff members, were charged with molesting over 350 children during a ten-year period. The investigation started with some mothers' suspicions that Raymond Buckey may have abused their children. When the mothers went to talk with Virginia McMartin's daughter and Raymond's mother, Peggy Buckey, she did not take their concerns seriously. However, a few weeks later when one child came home from the preschool with blood on his anus, his mother became concerned and took him to the Manhattan Beach Police Department and then to a local hospital. The doctors told her that her son had been sodomized, and a full-scale investigation of the McMartin Preschool began. During the ensuing investigation, investigators found that many of the children said that they had seen other children being sexually abused and they had been sexually abused themselves. Some of the allegations included fondling; exposure to vaginal, oral, and anal sex; and ritualistic and satanic acts of abuse. After seven years of legal proceedings and lots of media attention, no one was convicted.

Prior to these allegations, Virginia McMartin had been considered an upstanding member of the community. She was a member of an established Manhattan Beach family, she had received many awards from the city for her civic service, and her preschool had received great praise from child-care inspectors, who described the school as well run, well staffed, and well equipped. Most parents were impressed with the way she operated her school, including birthday parties, field trips, and educational projects.

Alice Miller

With a Ph.D. in psychology and sociology, Alice Miller has been a practicing psychoanalyst and instructor in psychoanalysis for over 20 years. When *Thou Shalt Not Be Aware* was first published in Germany in 1981, Miller was virtually the only person in Europe to write about the sexual abuse of children. She visited the United States in 1982 and was delighted to see that this topic was written about openly in this country. She believes that children are "used and misused for adults' needs, including sexual needs, to a much greater extent than we realize" (Miller 1986, 309). She thought that emotions blocked because of this abuse inevitably lead to emotional and physical problems. While she attempted to integrate her theories into the mainstream of psychoanalytic theory, she realized that this was an impossible task. She believes that psychoanalysts tend to ignore the prevalence of sexual abuse of children and to deny the serious effects of this abuse. She argues that therapists must start listening to the children and identify with them in order to understand them. Therapists must become advocates for their clients instead of representing current societal theories and values. They must not spare the parents at any cost, but must understand the ways in which sexuality can be used to control or have power over those weaker in society.

Richard Ofshe

Richard Ofshe is a professor of sociology at the University of California, Berkeley. An expert on mind control and cults, he is well known for his research into extreme techniques of influence and social control. Ofshe is quick to admit that no one knows for certain that cults that kill babies and sexually abuse children and adults even exist, because no one has found any concrete proof. He is quite aware of all the rumors of satanic ritual abuse, of the people who believe in or claim to have participated, usually against their will, in such rituals. He doubts that multiple personality exists as a separate and readily identifiable disorder; he tends to believe that these are highly suggestible people, that therapists suggest, unwittingly, symptoms that these patients will start manifesting. However, he is not willing to rule out the possibility that satanic cults exist. Ofshe shared a Pulitzer Prize in 1979 for his research on the Synanon cult in southern California. Other subjects he has written about include the thought-control techniques developed in Communist China, North Korea, and the Soviet Union and how these techniques have been used by religious cults in the United States.

Ofshe testified for the prosecution in the trial of Paul Ingram, one of the better-known cases involving repressed memories of childhood sexual abuse (see Chapter 6, p. 276, *Remembering Satan*, by Lawrence Wright). While Ofshe did not discount the possibility of the existence of a satanic cult, he still had not seen any conclusive evidence of one. The Ingram case was no exception. Ofshe believed that Ingram was visualizing events that had not occurred; nonetheless these visualizations were real to him. Ofshe continues to search for verifiable evidence that satanic cults do exist.

Florence Rush

As a social worker working in a residence for neglected and dependent girls, an activist in the Congress of Racial Equality, and a member of Older Women's Liberation, Florence Rush was no newcomer to many social issues during the 1960s. However, after attending a speakout on rape in New York City in which women had a open forum to tell their stories and share their emotions concerning rape, she realized the impact of sexual assault on women. Drawing on her experience as a social worker, she spoke at a subsequent conference on rape about her theories concerning the sexual abuse of children. Much of the information that she shared that day was later developed into her book, *The Best Kept Secret: Sexual Abuse of Children*. This book, which quickly became a classic in the field, was one of the first to counter the common beliefs about the sexual abuse of children that were held prior to the 1980s. She exposed the historical abuse of children and argued against the common beliefs that children usually were not seriously harmed by sexual abuse and that they were often the instigators of the abuse. According to many in the field, she was the first theorist to believe absolutely that the child was innocent in cases of sexual abuse.

Diana Russell

Born in Cape Town, South Africa, Diana Russell is a naturalized U.S. citizen. She received her B.A. from the University of Cape Town in 1958, a postgraduate diploma from the London School of Economics and Political Science in 1961, and her M.A. and Ph.D. in sociology from Harvard University. She is currently a professor of sociology at Mills College in Oakland, California. She has been a member of the coordinating committee of the International Tribunal on Crimes against Women, a research consultant for the California Commission on Crime Control and Violence Prevention, and a founding member of Women against Violence in Pornography and Media.

Much of her early research was on women and rape. In *The Politics of Rape: The Victim's Perspective,* she presented a comprehensive study on sexual assault against women, dispelling many of the myths that surrounded rape. Her interviews with rape victims revealed that rapes could be perpetrated by men the victims knew, including friends and lovers, not just by strangers, as had been widely believed. In *Rape in Marriage,* she wrote about the sexual abuse of women by their husbands, presenting information gathered from almost 1,000 women.

The Secret Trauma: Incest in the Lives of Girls and Women detailed her findings in a study of women who had been sexually abused as children. Many of her findings were important to the study of incest. She found that 73 percent of those women whose abuse lasted for more than five years considered the experience extremely or considerably traumatic, compared with 62 percent of those whose abuse lasted from one week to five years and 46 percent of those who were abused only once; no relationship existed between the occurrence of sexual abuse and the father's level of education or his occupation; girls who lived with their natural mother but without their natural father were more likely to be sexually abused; similar rates of abuse occurred for blacks and whites; and if a mother works outside the home, the children are at higher risk of sexual abuse. While earlier research had indicated that incest is relatively harmless to the child, Russell found that women who had experienced incest as children were more likely to experience problems later in life than women who had not been sexually abused as children. Her study was one of the first to combine stringent scholarship with an empathetic understanding of the incest victim.

Suzanne Sgroi

Suzanne Sgroi received her B.A. from Syracuse University in 1964 and her M.D. at the State University of New York in 1968. She was assistant project director and then health director for the Connecticut Child Welfare Association Children's Advocacy Center in Hartford, and she was a member of the advisory board and steering committee of the Sex Crimes Analysis Unit of the Connecticut State Police. She currently is executive director of New England Clinical Associates, a private office devoted to the treatment of child sexual abuse, and director of the Saint Joseph College Institute for Child Sexual Abuse Intervention, both in West Hartford, Connecticut.

In assessing the sexually abused child and determining the appropriate treatment, ten impact issues should be kept in mind, according to Sgroi. These include the "damaged goods" syndrome, guilt, fear, depression, low self-esteem and poor social skills, repressed anger and hostility, inability to trust, blurred role boundaries and role confusion, pseudomaturity, and self-mastery and control (Sgroi 1988). She is well known in the field of child sexual abuse and has written extensively on the subject.

References

Hechler, David. 1988. *The Battle and the Backlash: The Child Sexual Abuse War.* Lexington, MA: Lexington Books.

Loftus, Elizabeth, and Katherine Ketcham. 1994. *The Myth of Repressed Memory: False Memories and Allegations of Sexual Abuse.* New York: St. Martin's Press.

Miller, Alice. 1986. *Thou Shalt Not Be Aware: Society's Betrayal of the Child.* Trans. Hildegarde and Hunter Hannum. New York: Meridian.

Sgroi, Suzanne. 1988. *Vulnerable Populations: Evaluation and Treatment of Sexually Abused Children and Adult Survivors.* Lexington, MA: Lexington Books.

Data and Documents 4

This chapter presents general facts and statistics on the prevalence and incidence of childhood sexual abuse, children who may be most at risk for abuse, and signs and symptoms of sexual abuse. Documents included are a statement on false memories from the American Psychiatric Association, policies on sexual abuse of the Catholic Church, and recommendations for the multidisciplinary treatment of childhood sexual abuse, the result of a symposium sponsored by the National Institute of Justice, the Office of Juvenile Justice and Delinquency Prevention, the Office for Victims of Crime, and the National Center on Child Abuse and Neglect. Excerpts are included from relevant federal laws: the Child Abuse Prevention and Treatment Act, the Victims of Child Abuse Act, and the Protection of Children against Sexual Exploitation Act of 1977. Court decisions, including *Globe Newspaper Co. v. Superior Court* and *Idaho v. Wright*, are also excerpted.

Data

Prevalence and Incidence

Studies to determine the prevalence of child sexual abuse focus on estimating the proportion of the population who will be sexually abused as children, while studies to determine the incidence of child sexual abuse focus on determining the number of new cases arising during a given time period, usually one year.

Experts and researchers often differ in their estimates of the extent of child sexual abuse. Many reasons for this difference exist, but most experts will agree that the reporting of child sexual abuse incidents probably underestimates the extent of abuse, based on our assumptions about incest and the incest taboo, on research conducted on adults who were sexually abused as children but did not report this abuse to anyone, and on societal factors such as differing expectations of male and female sexual behavior. Most estimates come from three sources: research studies conducted on adults who were sexually abused as children, annual reports of sexual abuse made to child protection agencies, and the National Incidence Studies, two federally funded studies.

Prevalence

Most prevalence studies start with the assumption that the majority of cases of child sexual abuse are never reported to authorities and that the most reliable method of estimating the prevalence is to gather information from victim or perpetrator self-reports. Many factors influence the reporting of child sexual abuse. Parents, other family members, and other professionals may hesitate to report incidents to the authorities because of the stigma and the resulting trauma to the family; they may also fear breaking up the family or they may believe that they can deal with it themselves. Our society traditionally and legally supports the integrity and sanctity of the family, offering many families protection from the public eye and public censure. Children often will keep their abuse to themselves, not even telling parents or other close family members; they may reveal the abuse later in life, either while in therapy or when trying to overcome the trauma it inflicted in their lives. Studies of the prevalence of child sexual abuse often discover that adults admit that they never reported the abuse when it was happening to them.

For the purpose of determining the prevalence of child sexual abuse, researchers have defined child sexual abuse in various ways; some include acts such as exhibitionism, while others limit their definitions to actual physical contact. Some include only adults as perpetrators, while others include peers as well as adults, believing that children are capable of sexually abusing other children. These definitions usually exclude sexual exploration between teenagers.

Finkelhor and his colleagues conducted a national survey of a random sample of respondents in 1985 to determine the prevalence of child sexual abuse. They found that 27 percent of the women (out of 1,481 women) and 16 percent of men (out of 1,145 men) disclosed some form of sexual abuse while they were children; the median age for boys was 9.9 years and the median age for girls was 9.6 years (Finkelhor, Hotaling, Lewis, & Smith 1990). Diana Russell studied prevalence using a random sample of over 900 households in San Francisco. She found that 54 percent reported at least one instance of incestuous and/or extrafamilial sexual abuse before the age of 18, and 48 percent reported some type of sexual abuse before the age of 14 (Russell 1986). Wyatt sampled 248 women in Los Angeles County and found that 62 percent reported at least one instance of sexual abuse before the age of 18 (Wyatt 1985).

The Committee for Children estimates that "at least one in four girls and one in ten boys will be sexually abused before reaching the age of 18. The actual incidence is probably much greater, especially for boys" (Committee for Children 1993, 8).

Christine Courtois believes that "a very substantial percentage of the female population, possibly as high as twenty percent, has had an experience of incestuous abuse at some time in their lives, twelve percent before the age of fourteen, sixteen percent before the age of eighteen. Possibly five percent of all women have been abused by their fathers. Boys are also sexually victimized within the family, but in smaller numbers" (Courtois 1988, 5).

In his landmark study of sexual behavior, Alfred Kinsey and his colleagues found that one in four women interviewed for his research study had reported experiencing as children some sort of undesired sexual contact or other sexual experience initiated by an adult male. Kinsey was surprised that most of the women reported that they were frightened by this contact:

> It is difficult to understand why a child, except for its cultural conditioning, should be disturbed by having its genitalia touched, or disturbed by seeing the genitalia of another person. . . . Some of the more experienced

students of juvenile problems have come to believe
that the emotional reactions of the parents, police and
other adults . . . may disturb the child more seriously
than the contacts themselves. The current hysteria
over sex offenders may well have serious effects on
the ability of many of these children to work out sexual adjustments some years later in their marriages.
(Kinsey, Pomeroy, Martin, & Gebhard 1953, 121)

Kinsey also believed that males were in danger of being persecuted by females intent on protecting the children and themselves. He claimed that the law, by prosecuting offenders, hurts
more people than

was ever done by the individual in his illicit sexual activity. The histories which we have accumulated contain many such instances. The intoxicated male who
accidentally exposes his genitalia before a child may
receive a prison sentence which leaves his family destitute for some period of years, breaks up his marriage, and leaves three or four children wards of the
state and without the sort of guidance which the parents might well have supplied. . . . The child who has
been raised in fear of all strangers and all physical
manifestations of affection may ruin the lives of the
married couple who had lived as useful and honor-
able citizens through half or more of a century, by giving her parents and the police a distorted version of
the old man's attempt to bestow grandfatherly affection upon her. (Kinsey, Pomeroy, Martin, & Gebhard
1953, 20–21)

Sandra Butler, in the research for her book, *Conspiracy of Silence: The Trauma of Incest,* started to understand the reasons why
incest was kept a secret, but was appalled at the level of denial
and lack of services provided by the professional community to
incest victims and their families. She says:

Priests, ministers and rabbis insisted "that" [incest]
did not happen among their parishioners. Although
there were a few men who did admit "that" was mentioned in the sanctity of the confessional or in private
conversation, they felt untrained and unskilled in

ways to deal with incestuous assault and seldom attempted counseling or intervention with the members of such troubled families. Pediatricians, other doctors and nurses did not see "that" in their practices, and one young resident in a midwestern city assured me that contrary to all the medical literature I had read, "Seven-year-olds can catch gonorrhea from dirty sheets." Occasionally I found a clinical report of "that" published in a medical journal or a paper presented to a group of psychiatrists by a peer who was working with a sexually abused client. But overwhelmingly I encountered silence. (Butler 1985, 8–9)

Butler goes on to say that

[a]s long as we continue to believe that incestuous assault can happen only in other families, we can avoid examining our own lives. As long as we insist upon imagining the incestuous aggressor to be an easily identifiable, skulking, lascivious male who ravishes his luscious and budding daughter across town, we can keep a safe distance. This distance protects us from sexual feelings we may have experienced for older family members and any possible interplay that may have occurred in our own childhood as well as feelings we may have toward our children as we watch them developing to young men and women. While most of us do not act upon these feelings, it is our refusal to acknowledge to ourselves that we have ever had such feelings that creates our silence, aversion and unwillingness to openly discuss the issues involved in incestuous abuse. (Butler 1985, 11)

Incidence

The National Center on Child Abuse and Neglect (NCCAN), in 1976, supported the first comprehensive incidence study of child abuse and neglect. Known as the National Incidence Study, it estimated that 44,700 cases of child sexual abuse, or 0.7 per 1,000 children, were known to professionals during the period from April 1979 to March 1980 (NCCAN 1981). Repeated in 1986, the study revealed a threefold increase, estimating that 138,000, or 2.2 cases per 1,000 children, were known to authorities during that year. When they expanded the definition of child sexual abuse to include those acts committed by caretakers, the researchers found that the number jumped to 155,000, or 2.5 per 1,000 children (Sedlak 1987).

The National Committee for Prevention of Child Abuse, since 1989, has conducted an annual survey of all 50 states to examine the trends in reports of child abuse and neglect. In 1993, the researchers estimated that 2,989,000 children were reported to child protective services as alleged victims of abuse or neglect, and of these 15 percent, or approximately 450,000, were cases of child sexual abuse (McCurdy & Daro 1994).

According to the FBI, 109,062 females were forcibly raped in 1992. The U.S. Bureau of Justice Statistics survey of the states and the District of Columbia examined forcible rape by the age of the victim. While 36 states reported that they did not break down their statistics by age, the remaining 15 percent provided information on 26,427 cases of forcible rape. According to their findings, approximately one-third of all rape victims were under the age of 13 in Delaware, Michigan, and North Dakota; under the age of 16 in Nebraska, Pennsylvania, and Wisconsin; under the age of 17 in Alabama; and under the age of 18 in the District of Columbia and Idaho (Langan & Harlow 1994).

Many of these studies do not include the incidence of sexual abuse of children while in day care or by nonparental caretakers, such as teachers, priests, or babysitters. David Finkelhor and his colleagues examined all cases of sexual abuse of children while in day care reported from 1983 through 1985. They identified 270 cases and estimated the incidence of child sexual abuse in day-care settings to be 5.5 per 10,000 children enrolled, They concluded that children attending day care are not disproportionately at higher risk of child sexual abuse than other children in other settings. The high number of abuse reports from day-care settings, they believe, is a reflection of the large numbers of children placed in day care in this country today rather than an indication that these children are at higher risk of abuse because they are in day care (Finkelhor, Williams, & Burns 1989).

Children Most at Risk

Who are the children most at risk for becoming victims of child sexual abuse? According to the statistics, girls are more likely to experience sexual abuse than boys. Most studies indicate that girls are between two and ten times more likely to be abused than boys. In a study of the records from the Child Protection Center for Children's Hospital National Medical Center between 1978 and 1981, researchers found that in those cases in which the parents or guardians were the perpetrators, 41 percent of the children were under the age of 9 years and 25 percent of the children were male (Rogers & Thomas 1984). Most studies suggest that children are most at risk for sexual abuse when they are between the ages of 8 and 12.

While statistics have indicated for many years that most victims of child sexual abuse were girls, that view has changed over the years, with many experts now believing that boys are abused almost as often as girls. In one research study using random probability samples in Los Angeles, Denver, Omaha, Louisville, and Washington, D.C., of 4,340 adults, approximately equal percentages of women and men (16 percent) admitted to having sexual relations with an adult before they turned 16 years old. Under the age of 13 years, 9 percent of the boys and 7 percent of the girls claimed to have had sexual relations with an adult (Grayson 1989).

Johnson and Shrier compared the demographic and psychosocial characteristics of 40 adolescent males who reported that they were sexually molested as preadolescents with 40 adolescent males who reported no prior sexual abuse. They found that sexual abuse of boys is greatly underreported: only 6 out of the 40 boys who had been sexually abused had reported the abuse before revealing it in this study (Johnson & Shrier 1985). In a study of childhood sexual abuse among college men, Fromuth and Burkhart surveyed 253 male students at a large midwestern university and 329 male students at a southeastern university and found prevalence rates between 4 and 24 percent, depending on the definitions of child sexual abuse (Fromuth & Burkhart 1987).

While many people believe that children are most likely to be molested by strangers, the statistics show that children are more likely to be sexually abused by someone they know. In 1989, the Office of Juvenile Justice and Delinquency Prevention in the U.S. Department of Justice reported that researchers estimate that between 52 and 158 children were kidnapped and murdered by nonfamily members each year (U.S. Department of Justice 1989). According to the 1990 National Incidence Studies on Missing, Abducted, Runaway, and Thrownaway Children in America (NISMART), between 200 and 300 children each year are abducted, with the number abducted by strangers and murdered being between 43 and 147 each year (U.S. Department of Justice 1990).

Signs and Symptoms of Sexual Abuse

Most professionals generally agree on the typical symptoms that children display when they have been sexually abused, although they readily agree that a child displaying any of these symptoms has not necessarily been sexually abused; any of these symptoms may also be caused by other conditions or situations. The following material is excerpted from material issued by the Victim Services Agency in New York. They suggest the following signs and symptoms:

Signs of Possible Sexual Abuse (by age group):

Children 18 months and under:
- urinary and bowel problems
- fretful behavior
- flat affect
- lacerations of sex organs
- bleeding, discharge, or odors from sex organs
- inappropriate fear of adults
- fear of being abandoned
- excessive clinging behavior or the opposite
- failure to thrive
- excessive crying
- extreme behavior change
- sleep disturbances

Toddlers and Preschool:
- fear of particular adult or specific places
- sex play with toys
- poor peer relationships
- lacerations of sex organs
- bleeding, discharge, or odors from sex organs
- depersonalization
- fear, guilt, or anxiety
- regressive or non–age appropriate behavior
- increase in genital play
- toileting issues
- fear of refusal
- new problems in bowel or bladder control
- sexual acting out that is age inappropriate
- advanced knowledge of detailed adult sexual activity

School Age Children:
- sleep disturbances
- school problems
- poor peer relationships (feel older than peers)
- depersonalization
- school phobias
- anorexia
- role confusion
- self-blame
- fear
- low self-esteem
- wish for normal family
- responsible for family
- running away

Adolescents
- school problems
- drugs and/or alcohol
- clinical depression
- promiscuity
- prostitution
- suicide attempts
- overly compliant behavior
- poor body image
- eating disorders

Adults (effects from being sexually abused as a child)
- problems with intimacy
- confusion in sexual identity
- lack of trust
- poor body image
- sexual dysfunction

(From Victim Services Agency. *Incest Treatment: A Curriculum for Training Mental Health Professionals.* New York: Victim Services Agency, 1991, pp. 61–63.)

Documents

Statement on Memories of Sexual Abuse by the American Psychiatric Association

The American Psychiatric Association has issued the following statement on false memories of childhood sexual abuse.

American Psychiatric Association
Approved by the Board of Trustees on December 12, 1993

This Statement is in response to the growing concern regarding memories of sexual abuse. The rise in reports of documented cases of child sexual abuse has been accompanied by a rise in reports of sexual abuse that cannot be documented. Members of the public, as well as members of mental health and other professions, have debated the validity of some memories of sexual abuse, as well as some of the therapeutic techniques which have been used. The American Psychiatric Association has been concerned that the passionate debates about these issues have obscured the recognition of a body of scientific evidence that underlies widespread agreement among psychiatrists regarding psychiatric treatment in this area. We are especially concerned that the public confusion and dismay over this issue and the possibility of false accusations not discredit the reports of patients who have indeed been traumatized by actual previous abuse. While much more needs to be known, this Statement summarizes information about this topic that is important for psychiatrists in their work with patients for whom sexual abuse is an issue.

Sexual abuse of children and adolescents leads to severe negative consequences. Child sexual abuse is a risk factor for many classes of psychiatric disorders, including anxiety disorders, affective disorders, dissociative disorders and personality disorders.

Children and adolescents may be abused by family members, including parents and siblings, and by individuals outside of their families, including adults in trusted positions (e.g., teachers, clergy, camp counselors). Abusers come from all walks of life. There is no uniform "profile" or other method to accurately distinguish those who have sexually abused children from those who have not.

Children and adolescents who have been abused cope with the trauma by using a variety of psychological mechanisms. In some instances, these coping mechanisms result in a lack of conscious awareness of the abuse for varying periods of time. Conscious thoughts and feelings stemming from the abuse may emerge at a later date.

It is not known how to distinguish, with complete accuracy, memories based on true events from those derived from other sources. The following observations have been made:

• Human memory is a complex process about which there is a substantial base of scientific knowledge. Memory can be divided into four stages: input (encoding), storage, retrieval, and recounting. All of these processes can be influenced by a variety of factors, including developmental stage, expectations and knowledge base prior to an event; stress and bodily sensations experienced during an event; post-event questioning; and the experience and context of the recounting of the event. In addition, the retrieval and recounting of a memory can modify the form of the memory, which may influence the content and the conviction about the veracity of the memory in the future. Scientific knowledge is not yet precise enough to predict how a certain experience or factor will influence a memory in a given person.

• Implicit and explicit memory are two different forms of memory that have been identified. Explicit memory (also termed declarative memory) refers to the ability to consciously recall facts or events. Implicit memory (also termed procedural memory) refers to behavioral knowledge of an experience without conscious recall. A child who demonstrates knowledge of a skill (e.g., bicycle riding) without recalling how he/she learned it, or an adult who has an affective reaction to an event without understanding the basis for that reaction (e.g., a combat veteran who panics when he hears the sound of a helicopter, but cannot remember that he was in a helicopter crash which killed his best friend) are demonstrating implicit memories in the absence of explicit recall.

This distinction between explicit and implicit memory is fundamental because they have been shown to be supported by different brain systems, and because their differentiation and identification may have important clinical implications.

• Some individuals who have experienced documented traumatic events may nevertheless include some false or inconsistent elements in their reports. In addition, hesitancy in making a report, and recanting following the report can occur in victims of documented abuse. Therefore, these seemingly contradictory findings do not exclude the possibility that the report is based on a true event.

    • Memories can be significantly influenced by questioning, especially in young children. Memories also can be significantly influenced by a trusted person (e.g., therapist, parent involved in a custody dispute) who suggests abuse as an explanation for symptoms/problems, despite initial lack of memory of such abuse. It has also been shown that repeated questioning may lead individuals to report "memories" of events that never occurred.

It is not known what proportion of adults who report memories of sexual abuse were actually abused. Many individuals who recover memories of abuse have been able to find corroborating information about their memories. However, no such information can be found, or is possible to obtain, in some situations. While aspects of the alleged abuse situation, as well as the context in which the memories emerge, can contribute to the assessment, there is no completely accurate way of determining the validity of reports in the absence of corroborating information.

Psychiatrists are often consulted in situations in which memories of sexual abuse are critical issues. Psychiatrists may be involved in a variety of capacities, including as the treating clinician for the alleged victim, for the alleged abuser, or for other family member(s); as a school consultant; or in a forensic capacity.

Basic clinical and ethical principles should guide the psychiatrist's work in this difficult area. These include the need for role clarity. It is essential that the psychiatrist and the other involved parties understand and agree on the psychiatrist's role.

Psychiatrists should maintain an empathic, non-judgmental, neutral stance towards reported memories of sexual abuse. As in the treatment of all patients, care must be taken to avoid prejudging the cause of the patient's difficulties, or the veracity of the patient's reports. A strong prior belief by the psychiatrist that sexual abuse, or other factors, are or are not the cause of the patient's problems is likely to interfere with appropriate assessment and treatment. Many individuals who have experienced sexual abuse have a history of not being believed by their parents, or others in whom they have put their trust. Expression of disbelief is likely to cause the patient further pain and decrease his/her willingness to seek needed psychiatric treatment. Similarly, clinicians should not exert pressure on patients to believe in events that may not have occurred, or to prematurely disrupt important relationships or make other important decisions based on these speculations. Clinicians who have not had the training necessary to evaluate and treat patients with a broad range of psychiatric disorders are at risk of causing harm by providing inadequate care for the patient's psychiatric problems and by increasing the patient's resistance to obtaining and responding to appropriate treatment in the future. In addition, special knowledge and experience are necessary to properly evaluate and/or treat patients who report the emergence of memories during the use of specialized interview techniques (e.g., the use of hypnosis or amytal), or during the course of litigation.

The treatment plan should be based on a complete psychiatric assessment, and should address the full range of the patient's clinical needs. In addition to specific treatments for any primary psychiatric condition, the patient may need help recognizing and integrating data that informs and defines the issues related to the memories of abuse. As in the treatment of patients with any psychiatric disorder, it may be important to caution the patient against making major life decisions during the acute phase of treatment. During the acute and later phases of treatment, the issues of breaking off relationships with important attachment figures, of pursuing legal actions, and of making public disclosures may need to be addressed. The psychiatrist should help the patient assess the likely impact (including emotional) of such decisions, given the patient's overall clinical and social situation. Some patients will be left with unclear memories of abuse and no corroborating information. Psychiatric treatment may help these patients adapt to the uncertainty regarding such emotionally important issues.

The intensity of public interest and debate about these topics should not influence psychiatrists to abandon their commitment to basic principles of ethical practice, delineated in The Principles of Medical Ethics with Annotations Especially Applicable to Psychiatry. The following concerns are of particular relevance:

• Psychiatrists should refrain from making public statements about the veracity or other features of individual reports of sexual abuse.

• Psychiatrists should vigilantly assess the impact of their conduct on the boundaries of the doctor/patient relationship. This is especially critical when treating patients who are seeking care for conditions that are associated with boundary violations in their past.

The APA will continue to monitor developments in this area in an effort to help psychiatrists provide the best possible care for their patients.

Sexual Abuse Policies of the Catholic Church

The Ad Hoc Committee on Sexual Abuse of the Roman Catholic National Catholic Conference of Bishops suggested 28 specific recommendations for the church's policy on sexual abuse. Here are their recommendations:

General Guidelines

1. That all dioceses consider having a written policy on sexual abuse of minors.
2. That the tone of the diocesan policy, particularly in its introduction, be clearly pastoral while appropriately dealing with the legal (civil and canonical) and financial obligations of the diocese.
3. That the policy be a public document, thereby indicating that the local church is open to the accountability implied in it.
4. That any qualifying statements required in a policy be appropriately presented so that the pastoral tone not be diminished.
5. That a glossary be provided of the technical terms used in the policy.

Prevention–Education

6. That policies make special reference to prevention and education measures in place.
7. That policies include a reference to appropriate screening procedures for seminarians, employees and volunteers with responsibilities for dealing with the young.
8. That the policy be communicated to priests and religious, and to employees if applicable, and that all acknowledge acceptance in a formal manner.
9. That in educational sessions priests be provided with regular opportunities for updating their knowledge on child sexual abuse from viewpoints such as

new scientific knowledge, church policy and canon
law, civil laws and of moral theology, professional
ethics, the theology of sexuality, the pastoral care of
victims and coping with the disclosure of misconduct by a colleague.

10. That consideration be given to setting up a diocesan
advisory body to evaluate periodically the effectiveness of the policy in place and to propose revisions
as indicated.

Administrative Guidelines
In General

11. That consideration be given to having the diocesan
policy apply to clergy, religious and employees in
the context of sexual abuse, misconduct, exploitation
and harassment.

12. That in the principal diocesan policy dealing with
sexual abuse there be mainly general references to
the manner of dealing with clergy and religious, and
there be developed a subpolicy to cover the intrica-
cies of canon law in their regard.

13. That each diocese examine its history in this regard
and, based on the risk to the innocent and the vulnerable, consider having a risk track and a non–risk
track approach to implementing the procedures.

14. That because of the special skills required to do a
proper and expeditious investigation, individuals
with the primary responsibility for this role be given
appropriate training before assuming the position.

15. That there be identified in each diocese experts from
the many disciplines involved in the serious study of
issues connected with sexual abuse in order to approach the problem in its pastoral, legal, psychological, sociological, medical and educational dimensions.

Civil Law

16. That policies be reviewed to assure that this principle of honoring civil law obligations is articulated in
a practical manner.

17. That policies clearly state a willingness to cooperate
with government authorities (civil and criminal proceedings) to the extent possible in the circumstances.

18. That there be an explicit reference in the policy regarding coverage of the accused's legal expenses.
19. That, while maintaining a pastoral tone, the policy be clear that there could be occasions when the church may in justice defend itself.

Insurance

20. That to the extent possible the pastoral and educational tone of the policy be maintained with reference to the insurance aspects that must be included with it.
21. That dioceses seek insurance contracts to provide pastoral and clinical support to those in need.

Victims

22. That every policy recognize that primary attention be given to the person alleged to have been offended, to the family and to the parish community.
23. That the policy indicate there is some kind of multidisciplinary body available to provide concrete, direct and individualized assistance to victims, their families and the affected parish community.
24. That the diocese seek ways to involve the people in general in the whole process of healing the often serious and long-lasting aftereffects of child sexual abuse.
25. That the diocese promote sessions to affirm and encourage the body of priests, whose morale can be adversely affected by the actions of relatively few of their colleagues.

Accused

26. That, given the complexity inherent in the reassignment question, the diocesan policy make provision for some type of advisory body to assist the bishop in this regard.
27. That the policy of the diocese be as detailed as feasible on the possibilities and types of reassignment that may or may not be open to a priest guilty of sexual abuse.

Media

28. That the diocesan policy make reference to an approach for consistently relating with the media and to a designated, well-informed and experienced spokesperson (with substitute) for all inquiries and news conferences.

Multidisciplinary Approaches to Treatment of Child Victims of Sexual Abuse

The National Institute of Justice, the Office of Juvenile Justice and Delinquency Prevention, the Office for Victims of Crime, and the National Center on Child Abuse and Neglect sponsored a symposium, "Joint Investigations of Child Abuse." Their recommendations to enhance investigations at all levels of government are excerpted below.

For the Future: Symposium Recommendations

To speed the adoption of effective multidisciplinary approaches, symposium participants recommended strategies at the Federal, State, and local levels.

1. Provide comprehensive training that includes multidisciplinary and discipline-specific components.
- Identify Federal, State, and private funding sources for training.
- Base training curriculums on models that have been evaluated and found to work.
- Require that training conferences include participation of many disciplines.
- Make certain that the training curriculums cover such issues as cultural competency (that is, intervention sensitive to a family's cultural background), team-building, gender sensitivity, and compliance with laws affecting disabled individuals.
- Offer training at two levels, basic and advanced.

2. Promote joint investigations in local jurisdictions.
- Elicit support from community groups.
- Conduct a needs assessment to document the effectiveness of existing resources.

- Cultivate media contacts to create public awareness of the need for team investigations.
- Maximize the use of existing task forces, including those with representatives of CPS [Child Protective Services] and law enforcement agencies.
- Solicit the support of elected officials, agency administrators, opinion leaders, and policymakers.

3. Implement Federal and State incentives to establish community-based multidisciplinary teams.
- To the extent permitted by statutory authorizations, provide Federal funds allocated to the U.S. Department of Health and Human Services and the U.S. Department of Justice for training in joint investigation, "marketing" of model site programs, and program assessments.
- Convene a meeting of the Consortium of Federal Clearinghouses and the national resource centers to develop a unified strategy for disseminating information about the benefits of joint investigations. (The target audiences are public and private agencies that deal with child abuse.)
- Convene a "summit" of organizations representing child welfare, law enforcement, and prosecution professionals to communicate the results of the national clearinghouse meeting.
- Implement activities that will persuade policymakers and elected officials to expand the use of joint investigations.
- Require joint training under legislative and administrative mandates and follow up with advanced training, on-site support, and funding for personnel and equipment.
- Allow flexibility in the use of funds, avoiding narrowly prescribed purposes and instead permitting States to develop creative solutions.
- Furnish support for evaluating various types of joint investigations, identifying best practices, and establishing minimum guidelines.

4. Promote legislative reform by enhancing the Children's Justice Act and requiring ongoing evaluation of joint responses to child abuse and neglect by interagency task forces.
- Encourage States to apply for Children's Justice Act funds and ensure that federally funded activities meet the Act's requirement of providing team training in investigation and prosecution.

- Require that grantees who receive State aid disseminate information about their activities statewide.
- Amend the Act or promulgate regulations defining operational guidelines for the use of funds made available through it.
- Work to develop uniform nationwide standards in CPS and law enforcement for thorough investigations in which all agencies are informed and coordinate efforts.
- Identify existing State laws that can serve as models for joint investigations, determine gaps in services to victims and by agency, and examine data tracking needs.

Federal Laws

Excerpts from several laws are included here. The Child Abuse Prevention and Treatment Act, initially passed in 1974, has been amended several times. It required the establishment of the National Center on Child Abuse and Neglect and helped bring national attention to these problems. The Victims of Child Abuse Act, originally passed in 1990, has also been amended several times and contributed to the improvement of the investigation and prosecution of child abuse cases. It also helped establish court-appointed special advocate programs throughout the country. Finally, the Protection of Children against Sexual Exploitation Act of 1977 was passed to focus attention and resources on the problem of sexual exploitation of children, specifically through the use of child pornography.

The Child Abuse Prevention and Treatment Act, as amended November 4, 1992

SEC. 1. SHORT TITLE
This Act may be cited as the "Child Abuse Prevention and Treatment Act."
SEC. 2. FINDINGS.
Congress finds that—
(1) each year, hundreds of thousands of American children are victims of abuse and neglect with such numbers having increased dramatically over the past decade;

(2) many of these children and their families fail to receive adequate protection or treatment;

(3) the problem of child abuse and neglect requires a comprehensive approach that—

   (A) integrates the work of social service, legal, health, mental health, education, and substance abuse agencies and organizations;

   (B) strengthens coordination among all levels of government, and with private agencies, civic, religious, and professional organizations, and individual volunteers;

   (C) emphasizes the need for abuse and neglect prevention, investigation, and treatment at the neighborhood level;

   (D) ensures properly trained and support staff with specialized knowledge, to carry out their child protection duties; and

   (E) is sensitive to ethnic and cultural diversity;

(4) the failure to coordinate and comprehensively prevent and treat child abuse and neglect threatens the futures of tens of thousands of children and results in a cost to the Nation of billions of dollars in direct expenditures for health, social, and special educational services and ultimately in the loss of work productivity;

(5) all elements of American society have a shared responsibility in responding to this national child and family emergency;

(6) substantial reductions in the prevalence and incidence of child abuse and neglect and the alleviation of its consequences are matters of the highest national priority;

(7) national policy should strengthen families to remedy the causes of child abuse and neglect, provide support for intensive services to prevent the unnecessary removal of children from families, and promote the reunification of families if removal has taken place;

(8) the child protection system should be comprehensive, child-centered, family-focused, and community-based, should incorporate all appropriate measures to prevent the occurrence or recurrence of child abuse and neglect, and should promote physical and psychological recovery and social re-integration in an environment that fosters the health, self-respect, and dignity of the child;

(9) because of the limited resources available in low-income communities, Federal aid for the child protection system should be distributed with due regard to the relative financial need of the communities;

(10) the Federal government should ensure that every

community in the United States has the fiscal, human, and technical resources necessary to develop and implement a successful and comprehensive child protection strategy;

(11) the Federal government should provide leadership and assist communities in their child protection efforts by—

(A) promoting coordinated planning among all levels of government;

(B) generating and sharing knowledge relevant to child protection, including the development of models for service delivery;

(C) strengthening the capacity of States to assist communities;

(D) allocating sufficient financial resources to assist States in implementing community plans;

(E) helping communities to carry out their child protection plans by promoting the competence of professional, paraprofessional, and volunteer resources; and

(F) providing leadership to end the abuse and neglect of the nation's children and youth.

I—General Program

NATIONAL CENTER ON CHILD ABUSE AND NEGLECT
Sec. 101. [42 U.S.C. 5101]
(a) ESTABLISHMENT.—The Secretary of Health and Human Services shall establish an office to be known as the National Center on Child Abuse and Neglect.
(b) APPOINTMENT OF DIRECTOR
(c) OTHER STAFF AND RESOURCES.—The Secretary shall make available to the Center such staff and resources as are necessary for the Center to carry out effectively its functions under this Act. The Secretary shall require that professional staff have experience relating to child abuse and neglect. The Secretary is required to justify, based on the priorities and needs of the Center, the hiring of any professional staff member who does not have experience relating to child abuse and neglect.

Inter-Agency Task Force on Child Abuse and Neglect

Sec. 103. [42 U.S.C. 5103]
(a) ESTABLISHMENT.—The Secretary shall establish a task force to be known as the Inter-Agency Task Force on Child Abuse and Neglect.

(b) COMPOSITION.—The Secretary shall request representation for the task force from Federal agencies with responsibility for programs and activities related to child abuse and neglect.
(c) CHAIRPERSON.—The Task Force shall be chaired by the Director.
(d) DUTIES.—The task force shall—

(1) coordinate Federal efforts with respect to child abuse prevention and treatment programs;
(2) encourage the development by other Federal agencies of activities relating to child abuse prevention and treatment;
(3) coordinate the use of grants received under this Act with the use of grants received under other programs;
(4) prepare a comprehensive plan for coordinating the goals, objectives, and activities of all Federal agencies and organizations which have responsibilities for programs and activities related to child abuse and neglect, and submit such plan to such Advisory Board not later than 12 months after the date of enactment of the Child Abuse Prevention, Adoption and Family Services Act of 1988; and
(5) coordinate adoption related activities, develop Federal standards with respect to adoption activities under this Act, and prevent duplication with respect to the allocation of resources to adoption activities.

National Clearinghouse for Information Relating to Child Abuse

Sec. 104. [42 U.S.C. 5104]
(a) ESTABLISHMENT.—Before the end of the 2-year period beginning on the date of the enactment of the Child Abuse Prevention, Adoption and Family Services Act of 1988, the Secretary shall through the Center, or by contract of no less than 3 years duration let through a competition, establish a national clearinghouse for information relating to child abuse.
(b) FUNCTIONS.—The Director shall, through the clearinghouse established by subsection (a)—

(1) maintain, coordinate, and disseminate information on all programs, including private programs, that show promise of success with respect to the prevention, identification, and treatment of child abuse and neglect, including the information provided by the National Center for Child Abuse and Neglect under section 105(b);
(2) maintain and disseminate information relating to—

(A) the incidence of cases of child abuse and neglect in the general population;

(B) the incidence of such cases in populations determined by the Secretary under section 105(a)(1) of the Child Abuse Prevention, Adoption, and Family Services Act of 1988;

(C) the incidence of any such cases related to alcohol or drug abuse; and

(D) State and local recordkeeping with respect to such cases; and

(3) directly or through contract, identify effective programs carried out by the States pursuant to title II and provide technical assistance to the States in the implementation of such programs.

(c) COORDINATION WITH AVAILABLE RESOURCES.—In establishing a national clearinghouse as required by subsection (a), the Director shall—

(1) consult with other Federal agencies that operate similar clearinghouses;

(2) consult with the head of each agency that is represented on the task force on the development of the components for information collection and management of such clearing house;

(3) develop a Federal data system involving the elements under subsection (b) which, to the extent practicable, coordinates existing State, regional, and local data systems; and

(4) solicit public comment on the components of such clearinghouse.

Research and Assistance Activities of the National Center on Child Abuse and Neglect

Sec. 105. [42 U.S.C. 5105]

(a) RESEARCH.—

(1) TOPICS.— The Secretary shall, through the Center, conduct research on—

(A) the causes, prevention, identification, treatment, and cultural distinctions of child abuse and neglect;

(B) appropriate, effective and culturally sensitive investigative, administrative, and judicial procedures with respect to cases of child abuse; and

(C) the national incidence of child abuse and neglect, including—

(i) the extent to which incidents of child abuse are increasing or decreasing in number and severity;

(ii) the relationship of child abuse and neglect to nonpayment of child support, cultural diversity, disabilities, and various other factors; and

(iii) the incidence of substantiated reported child abuse cases that result in civil child protection proceedings or criminal proceedings, including the number of such cases with respect to which the court makes a finding that abuse or neglect exists in the disposition of such cases.

(b) PUBLICATION AND DISSEMINATION OF INFORMATION.—The Secretary shall, through the Center—

(1) as a part of research activities, establish a national data collection and analysis program—

(A) which, to the extent practicable, coordinates existing State child abuse and neglect reports and which shall include—

(i) standardized data on false, unfounded, or unsubstantiated reports; and

(ii) information on the number of deaths due to child abuse and neglect; and

(B) which shall collect, compile, analyze, and make available State child abuse and neglect reporting information which, to the extent practical, is universal and case specific, and integrated with other case-based foster care and adoption data collected by the Secretary;

(2) annually compile and analyze research on child abuse and neglect and publish a summary of such research;

(3) compile, evaluate, publish, and disseminate to the States and to the clearinghouse . . . materials and information designed to assist the States in developing, establishing, and operating the programs described in section 109, including an evaluation of—

(A) various methods and procedures for the investigation and prosecution of child physical and sexual abuse cases; and

(B) resultant psychological trauma to the child victim;

(4) compile, publish, and disseminate training materials

(A) for persons who are engaged in or intend to engage in the prevention, identification, and treatment of child abuse and neglect; and

(B) to appropriate State and local officials to assist in

training law enforcement, legal, judicial, medical, mental health, and child welfare personnel in appropriate methods of interacting during investigative, administrative, and judicial proceedings with children who have been subjected to abuse; and

(5) establish model information collection systems, in consultation with appropriate State and local agencies and professionals.

(c) PROVISION OF TECHNICAL ASSISTANCE.—The Secretary shall, through the Center, provide technical assistance to public and non-profit private agencies and organizations, including disability organizations and persons who work with children with disabilities, to assist such agencies and organizations in planning, improving, developing and carrying out programs and activities relating to the prevention, identification, and treatment of child abuse and neglect.

Grants to Public Agencies and Nonprofit Private Organizations for Demonstration or Service Programs and Projects

Sec. 106 [42 U.S.C. 5106]

(a) GENERAL AUTHORITY

(1) DEMONSTRATION OR SERVICE PROGRAMS AND PROJECTS.— The Secretary, through the Center, shall . . . make grants to, and enter into contracts with, public agencies or nonprofit private organizations (or combinations of such agencies or organizations) for demonstration or service programs and projects designed to prevent, identify, and treat child abuse and neglect.

(2) EVALUATIONS.— In making grants or entering into contracts for demonstration projects, the Secretary shall require all such projects to be evaluated for their effectiveness. Funding for such evaluations shall be provided either as a stated percentage of a demonstration grant or contract, or as a separate grant or contract entered into by the Secretary for the purpose of evaluating a particular demonstration project or group of projects.

(b) GRANTS FOR RESOURCE CENTERS.—The Secretary shall, directly or through grants or contracts with public or private nonprofit organizations under this section, provide for the establishment of resource centers—

(1) serving defined geographic areas;

(2) staffed by multidisciplinary teams of personnel trained in the prevention, identification, and treatment of child abuse and neglect; and

(3) providing advice and consultation to individuals, agencies, and organizations which request such services.

(c) DISCRETIONARY GRANTS.— In addition to grants or contracts made under subsection (b), grants or contracts under this section may be used for the following:

(1) TRAINING PROGRAMS.—

(A) for professional and paraprofessional personnel in the fields of medicine, law, education, social work, and other relevant fields who are engaged in, or intend to work in, the field of prevention, identification, and treatment of child abuse and neglect;

(B) to provide culturally specific instruction in methods of protecting children from child abuse and neglect to children and to persons responsible for the welfare of children, including parents of and persons who work with disabilities; or

(C) to improve the recruitment, selection, and training of volunteers serving in private and public nonprofit children, youth and family service organizations in order to prevent child abuse and neglect through collaborative analysis of current recruitment, selection, and training programs and development of model programs for dissemination and replication nationally.

(2) Such other innovative programs and projects as the Secretary may approve, including programs and projects for parent self-help, for prevention and treatment of alcohol and drug-related child abuse and neglect, and for home health visitor programs designed to reach parents of children in populations in which risk is high, that show promise of successfully preventing and treating cases of child abuse and neglect, and for a parent self-help program of demonstrated effectiveness which is national in scope.

(3) Projects which provide educational identification, prevention, and treatment services in cooperation with preschool and elementary and secondary schools.

(4) Respite and crisis nursery programs provided by community-based organizations under the direction and supervision of hospitals.

(5) Respite and crisis nursery programs provided by community-based organizations.

(6)(A) Providing hospital-based information and referral services to—
>(i) parents of children with disabilities; and
>(ii) children who have been neglected or abused and their parents.

(B) Except as provided in subparagraph (C)(iii), services provided under a grant received under this paragraph shall be provided at the hospital involved—
>(i) upon the birth or admission of a child with disabilities; and
>(ii) upon the treatment of a child for abuse or neglect.

(C) Services, as determined as appropriate by the grantee, provided under a grant received under this paragraph shall be hospital-based and shall consist of—
>(i) the provision of notice to parents that information relating to community services is available;
>(ii) the provision of appropriate information to parents of a child with disabilities regarding resources in the community, particularly parent training resources, that will assist such parents in caring for their child;
>(iii) the provision of appropriate information to parents of a child who has been neglected or abused regarding resources in the community, particularly parent training resources, that will assist such parents in caring for their child and reduce the possibility of abuse or neglect;
>(iv) the provision of appropriate follow-up services to parents of a child described in subparagraph (B) after the child has left the hospital; and
>(v) where necessary, assistance in coordination of community services available to parents of children described in subparagraph (B).

The grantee shall assure that parental involvement described in this subparagraph is voluntary.

Grants to States for Child Abuse and Neglect Prevention and Treatment Programs

Sec. 107. [42 U.S.C. 5106a]
(a) DEVELOPMENT AND OPERATION GRANTS. —The Secretary, acting through the Center, shall make grants to the States, based on the population of children under the age of 18 in each State that applies for a grant under this section, for purposes of

assisting the States in improving the child protective service system of each such State in—

(1) the intake and screening of reports of abuse and neglect through the improvement of the receipt of information, decisionmaking, public awareness, and training of staff;

(2)(A) investigating such reports through improving response time, decisionmaking, referral to services, and training of staff;

(B) creating and improving the use of multidisciplinary teams and interagency protocols to enhance investigations; and

(C) improving legal preparation and representation;

(3) case management and delivery services provided to families through the improvement of response time in service provision, improving the training of staff, and increasing the numbers of families to be served;

(4) enhancing the general child protective system by improving assessment tools, automation systems that support the program, information referral systems, and the overall training of staff to meet minimum competencies; or

(5) developing, strengthening, and carrying out child abuse and neglect prevention, treatment, and research programs.

(b) ELIGIBILITY REQUIREMENTS.— In order for a State to qualify for a grant under subsection (a), such State shall—

(1) have in effect a State law relating to child abuse and neglect, including—

(A) provisions for the reporting of known and suspected instances of child abuse and neglect, and

(B) provisions for immunity from prosecution under State and local laws for persons who report instances of child abuse or neglect for circumstances arising from such reporting;

(2) provide that upon receipt of a report of known or suspected instances of child abuse or neglect an investigation shall be initiated promptly to substantiate the accuracy of the report, and, upon a finding of abuse or neglect, immediate steps shall be taken to protect the health and welfare of the abused or neglected child and of any other child under the same care who may be in danger of abuse or neglect;

(3) demonstrate that there are in effect throughout the State, in connection with the enforcement of child abuse and neglect laws and with the reporting of suspected instances of

child abuse and neglect, such—
    (A) administrative procedures;
    (B) personnel trained in child abuse and neglect prevention and treatment;
    (C) training procedures;
    (D) institutional and other facilities (public and private); and
    (E) such related multidisciplinary programs and services;
    as may be necessary or appropriate to ensure that the State will deal effectively with child abuse and neglect cases in the State;
(4) provide for—
    (A) methods to preserve the confidentiality of all records in order to protect the rights of the child and of the child's parents or guardians, including methods to ensure that disclosure (and redisclosure) of information concerning child abuse or neglect involving specific individuals is made only to persons or entities that the State determines have a need for such information directly related to purposes of this Act; and
    (B) requirements for the prompt disclosure of all relevant information to any Federal, State, or local governmental entity, or any agent of such entity, with a need for such information in order to carry out its responsibilities under law to protect children from abuse and neglect.
(5) provide for the cooperation of law enforcement officials, courts of competent jurisdiction, and appropriate State agencies providing human services;
(6) provide that in every case involving an abused or neglected child which results in a judicial proceeding a guardian ad litem shall be appointed to represent the child in such proceedings;
(7) provide that the aggregate of support for programs or projects related to child abuse and neglect assisted by State funds shall not be reduced below the level provided during fiscal year 1973, and set forth policies and procedures designed to ensure that Federal funds made available under this Act for any fiscal year shall be so used as to supplement and, to the extent practicable, increase the level of State funds which would, in the absence of Federal funds, be available for such programs and projects;
(8) provide for dissemination of information, including efforts to encourage more accurate reporting, to the general

public with respect to the problem of child abuse and neglect and the facilities and prevention and treatment methods available to combat instances of child abuse and neglect;

(9) to the extent feasible, ensure that parental organizations combating child abuse and neglect receive preferential treatment; and

(10) have in place for the purpose of responding to the reporting of medical neglect (including instances of withholding of medically indicated treatment from disabled infants with life-threatening conditions), procedures or programs, or both (within the State child protective services system) . . .

(c) STATE PROGRAM PLAN.—To be eligible to receive a grant under this section, a State shall submit every four years a plan to the Secretary that specifies the child protective service system area or areas described in subsection (a) that the State intends to address with funds received under the grant. The plan shall describe the current system capacity of the State in the relevant area or areas from which to assess programs with grant funds and specify the manner in which funds from the State's programs will be used to make improvements. The plan required under this subsection shall contain, with respect to each area in which the State intends to use funds from the grant, the following information with respect to the State:

(1) INTAKE AND SCREENING.—

(A) STAFFING.— The number of child protective service workers responsible for the intake and screening of reports of abuse and neglect relative to the number of reports filed in the previous year.

(B) TRAINING.— The types and frequency of pre-service and in-service training programs available to support direct line and supervisory personnel in report-taking, screening, decision-making, and referral for investigation.

(C) PUBLIC EDUCATION.—An assessment of the State or local agency's public education program with respect to—

(i) what is child abuse and neglect;

(ii) who is obligated to report and who may choose to report; and

(iii) how to report,

(2) INVESTIGATION OF REPORTS.—

(A) RESPONSE TIME.— The number of reports of child abuse and neglect filed in the State in the previous year where appropriate, the agency response time to each with respect to initial investigation, the number of substantiated and unsubstantiated reports, and where appropriate, the response time with respect to the provision of services.

(B) STAFFING.—The number of child protective service workers responsible for the investigation of child abuse and neglect reports relative to the number of reports investigated in the previous year.

(C) INTERAGENCY COORDINATION.—A description of the extent to which interagency coordination processes exist and are available Statewide, and whether protocols or formal policies governing interagency relationships exist in the following areas—

(i) multidisciplinary investigation teams among child welfare and law enforcement agencies;

(ii) interagency coordination for the prevention, intervention and treatment of child abuse and neglect among agencies responsible for child protective services, criminal justice, schools, health, mental health, and substance abuse; and

(iii) special interagency child fatality review panels, including a listing of those agencies that are involved.

(D) TRAINING.—The types and frequency of pre-service and in-service training programs available to support direct line and supervisory personnel in such areas as investigation, risk assessment, court preparation, and referral to and provision of services.

(E) LEGAL REPRESENTATION.— A description of the State agency's current capacity for legal representation, including the manner in which workers are prepared and trained for court preparation and attendance, including procedures for appealing substantiated reports of abuse and neglect.

(3) CASE MANAGEMENT AND DELIVERY OF ONGOING FAMILY SERVICES.— For children for whom a report of abuse and neglect has been substantiated and the children remain in their own homes and are not currently at risk of removal, the State shall assess the activities and the outcomes of the following services:

(A) RESPONSE TIME.—The number of cases opened for services as a result of investigation of child abuse and neglect reports filed in the previous year, including the response time with respect to the provision of services from the time of initial report and initial investigation.

(B) STAFFING.— The number of child protective services workers responsible for providing services to children and their families in their own homes as a result of investigation of reports of child abuse and neglect.

(C) TRAINING.—The types and frequency of pre-service and in-service training programs available to support direct line and supervisory personnel in such areas as risk assessment, court preparation, provision of services and determination of case disposition, including how such training is evaluated for effectiveness.

(D) INTERAGENCY COORDINATION.—The extent to which treatment services for the child and other family members are coordinated with child welfare, social service, mental health, education, and other agencies.

(4) GENERAL SYSTEM ENHANCEMENT.—

(A) AUTOMATION.—A description of the capacity of current automated systems for tracking reports of child abuse and neglect from intake through final disposition and how personnel are trained in the use of such system.

(B) ASSESSMENT TOOLS.—A description of whether, how, and what risk assessment tools are used for screening reports of abuse and neglect, determining whether child abuse and neglect has occurred, and assessing the appropriate level of State agency protection and intervention, including the extent to which such tool is used statewide and how workers are trained in its use.

(C) INFORMATION AND REFERRAL.—A description and assessment of the extent to which a State has in place—

(i) information and referral systems, including their availability and ability to link families to various child welfare services such as homemakers, intensive family-based services, emergency caretakers, home health visitors, daycare and services outside the child welfare system such as housing, nutrition, health care, special education, income support, and emergency resource assistance; and

(ii) efforts undertaken to disseminate to the public information concerning the problem of child abuse and neglect and the prevention and treatment programs and services available to combat instances of such abuse and neglect.

(D) STAFF CAPACITY AND COMPETENCE.—An as
sessment of basic and specialized training needs of all
staff and current training provided staff. Assessment of
the competencies of staff with respect to minimum
knowledge in areas such as child development, cultural
and ethnic diversity, functions and relationship of other
systems to child protective services and in specific skills
such as interviewing, assessment, and decisionmaking
relative to the child and family, and the need for training
consistent with such minimum competencies.
(5) INNOVATIVE APPROACHES.—A description of—
(A) research and demonstration efforts for developing,
strengthening, and carrying out child abuse and neglect
prevention, treatment, and research programs, including
the interagency efforts at the State level; and
(B) the manner in which proposed research and development activities build on existing capacity in the programs
being addressed.

Emergency Child Abuse Prevention Services Grant

Sec. 107A. [42 U.S.C. 5106a-1]
(a) ESTABLISHMENT.—The Secretary shall establish a grant program to make grants to eligible entities to enable such entities to
provide services to children whose parents are substance abusers.
(b) ELIGIBLE ENTITIES.—Entities eligible to receive a grant
under this section shall be—
(1) State and local agencies that are responsible for administering child abuse or related child abuse intervention services; and
(2) community and mental health agencies and nonprofit
youth-serving organizations with experience in providing
child abuse prevention services.
(c) APPLICATION.—
(1) IN GENERAL.—To be eligible to receive a grant under
this section, an entity shall submit an application to the Secretary at such time, in such manner, and containing such information as the Secretary may by regulation require. . . .
(d) USE OF FUNDS.—Funds received by an entity under this
section shall be used to improve the delivery of services to children whose parents are substances abusers. Such services may
include—

(1) the hiring of additional personnel by the entity to reduce caseloads;

(2) the provision of additional training for personnel to improve their ability to provide emergency child abuse prevention services related to substance abuse by the parents of such children;

(3) the provision of expanded services to deal with family crises created by substance abuse; and

(4) the establishment or improvement of coordination between the agency administering the grant, and—

(A) child advocates;

(B) public educational institutions;

(C) community-based organizations that serve substance abusing parents, including pregnant and post-partum females and their infants; and

(D) parents and representatives of parent groups and related agencies.

Technical Assistance to States for Child Abuse Prevention and Treatment Programs

Sec. 108. [42 U.S.C. 5106b]

(a) TRAINING AND TECHNICAL ASSISTANCE.—The Secretary shall provide, directly or through grants or contracts with public or private nonprofit organizations, for—

(1) training and technical assistance programs to assist States in developing, implementing, or operating programs and procedures meeting the requirements of section 107(b)(10); and

(2) the establishment and operation of national and regional information and resource clearinghouses for the purpose of providing the most current and complete information regarding medical treatment procedures and resources and community resources for the provision of services and treatment to disabled infants with life-threatening conditions, in cluding—

(A) compiling, maintaining, updating, and disseminating regional directories of community services and resources (including the names and phone numbers of State and local medical organizations) to assist parents, families, and physicians; and

(B) attempting to coordinate the availability of appropriate regional education resources for health-care personnel.

(b) LIMITATION ON FUNDING.—Not more than $1,000,000 of the funds appropriated for any fiscal year for purposes of carrying out this title may be used to carry out this section.

Sec. 109. GRANTS TO STATES FOR PROGRAMS RELATING TO THE INVESTIGATION AND PROSECUTION OF CHILD ABUSE AND NEGLECT CASES.

Sec. 109. [42 U.S.C. 5106C]

(a) GRANTS TO STATES.—The Secretary, acting through the Center and in consultation with the Attorney General, is authorized to make grants to the States for the purpose of assisting States in developing, establishing, and operating programs designed to improve—

(1) the handling of child abuse and neglect cases, particularly cases of child sexual abuse and exploitation, in a manner which limits additional trauma to the child victim;

(2) the handling of cases of suspected child abuse or neglect related fatalities; and

(3) the investigation and prosecution of cases of child abuse and neglect, particularly child sexual abuse and exploitation.

(b) ELIGIBILITY REQUIREMENTS.—In order for a State to qualify for assistance under this section, such State shall—

(1) fulfill the requirements of section 107(b);

(2) establish a task force as provided in subsection (c);

(3) fulfill the requirements of subsection (d);

(4) submit annually an application to the Secretary at such time and containing such information and assurances as the Secretary considers necessary, including an assurance that the State will—

(A) make such reports to the Secretary as may reasonably be required; and

(B) maintain and provide access to records relating to activities under subsections (a) and (b); and

(5) submit annually to the Secretary a report on the manner in which assistance received under this program was expended throughout the State, with particular attention focused on the areas described in paragraphs (1) through (3) of subsection (a).

(c) STATE TASK FORCES.—

(1) GENERAL RULE.—Except as provided in paragraph (2),

a State requesting assistance under this section shall establish or designate and maintain a State multidisciplinary task force on children's justice (hereinafter referred to as State task force) composed of professionals with knowledge and experience relating to the criminal justice system and issues of child physical abuse, child neglect, child sexual abuse and exploitation, and child maltreatment related fatalities. The State task force shall include—

(A) individuals representing the law enforcement community;

(B) judges and attorneys involved in both civil and criminal court proceedings related to child abuse and neglect (including individuals involved with the defense as well as the prosecution of such cases);

(C) child advocates, including both attorneys for children and, where such programs are in operation, court appointed special advocates;

(D) health and mental health professionals;

(E) individuals representing child protective service agencies;

(F) individuals experienced in working with children with disabilities; and

(G) representatives of parents' groups.

(2) EXISTING TASK FORCE.—As determined by the Secretary, a State commission or task force established after January 1, 1983, with substantially comparable membership and functions, may be considered the State task force for the purposes of this subsection.

(d) STATE TASK FORCE STUDY.—Before a State receives assistance under this section, at three year intervals thereafter, the State task force shall comprehensively—

(1) review and evaluate State investigative, administrative and both civil and criminal judicial handling of cases of child abuse and neglect, particularly child sexual abuse and exploitation, as well as cases involving suspected child maltreatment related fatalities and cases involving a potential combination of jurisdictions, such as interstate, Federal-State, and State-Tribal;

(2) make policy and training recommendations in each of the categories described in subsection (e). The task force may make such other comments and recommendations as are considered relevant and useful.

(e) ADOPTION OF STATE TASK FORCE

RECOMMENDATIONS.—
    (1) GENERAL RULE.—Subject to the provisions of paragraph (2), before a State receives assistance under this section, a State shall adopt recommendations of the State task force in each of the following categories—
        (A) investigative, administrative, and judicial handling of cases of child abuse and neglect, particularly child sexual abuse and exploitation, as well as cases involving suspected child maltreatment related fatalities and cases involving a potential combination of jurisdictions, such as interstate, Federal-State, and State-Tribal, in a manner which reduces the additional trauma to the child victim and the victim's family and which also ensures procedural fairness to the accused;
        (B) experimental, model and demonstration programs for testing innovative approaches and techniques which may improve the prompt and successful resolution of civil and criminal court proceedings or enhance the effectiveness of judicial and administrative action in child abuse and neglect cases, particularly child sexual abuse and exploitation cases, including the enhancement of performance of court-appointed attorneys and guardians ad litem for children, and which also ensure procedural fairness to the accused; and
        (C) reform of State laws, ordinances, regulations, protocols and procedures to provide comprehensive protection for children from abuse, particularly sexual abuse and exploitation, while ensuring fairness to all affected persons.
    (2) EXEMPTION.—As determined by the Secretary, a State shall be considered to be in fulfillment of the requirements of this subsection if—
        (A) the State adopts an alternative to the recommendations of the State task force, which carries out the purpose of this section, in each of the categories under paragraph (1) for which the State task force's recommendations are not adopted; or
        (B) the State is making substantial progress toward adopting recommendations of the State task force or a comparable alternative to such recommendations.
(f) FUNDS AVAILABLE.—For grants under this section, the Secretary shall use the amount authorized by section 1404A of the Victims of Crime Act of 1984.

Coordination of Child Abuse and Neglect Programs

Sec. 111. [42 U.S.C. 51016e] The Secretary shall prescribe regulations and make such arrangements as may be necessary or appropriate to ensure that there is effective coordination among programs related to child abuse and neglect under this Act and other such programs which are assisted by Federal funds.

Definitions
Sec. 113. [42 U.S.C. 5106g] For purposes of this title—
(1) the term "board" means the Advisory Board on Child Abuse and Neglect established under section 102;
(2) the term "Center" means the National Center on Child Abuse and Neglect established under section 101;
(3) the term "child" means a person who has not attained the lesser of—
(A) the age of 18; or
(B) except in the case of sexual abuse, the age specified by the child protection law of the State in which the child resides;
(4) the term "child abuse and neglect" means the physical or mental injury, sexual abuse or exploitation, negligent treatment, or maltreatment of a child by a person who is responsible for the child's welfare, under circumstances which indicate that the child's health or welfare is harmed or threatened thereby, as determined in accordance with regulations prescribed by the Secretary;
(5) the term "person who is responsible for the child's welfare" includes—
(A) any employee of a residential facility; and
(B) any staff person providing out-of-home care;
(6) the term "Secretary" means the Secretary of Health and Human Services;
(7) the term "sexual abuse" includes—
(A) the employment, use, persuasion, inducement, enticement, or coercion of any child to engage in, or assist any other person to engage in, any sexually explicit conduct or simulation of such conduct for the purpose of producing a visual depiction of such conduct; or
(B) the rape, molestation, prostitution, or other form of sexual exploitation of children, or incest with children;
(8) the term "State" means each of the several States, the

District of Columbia, the Commonwealth of Puerto Rico, the Virgin Islands, Guam, American Samoa, the Commonwealth of the Northern Mariana Islands, and the Trust Territory of the Pacific Islands;

(9) the term "task force" means the Inter-Agency Task Force on Child Abuse and Neglect established under section 103; and

(10) the term "withholding of medically indicated treatment" means the failure to respond to the infant's life-threatening conditions by providing treatment (including appropriate nutrition, hydration, and medication) which, in the treating physician's or physicians' reasonable medical judgment, will be most likely to be effective in ameliorating or correcting all such conditions, except that the term does not include the failure to provide treatment (other than appropriate nutrition, hydration, or medication) to an infant when, in the treating physician's or physicians' reasonable medical judgment—

    (A) the infant is chronically and irreversibly comatose;

    (B) the provision of such treatment would—

        (i) merely prolong dying;

        (ii) not be effective in ameliorating or correcting all of the infant's life-threatening conditions; or

        (iii) otherwise be futile in terms of the survival of the infant; or

    (C) the provision of such treatment would be virtually futile in terms of the survival of the infant and the treatment itself under such circumstances would be inhumane.

The Victims of Child Abuse Act

P.L. 101-647, November 29, 1990
42 USCS §13001–§13041

Improving Investigation and Prosecution of Child Abuse Cases

§13001. Findings.
The Congress finds that—

    (1) over 2,000,000 reports of suspected child abuse and neglect are made each year, and drug abuse is associated with a significant portion of these;

    (2) the investigation and prosecution of child abuse cases is extremely complex, involving numerous agencies and dozens of personnel;

(3) traditionally, community agencies and professionals have different roles in the prevention, investigation, and intervention process;

(4) in such cases, too often the system does not pay sufficient attention to the needs and welfare of the child victim, aggravating the trauma that the child victim has already experienced;

(5) there is a national need to enhance coordination among community agencies and professionals involved in the intervention system;

(6) multidisciplinary child abuse investigation and prosecution programs have been developed that increase the reporting of child abuse cases, reduce the trauma to the child victim, and increase the successful prosecution of child abuse offenders; and

(7) such programs have proven effective, and with targeted Federal assistance, could be duplicated in many jurisdictions throughout the country.

§13001a. Definitions
For purposes of this subtitle—

(1) the term "Administrator" means the agency head designated under section 201(b) of the Juvenile Justice and Delinquency Prevention Act of 1974 (42 U.S.C. 5611(b));

(2) the term "applicant" means a child protective service, law enforcement, legal, medical and mental health agency or other agency that responds to child abuse cases;

(3) the term "board" means the Children's Advocacy Advisory Board established under section 213(e) [42 USCS 13001b(E)];

(4) the term "census region" means 1 of the 4 census regions (northeast, south, midwest, and west) that are designated as census regions by the Bureau of the Census as of the date of enactment of this section [enacted November 4, 1992];

(5) the term "child abuse" means physical or sexual abuse or neglect of a child;

(6) the term "Director" means the Director of the National Center on Child Abuse and Neglect;

(7) the term "multidisciplinary response to child abuse" means a response to child abuse that is based on mutually agreed upon procedures among the community agencies and professionals involved in the intervention, prevention, prosecution, and investigation systems that best meets the

needs of child victims and their nonoffending family members;

8) the term "nonoffending family member" means a member of the family of a victim of child abuse other than a member who has been convicted or accused of committing an act of child abuse; and

(9) the term "regional children's advocacy program" means the children's advocacy program established under section 213(a) [42 U.S.C. §13001b(a)].

§13001b. Regional children's advocacy centers.

(a) Establishment of regional children's advocacy program. The Administrator, in coordination with the Director and with the Director of the Office of Victims of Crime, shall establish a children's advocacy program to—

(1) focus attention on child victims by assisting communities in developing child-focused, community-oriented, facility-based programs designed to improve the resources available to children and families;

(2) provide support for nonoffending family members;

(3) enhance coordination among community agencies and professionals involved in the intervention, prevention, prosecution, and investigation systems that respond to child abuse cases; and

(4) train physicians and other health care and mental health care professionals in the multidisciplinary approach to child abuse so that trained medical personnel will be available to provide medical support to community agencies and professionals involved in the intervention, prevention, prosecution, and investigation systems that respond to child abuse cases.

(b) Activities of the regional children's advocacy program. (1) Administrator. The Administrator, in coordination with the Director, shall—

(A) establish regional children's advocacy program centers;

(B) fund existing regional centers with expertise in the prevention, judicial handling, and treatment of child abuse and neglect; and

(C) fund the establishment of freestanding facilities in multidisciplinary programs within communities that have yet to establish such facilities, for the purpose of enabling grant recipients to provide information, services and technical assistance to aid communities in establishing multidisciplinary programs that respond to child abuse.

(2) Grant recipients. A grant recipient under this section shall—
  (A) assist communities—
    (i) in developing a comprehensive, multidisciplinary response to child abuse that is designed to meet the needs of child victims and their families;
    (ii) in establishing a freestanding facility where interviews of and services for abused children can be provided;
    (iii) in preventing or reducing trauma to children caused by multiple contacts with community professionals;
    (iv) in providing families with needed services and assisting them in regaining maximum functioning;
    (v) in maintaining open communication and case coordination among community professionals and agencies involved in child protection efforts;
    (vi) in coordinating and tracking investigative, preventive, prosecutorial, and treatment efforts;
    (vii) in obtaining information useful for criminal and civil proceedings;
    (viii) in holding offenders accountable through improved prosecution of child abuse cases;
    (ix) in enhancing professional skills necessary to effectively respond to cases of child abuse through training; and
    (x) in enhancing community understanding of child abuse; and
  (B) provide training and technical assistance to local children's advocacy centers in its census region that are grant recipients under section 214 [42 USCS §13002].
(c) Operation of the regional children's advocacy program. (1) Solicitation of proposals. Not later than 1 year after the date of enactment of this section, the Administrator shall solicit proposals for assistance under this section.
  (2) Minimum qualifications. In order for a proposal to be selected, the Administrator may require an applicant to have in existence, at the time the proposal is submitted, 1 or more of the following:
    (A) A proven record in conducting activities of the kinds described in subsection (c).
    (B) A facility where children who are victims of sexual or physical abuse and their nonoffending family members can go for the purpose of evaluation, intervention, evidence gathering, and counseling.

(C) Multidisciplinary staff experienced in providing remedial counseling to children and families.

(D) Experience in serving as a center for training and education and as a resource facility.

(E) National expertise in providing technical assistance to communities with respect to the judicial handling of child abuse and neglect.

(3) Proposal requirements. . . .

(4) Selection of proposals. . . .

(d) Review.

(1) Evaluation of regional children's advocacy program activities. The Administrator, in coordination with the Director, shall regularly monitor and evaluate the activities of grant recipients and shall determine whether each grant recipient has complied with the original proposal and any modifications. . . .

(e) Children's advocacy advisory board.

(1) Establishment of board.

(A) In general. Not later than 120 days after the date of enactment of this section . . . the Administrator and the Director, after consulting with representatives of community agencies that respond to child abuse cases, shall establish a children's advocacy advisory board to provide guidance and oversight in implementing the selection criteria and operation of the regional children's advocacy program.

(B) Membership. (i) The board—

(I) shall be composed of 12 members who are selected by the Administrator, in coordination with the Director, a majority of whom shall be individuals experienced in the child abuse investigation, prosecution, prevention, and intervention systems;

(II) shall include at least 1 member from each of the 4 census regions; and

(III) shall have members appointed for a term not to exceed 3 years.

(ii) Members of the Board may be reappointed for successive terms.

(2) Review and recommendations. (A) Objectives. Not later than 180 days after the date of enactment of this section and annually thereafter, the Board shall develop and submit to the Administrator and the Director objectives for the implementation of the children's advocacy program activities described in subsection (b).

(B) Review. The board shall annually—
(i) review the solicitation and selection of children's advocacy program proposals and make recommendations concerning how each such activity can be altered so as to better achieve the purposes of this section; and
(ii) review the program activities and management plan of each grant recipient and report its findings and recommendations to the Administrator and the Director.

(3) Rules and regulations. The Board shall promulgate such rules and regulations as it deems necessary to carry out its duties under this section.

(f) Reporting. The Attorney General and the Secretary of Health and Human Services shall submit to Congress, by March 1 of each year, a detailed review of the progress of the regional children's advocacy program activities.

§13002. Local children's advocacy centers.
(a) In general. The Administrator, in coordination with the Director and with the Director of the Office of Victims of Crime, shall make grants to develop and implement multidisciplinary child abuse investigation and prosecution programs.
(b) Grant criteria. (1) The Director shall establish the criteria to be used in evaluating applications for grants under this section consistent with sections 262, 293, and 296 of subpart II of title II of the Juvenile Justice and Delinquency Prevention Act of 1974.

(2) In general, the grant criteria established pursuant to paragraph (1) may require that a program include any of the following elements:
(A) A written agreement between local law enforcement, social service, health, and other related agencies to coordinate child abuse investigation, prosecution, treatment, and counseling services.
(B) An appropriate site for referring, interviewing, treating, and counseling child victims of sexual and serious physical abuse and neglect and nonoffending family members (referred to as the "counseling center").
(C) Referral of all sexual and serious physical abuse and neglect cases to the counseling center not later than 24 hours after notification of an incident of abuse.
(D) Joint initial investigative interviews of child victims by personnel from law enforcement, health, and social service agencies.

(E) A requirement that, to the extent practicable, the same agency representative who conducts an initial interview conduct all subsequent interviews.

(F) A requirement that, to the extent practicable, all interviews and meetings with a child victim occur at the counseling center.

(G) Coordination of each step of the investigation process to minimize the number of interviews that a child victim must attend.

(H) Designation of a director for the multidisciplinary program.

(I) Assignment of a volunteer or staff advocate to each child in order to assist the child and, when appropriate, the child's family, throughout each step of judicial proceedings.

(J) Such other criteria as the Director shall establish by regulation.

(c) Distribution of grants. . . .

(d) Consultation with regional children's advocacy centers. A grant recipient under this section shall consult from time to time with regional children's advocacy centers in its census region that are grant recipients under section 213 [42 USCS §13001b].

§13003. Grants for specialized technical assistance and training programs.

(a) In general. The Administrator shall make grants to national organizations to provide technical assistance and training to attorneys and others instrumental to the criminal prosecution of child abuse cases in State or Federal courts, for the purpose of improving the quality of criminal prosecution of such cases.

(b) Grantee organizations. An organization to which a grant is made pursuant to subsection(a) shall be one that has, or is affiliated with one that has, broad membership among attorneys who prosecute criminal cases in State courts and has demonstrated experience in providing training and technical assistance for prosecutors.

(c) Grant criteria. . . .

§ 13004. Authorizations of appropriations. . . .

Court-Appointed Special Advocate Program.

§13011. Findings.

The Congress finds that—

(1) the National Court-Appointed Special Advocate provides training and technical assistance to a network of 13,000 volunteers in 377 programs operating in 47 States; and
(2) in 1988, these volunteers represented 40,000 children, representing approximately 15 percent of the estimated 270,000 cases of child abuse and neglect in juvenile and family courts.

§13012. Purpose
The purpose of this chapter . . . is to ensure that by January 1, 1995, a court-appointed special advocate shall be available to every victim of child abuse or neglect in the United States that needs such an advocate.

§13013. Strengthening of the court-appointed special advocate program
(a) In general. The Administrator of the Office of Juvenile Justice and Delinquency Prevention shall make grants to expand the court-appointed special advocate program.
(b) Grantee organizations. (1) An organization to which a grant is made pursuant to subsection (a) shall be a national organization that has broad membership among court-appointed special advocates and has demonstrated experience in grant administration of court-appointed special advocate programs and in providing training and technical assistance to court-appointed special advocate programs; or
    (2) may be a local public or not-for-profit agency that has demonstrated the willingness to initiate or expand a court-appointed special advocate program. . . .
(c) Grant criteria. (1) The Administrator shall establish criteria to be used in evaluating applications for grants under this section . . .
    (2) In general, the grant criteria established pursuant to paragraph (1) shall require that a court-appointed special advocate program provide screening, training, and supervision of court-appointed special advocates in accordance with standards developed by the National Court-Appointed Special Advocate Association. Such criteria may include the requirements that—
        (A) a court-appointed special advocate association program have a mission and purpose in keeping with the mission and purpose of the National Court-Appointed Special Advocate Association and that it abide by the National Court-Appointed Special Advocate Association Code of Ethics.

(B) a court-appointed special advocate association program operate with access to legal counsel;

(C) the management and operation of a court-appointed special advocate program assure adequate supervision of court-appointed special advocate volunteers;

(D) a court-appointed special advocate program keep written records on the operation of the program in general and on each applicant, volunteer, and case;

(E) a court-appointed special advocate program have written management and personnel policies and procedures, screening requirements, and training curriculum;

(F) a court-appointed special advocate program not accept volunteers who have been convicted of, have charges pending for, or have in the past been charged with, a felony or misdemeanor involving a sex offense, violent act, child abuse or neglect, or related acts that would pose risks to children or to the court-appointed special advocate program's credibility;

(G) a court-appointed special advocate program have an established procedure to allow the immediate reporting to a court or appropriate agency of a situation in which a court-appointed special advocate volunteer has reason to believe that a child is in imminent danger;

(H) a court-appointed special advocate volunteer be an individual who has been screened and trained by a recognized court-appointed special advocate program and appointed by the court to advocate for children who come into the court system primarily as a result of abuse or neglect; and

(I) a court-appointed special advocate volunteer serve the function of reviewing records, facilitating prompt, thorough review of cases, and interviewing appropriate parties in order to make recommendations on what would be in the best interests of the child.

(3) In awarding grants under this section, the Administrator shall ensure that grants are distributed to localities that have no existing court-appointed special advocate program and to programs in need of expansion.

§13014 Authorization of appropriations. . . .

Child Abuse Training Programs for Judicial Personnel and Practitioners

§13021. Findings and purpose

(a) Findings. The Congress finds that—

(1) a large number of juvenile and family courts are inundated with increasing numbers of cases due to increased reports of abuse and neglect, increasing drug-related maltreatment, and insufficient court resources;

(2) the amendments made to the Social Security Act by the Adoption Assistance and Child Welfare Act of 1980 make substantial demands on the courts handling abuse and neglect cases, but provide no assistance to the courts to meet those demands;

(3) the Adoption and Child Welfare Act of 1980 requires courts to—

(A) determine whether the agency made reasonable efforts to prevent foster care placement;

(B) approve voluntary nonjudicial placement; and

(C) provide procedural safeguards for parents when their parent-child relationship is affected;

(4) social welfare agencies press the courts to meet such requirements, yet scarce resources often dictate that courts comply pro forma without undertaking the meaningful judicial inquiry contemplated by Congress in the Adoption and Child Welfare Act of 1980;

(5) compliance with the Adoption and Child Welfare Act of 1980 and overall improvements in the judicial response to abuse and neglect cases can best come about through action by top level court administrators and judges with administrative functions who understand the unique aspects of decisions required in child abuse and neglect cases; and

(6) the Adoption and Child Welfare Act of 1980 provides financial incentives to train welfare agency staff to meet the requirements, but provides no resources to train judges.

(b) Purpose. The purpose of this chapter . . . is to provide expanded technical assistance and training to judicial personnel and attorneys, particularly personnel and practitioners in juvenile and family courts, to improve the judicial system's handling of child abuse and neglect cases with specific emphasis on the role of the courts in addressing reasonable efforts that can safely avoid unnecessary and unnecessarily prolonged foster care placement.

§13022. Grants for juvenile and family court personnel
In order to improve the judicial system's handling of child abuse and neglect cases, the Administrator of the Office of Juvenile Justice and Delinquency Prevention shall make grants for the purpose of providing—
  (1) technical assistance and training to judicial personnel and attorneys, particularly personnel and practitioners in juvenile and family courts; and
  (2) administrative reform in juvenile and family courts.

§13023. Specialized technical assistance and training programs
(a) Grants to develop model programs. (1) The Administrator shall make grants to national organizations to develop 1 or more model technical assistance and training programs to improve the judicial system's handling of child abuse and neglect cases.
  (2) an organization to which a grant is made pursuant to paragraph (1) shall be one that has broad membership among juvenile and family court judges and has demonstrated experience in providing training and technical assistance for judges, attorneys, child welfare personnel, and lay child advocates.
(b) Grants to juvenile and family courts. (1) In order to improve the judicial system's handling of child abuse and neglect cases, the Administrator shall make grants to State courts or judicial administrators for programs that provide or contract for, the implementation of—
    (A) training and technical assistance to judicial personnel and attorneys in juvenile and family courts; and
    (B) administrative reform in juvenile and family courts.
  (2) The criteria established for the making of grants pursuant to paragraph (1) shall give priority to programs that improve—
    (A) procedures for determining whether child service agencies have made reasonable efforts to prevent placement of children in foster care;
    (B) procedures for determining whether child service agencies have, after placement of children in foster care, made reasonable efforts to reunite the family; and
    (C) procedures for coordinating information and services among health professionals, social workers, law enforcement professionals, prosecutors, defense attorneys, and juvenile and family court personnel, consistent with subtitle A [42 USCS §13001 et seq.].

(c) Grant criteria. . . .

§13024. Authorization of appropriations. . . .

Federal Victims' Protections and Rights

§13031. Child abuse reporting

(a) In general. A person who while engaged in a professional capacity or activity described in subsection (b) on Federal land or in a federally operated (or contracted) facility learns of facts that give reason to suspect that a child has suffered an incident of child abuse, shall as soon as possible make a report of the suspected abuse to the agency designated under subsection (d).

(b) Covered professionals. Persons engaged in the following professions and activities are subject to the requirements of subsection (a):

(1) Physicians, dentists, medical residents or interns, hospital personnel and administrators, nurses, health care practitioners, chiropractors, osteopaths, pharmacists, optometrists, podiatrists, emergency medical technicians, ambulance drivers, undertakers, coroners, medical examiners, alcohol or drug treatment personnel, and persons performing a healing role or practicing the healing arts.

(2) Psychologists, psychiatrists, and mental health professionals.

(3) Social workers, licensed or unlicensed marriage, family, and individual counselors.

(4) Teachers, teacher's aides or assistants, school counselors and guidance personnel, school officials, and school administrators.

(5) Child care workers and administrators.

(6) Law enforcement personnel, probation officers, criminal prosecutors, and juvenile rehabilitation or detention facility employees.

(7) Foster parents.

(8) Commercial film and photo processors.

(c) Definitions. For the purposes of this section—

(1) the term "child abuse" means the physical or mental injury, sexual abuse or exploitation, or negligent treatment of a child;

(2) the term "physical injury" includes but is not limited to lacerations, fractured bones, burns, internal injuries, severe bruising or serious bodily harm;

(3) the term "mental injury" means harm to a child's psychological or intellectual functioning which may be exhibited by severe anxiety, depression, withdrawal or outward aggressive behavior, or a combination of those behaviors, which may be demonstrated by a change in behavior, emotional response or cognition;

(4) the term "sexual abuse" includes the employment, use, persuasion, inducement, enticement, or coercion of a child to engage in, or assist another person to engage in, sexually explicit conduct or the rape, molestation, prostitution, or other form of sexual exploitation of children, or incest with children;

(5) the term "sexually explicit conduct" means actual or simulated—

(A) sexual intercourse including sexual contact in the manner of genital-genital, oral-genital, anal-genital, or oral-anal contact, whether between persons of the same or of opposite sex; sexual contact means the intentional touching, either directly or through clothing, of the genitalia, anus, groin, breast, inner thigh, or buttocks of any person with an intent to abuse, humiliate, harass, degrade, or arouse or gratify sexual desire of any person;

(B) bestiality;

(C) masturbation;

(D) lascivious exhibition of the genitals or pubic area of a person or animal, or

(E) sadistic or masochistic abuse;

(6) the term "exploitation" means child pornography or child prostitution;

(7) the term "negligent treatment" means the failure to provide, for reasons other than poverty, adequate food, clothing, shelter, or medical care so as to seriously endanger the physical health of the child; and

(8) the term "child abuse" shall not include discipline administered by a parent or legal guardian to his or her child provided it is reasonable in manner and moderate in degree and otherwise does not constitute cruelty.

(d) Agency designated to receive report and action to be taken. For all Federal lands and all federally operated (or contracted) facilities in which children are cared for or reside, the Attorney General shall designate an agency to receive and investigate the reports described in subsection (a). By formal written agreement, the designated agency may be a non-Federal agency.

When such reports are received by social services or health care agencies, and involve allegations of sexual abuse, serious physical injury, or life-threatening neglect of a child, there shall be an immediate referral of the report to a law enforcement agency with authority to take emergency action to protect the child. All reports received shall be promptly investigated, and whenever appropriate, investigations shall be conducted jointly by social services and law enforcement personnel, with a view toward avoiding unnecessary multiple interviews with the child.
(e) Reporting form. In every federally operated (or contracted) facility, and on all Federal lands, a standard written reporting form, with instructions, shall be disseminated to all mandated reporter groups. Use of the form shall be encouraged, but its use shall not take the place of the immediate making of oral reports, telephonically or otherwise, when circumstances dictate.
(f) Immunity for good faith reporting and associated actions. All persons who, acting in good faith, make a report by subsection (a), or otherwise provide information or assistance in connection with a report, investigation, or legal intervention pursuant to a report, shall be immune from civil and criminal liability arising out of such actions. There shall be a presumption that any such persons acted in good faith. If a person is sued because of the person's performance of one of the above functions, and the defendant prevails in the litigation, the court may order that the plaintiff pay the defendant's legal expenses. Immunity shall not be accorded to persons acting in bad faith. . . .
(h) Training of prospective reporters. All individuals in the occupations listed in subsection (b)(1) who work on Federal lands, or are employed in federally operated (or contracted) facilities, shall receive periodic training in the obligation to report, as well as in the identification of abused and neglected children.

Child Care Worker Employee Background Checks

§13041. Requirement for background checks
(a) In general. (1) Each agency of the Federal Government, and every facility operated by the Federal Government (or operated under contract with the Federal Government), that hires (or contracts for hire) individuals involved with the provision to children under the age of 18 of child care services shall assure that all existing and newly-hired employees undergo a criminal history background check. All existing staff shall receive such

checks not later than May 29, 1991. Except as provided in sub-section (b)(3), no additional staff shall be hired without a check having been completed.

(2) For the purposes of this section, the term "child care ser-vices" means child protective services (including the investi-gation of child abuse and neglect reports), social services, health and mental health care, child (day) care, education (whether or not directly involved in teaching), foster care, residential care, recreational or rehabilitative programs, and detention, correctional, or treatment services.

(b) Criminal history check. (1) A background check required by subsection (a) shall be—

(A) Based on a set of the employee's fingerprints ob-tained by a law enforcement officer and on other identi-fying information;

(B) conducted through the Identification Division of the Federal Bureau of Investigation and through the State criminal history repositories of all States that an em-ployee or prospective employee lists as current and for-mer residences in an employment application; and

(C) initiated through the personnel programs of the ap-plicable Federal agencies.

(2) The results of the background check shall be communi-cated to the employing agency.

(3) An agency or facility described in subsection (a)(1) may hire a staff person provisionally prior to the completion of a background check if, at all times prior to receipt of the back-ground check during which children are in the care of the person, the person is within the sight and under the supervi-sion of a staff person with respect to whom a background check has been completed.

(c) Applicable criminal histories. Any conviction for a sex crime, an offense involving a child victim, or a drug felony, may be ground for denying employment or for dismissal of an em-ployee in any of the positions listed in subsection (a)(2). In the case of an incident in which an individual has been charged with one of those offenses, when the charge has not yet been disposed of, an employer may suspend an employee from hav-ing any contact with children while on the job until the case is resolved. Conviction of a crime other than a sex crime may be considered if it bears on an individual's fitness to have respon-sibility for the safety and well-being of children.

(d) Employment application. (1) Employment applications for

individuals who are seeking work for an agency of the Federal Government, or for a facility or program operated by (or through contract with) the Federal Government, in any of the positions listed in subsection (a)(1), shall contain a question asking whether the individual has ever been arrested for or charged with a crime involving a child, and if so requiring a description of the disposition of the arrest or charge. An application shall state that it is being signed under penalty of perjury, with the applicable Federal punishment for perjury stated on the application.

> (2) A Federal agency seeking a criminal history record check shall first obtain the signature of the employee or prospective employee indicating that the employee or prospective employee has been notified of the employer's obligation to require a record check as a condition of employment and the employee's right to obtain a copy of the criminal history report made available to the employing Federal agency and the right to challenge the accuracy and completeness of any information contained in the report.

(e) Encouragement of voluntary criminal history checks for others who may have contact with children. Federal agencies and facilities are encouraged to submit identifying information for criminal history checks on volunteers working in any of the positions listed in subsection (a) and on adult household members in places where child care or foster care services are being provided in a home.

Protection of Children Against Sexual Exploitation Act of 1977

P.L. 95-225
18 USCS §2251—§2257

Findings. The Congress finds that—
(1) child exploitation has become a multi-million dollar industry, infiltrated and operated by elements of organized crime, and by a nationwide network of individuals openly advertising their desire to exploit children;
(2) Congress has recognized the physiological, psychological, and emotional harm caused by the production, distribution, and display of child pornography by strengthening laws prescribing such activities;

(3) the Federal Government lacks sufficient enforcement tools to combat concerted efforts to exploit children prescribed by Federal law, and exploitation victims lack effective remedies under Federal law; and

(4) current rules of evidence, criminal procedure, and civil procedure and other courtroom and investigative procedures inhibit the participation of child victims as witnesses and damage their credibility when they do testify, impairing the prosecution of child exploitation offenses.

§2251. Sexual exploitation of children.

(a) Any person who employs, uses, persuades, induces, entices, or coerces any minor to engage in, or who has a minor assist any other person to engage in, or who transports any minor in interstate or foreign commerce, or in any Territory or Possession of the United States, with the intent that such minor engage in any sexually explicit conduct for the purpose of producing any visual depiction of such conduct, shall be punished as provided under subsection (d), if such person knows or has reason to know that such visual depiction will be transported in interstate or foreign commerce or mailed, or if such visual depiction has actually been transported in interstate or foreign commerce or mailed.

(b) Any parent, legal guardian, or person having custody or control of a minor who knowingly permits such minor to engage in, or to assist any other person to engage in, sexually explicit conduct for the purpose of producing any visual depiction of such conduct shall be punished as provided under subsection (d) of this section, if such parent, legal guardian, or person knows or has reason to know that such visual depiction will be transported in interstate or foreign commerce or mailed or if such visual depiction has actually been transported in interstate or foreign commerce or mailed.

(c)(1) Any person who, in a circumstance described in paragraph (2), knowingly makes, prints, or publishes, or causes to be made, printed, or published, any notice or advertisement seeking or offering—

    (A) to receive, exchange, buy, produce, display, distribute, or reproduce, any visual depiction, if the production of such visual depiction involves the use of a minor engaging in sexually explicit conduct and such visual depiction is of such conduct; or

    (B) participation in any act of sexually explicit conduct

by or with any minor for the purpose of producing a visual depiction of such conduct;

shall be punished as provided under subsection (d).

(2) The circumstance referred to in paragraph (1) is that—

(A) such person knows or has reason to know that such notice or advertisement will be transported in interstate or foreign commerce by any means including by computer or mailed; or

(B) such notice or advertisement is transported in interstate or foreign commerce by any means including by computer or mailed.

(d) Any individual who violates this section shall be fined not more than $100,000, or imprisoned not more than 10 years, or both, but, if such individual has a prior conviction under this section, such individual shall be fined not more than $200,000, or imprisoned not less than five years nor more than 15 years, or both. Any organization which violates this section shall be fined not more than $250,000.

§2251A. Selling or buying of children.

(a) A parent, legal guardian or other person having custody or control of a minor who sells or otherwise transfers custody or control of such minor, or offers to sell or otherwise transfer custody of such minor either—

(1) with knowledge that, as a consequence of the sale or transfer, the minor will be portrayed in a visual depiction engaging in, or assisting another person to engage in, sexually explicit conduct; or

(2) with intent to promote either—

(A) the engaging in of sexually explicit conduct by such minor for the purpose of producing any visual depiction of such conduct; or

(B) the rendering of assistance by the minor to any other person to engage in sexually explicit conduct for the purpose of producing any visual depiction of such conduct;

shall be punished by imprisonment for not less than 20 years or for life and by a fine under this title, if any of the circumstances described in subsection (c) of this section exist.

(b) Whoever purchases or otherwise obtains custody or control of a minor, or offers to purchase or otherwise obtain custody or control of a minor either—

(1) with knowledge that, as a consequence of the purchase or obtaining of custody, the minor will be portrayed in a

visual depiction engaging in, or assisting another person to engage in, sexually explicit conduct; or

(2) with intent to promote either—

(A) the engaging in of sexually explicit conduct by such minor for the purpose of producing any visual depiction of such conduct; or

(B) the rendering of assistance by the minor to any other person to engage in sexually explicit conduct for the purpose of producing any visual depiction of such conduct;

shall be punished by imprisonment for not less than 20 years or for life and by a fine under this title, if any of the circumstances described in subsection (c) of this section exist.

(c) The circumstances referred to in subsections (a) and (b) are that—

(1) in the course of the conduct described in such subsections the minor or the actor traveled in or was transported in interstate or foreign commerce;

(2) any offer described in such subsections was communicated or transported in interstate or foreign commerce by any means including by computer or mail; or

(3) the conduct described in such subsections took place in any territory or possession of the United States.

§2252. Certain activities relating to material involving the sexual exploitation of minors.

(a) Any person who—

(1) knowingly transports or ships in interstate or foreign commerce by any means including by computer or mails, any visual depiction, if—

(A) the producing of such visual depiction involves the use of a minor engaging in sexually explicit conduct; and

(B) such visual depiction is of such conduct; or

(2) knowingly receives, or distributes, any visual depiction that has been transported or shipped in interstate or foreign commerce by any means including by computer or mailed or knowingly reproduces any visual depiction for distribution in interstate or foreign commerce by any means including by computer or through the mails, if—

(A) the producing of such visual depiction involves the use of a minor engaging in sexually explicit conduct; and

(B) such visual depiction is of such conduct;

shall be punished as provided in subsection (b) of this section.

(b) Any individual who violates this section shall be fined not more than $100,000, or imprisoned not more than 10 years, or both, but, if such individual has a prior conviction under this section, such individual shall be fined not more than $200,000, or imprisoned not less than five years nor more than 15 years, or both. Any organization which violates this section shall be fined not more than $250,000.

§2253. Criminal forfeiture

(a) Property subject to criminal forfeiture. A person who is convicted of an offense under this chapter involving a visual depiction described in sections 2251, 2251A, or 2252 of this chapter shall forfeit to the United States such person's interest in—

> (1) any visual depiction described in sections 2251, 2251A, or 2252 of this chapter, or any book, magazine, periodical, film, videotape, or other matter which contains any such visual depiction, which was produced, transported, mailed, shipped, or received in violation of this chapter;
>
> (2) any property, real or personal, constituting or traceable to gross profits or other proceeds obtained from such offense; and
>
> (3) any property, real or personal, used or intended to be used to commit or to promote the commission of such offense.

(b) Third party transfers. All right, title, and interest in property described in subsection (a) of this section vests in the United States upon the commission of the act giving rise to forfeiture under this section. Any such property that is subsequently transferred to a person other than the defendant may be the subject of a special verdict of forfeiture and thereafter shall be ordered forfeited to the United States, unless the transferee establishes in a hearing pursuant to subsection (m) of this section that he is a bona fide purchaser for value of such property who at the time of purchase was reasonably without cause to believe that the property was subject to forfeiture under this section.

(c) Protective orders. (1) Upon application of the United States, the court may enter a restraining order or injunction, require the execution of a satisfactory performance bond, or take any other action to preserve the availability of property described in subsection (a) of this section for forfeiture under this section. . . .

(d) Warrant of seizure. The Government may request the issuance of a warrant authorizing the seizure of property subject to forfeiture under this section in the same manner as provided for a search warrant. If the court determines that there is probable cause to believe that the property to be seized would, in the event of conviction, be subject to forfeiture and that an order under subsection (c) of this section may not be sufficient to assure the availability of the property for forfeiture, the court shall issue a warrant authorizing the seizure of such property.

(e) Order of forfeiture. The court shall order forfeiture of property referred to in subsection (a) if the trier of fact determines, beyond a reasonable doubt, that such property is subject to forfeiture.

(f) Execution. Upon entry of an order of forfeiture under this section, the court shall authorize the Attorney General to seize all property ordered forfeited upon such terms and conditions as the court shall deem proper. . . .

(g) Disposition of property. Following the seizure of property ordered forfeited under this section, the Attorney General shall destroy or retain for official use any article described in paragraph (1) of subsection (a), and shall retain for official use or direct the disposition of any property described in paragraph (2) or (3) of subsection (a) by sale or any other commercially feasible means, making due provision for the rights of any innocent persons. . . .

§2254. Civil forfeiture

(a) Property subject to civil forfeiture. The following property shall be subject to forfeiture by the United States:

(1) Any visual depiction described in sections 2251, 2251A, or 2252 of this chapter, or any book, magazine, periodical, film, videotape, or other matter which contains any such visual depiction, which was produced, transported, mailed, shipped, or received in violation of this chapter.

(2) Any property, real or personal, used or intended to be used to commit or to promote the commission of an offense under this chapter involving a visual depiction described in sections 2251, 2251A, or 2252 of this chapter, except that no property shall be forfeited under this paragraph, to the extent of the interest of an owner, by reason of any act or omission established by that owner to have been committed or omitted without the knowledge or consent of that owner.

(3) Any property, real or personal, constituting or traceable to gross profits or other proceeds obtained from a violation of this chapter . . . involving a visual depiction described in sections 2251, 2251A, or 2252 of this chapter, except that no property shall be forfeited under this paragraph, to the extent of

the interest of an owner, by reason of any act or omission established by that owner to have been committed or omitted without the knowledge or consent of that owner. . . .

§2255. Civil remedy for personal injuries.
(a) Any minor who is a victim of a violation of section 2251 or 2251 of this title and who suffers a personal injury as a result of such violation may sue in any appropriate United States District Court and shall recover the actual damages such minor sustains and the cost of the suit, including a reasonable attorney's fee. Any minor as described in the preceding sentence shall be deemed to have sustained damages of no less than $50,000 in value.
(b) Any action commenced under this section shall be barred unless the complaint is filed within six years after the right of action first accrues or in the case of a person under a legal disability, not later than three years after the disability.

§2256. Definitions for chapter
For the purposes of this chapter . . . the term—
(1) "minor" means any person under the age of eighteen years;
(2) "sexually explicit conduct" means actual or simulated—
    (A) sexual intercourse, including genital-genital, oral-genital, anal-genital, or oral-anal, whether between persons of the same or opposite sex;
    (B) bestiality;
    (C) masturbation;
    (D) sadistic or masochistic abuse; or
    (E) lascivious exhibition of the genitals or pubic area of any person;
(3) "producing" means producing, directing, manufacturing, issuing, publishing, or advertising;
(4) "organization" means a person other than an individual;
(5) "visual depiction" includes undeveloped film and videotape;
(6) "computer" has the meaning given that term in section 1030 of this title; and
(7) "custody or control" includes temporary supervision over or responsibility for a minor whether legally or illegally obtained.

§2257. Record keeping requirements
(a) Whoever produces any book, magazine, periodical, film, videotape, or other matter which—

(1) contains one or more visual depictions made after February 6, 1978 of actual sexually explicit conduct; and

(2) is produced in whole or in part with materials which have been mailed or shipped in interstate or foreign commerce, or is shipped or transported or is intended for shipment or transportation in interstate or foreign commerce;

shall create and maintain individually identifiable records pertaining to every performer portrayed in such a visual depiction.

(b) Any person to whom subsection (a) applies shall, with respect to every performer portrayed in a visual depiction of actual sexually explicit conduct—

(1) ascertain, by examination of an identification document containing such information, the performer's name and date of birth, and require the performer to provide such other indicia of his or her identity as may be prescribed by regulations;

(2) ascertain any name, other than the performer's present and correct name, ever used by the performer including maiden name, alias, nickname, stage, or professional name; and

(3) record in the records required by subsection (a) the information required by paragraphs (1) and (2) of this subsection and such other identifying information as may be prescribed by regulation.

(c) Any person to whom subsection (a) applies shall maintain the records required by this section at his business premises, or at such other place as the Attorney General may by regulation prescribe and shall make such records available to the Attorney General for inspection at all reasonable times.

(d)(1) No information or evidence obtained from records required to be created or maintained by this section shall, except as provided in paragraphs (2) and (3), be used, directly or indirectly, as evidence against any person with respect to any violation of law.

(2) Paragraph (1) of this subsection shall not preclude the use of such information or evidence in a prosecution or other action for a violation of any applicable provision of law with respect to the furnishing of false information.

(3) In a prosecution of any person to whom subsection (a) applies for an offense in violation of subsection 2251(a) of this title which has as an element the production of a visual depiction of a minor engaging in or assisting another person to engage in sexually explicit conduct and in which that element is

sought to be established by showing that a performer within the meaning of this section is a minor—

(A) proof that the person failed to comply with the provisions of subsection (a) or (b) of this section concerning the creation and maintenance of records, or a regulation issued pursuant thereto, shall raise a rebuttable presumption that such performer was a minor; and

(B) proof that the person failed to comply with the provisions of subsection (e) of this section concerning the statement required by that subsection shall raise the rebuttable presumption that every performer in the matter was a minor.

(e)(1) Any person to whom subsection (a) applies shall cause to be affixed to every copy of any matter described in paragraph (1) of subsection (a) of this section, in such manner and in such form as the Attorney General shall by regulations prescribe, a statement describing where the records required by this section with respect to all performers depicted in that copy of the matter may be located.

(2) If the person to whom subsection (a) applies is an organization the statement required by this subsection shall include the name, title, and business address of the individual employed by such organization responsible for maintaining the records required by this section.

(3) In any prosecution of a person for an offense in violation of section 2252 of this title which has as an element the transporting, mailing, or distribution of a visual depiction involving the use of a minor engaging in sexually explicit conduct, and in which that element is sought to be established by a showing that a performer within the meaning of this section is a minor, proof that the matter in which the visual depiction is contained did not contain the statement required by this section shall raise a rebuttable presumption that such performer was a minor.

(f) The Attorney General shall issue appropriate regulations to carry out this section.

(g) As used in this section—

(1) the term "actual sexually explicit conduct" means actual but not simulated conduct as defined in subparagraphs (A) through (E) of paragraph (2) of section 2256 of this title;

(2) "identification document" has the meaning given that term in subsection 1028(d) of this title;

(3) the term "produces" means to produce, manufacture, or

publish and includes the duplication, reproduction, or reissuing of any material; and

(4) the term "performer" includes any person portrayed in a visual depiction engaging in, or assisting another person to engage in, actual sexually explicit conduct.

Court Decisions

Globe Newspaper Co. v. Superior Court for the County of Norfolk

457 U.S. 596

Section 16A of Chapter 278 of the Massachusetts General Laws, as construed by the Massachusetts Supreme Judicial Court, requires trial judges, at trials for specified sexual offenses involving a victim under the age of 18, to exclude the press and general public from the courtroom during the testimony of that victim. The question presented is whether the statute thus construed violates the First Amendment as applied to the States through the Fourteenth Amendment.

I

The case began when appellant, Globe Newspaper Co. (Globe), unsuccessfully attempted to gain access to a rape trial conducted in the Superior Court for the County of Norfolk, Commonwealth of Massachusetts. The criminal defendant in that trial had been charged with the forcible rape and forced unnatural rape of three girls who were minors at the time of trial—two 16 years of age and one 17. In April 1979, during hearings on several preliminary motions, the trial judge ordered the courtroom closed. Before the trial began, Globe moved that the court revoke this closure order, hold hearings on any future such orders, and permit appellant to intervene "for the limited purpose of asserting its rights to access to the trial and hearings on related preliminary motions." . . . The trial court denied Globe's motions, relying on Mass. Gen. Laws Ann., ch. 278, §16A (West 1981), and ordered the exclusion of the press and general public from the courtroom during the trial. The defendant immediately objected to that exclusion order, and the prosecution stated for purposes of the record that the order was issued on the court's "own motion and not at the request of the Commonwealth."

Within hours after the court had issued its exclusion order, Globe sought injunctive relief from a justice of the Supreme Judicial Court of Massachusetts. The next day the justice conducted a hearing, at which the Commonwealth, "on behalf of the victims," waived "whatever rights it [might] have [had] to exclude the press."*Id.*, at 28a. Nevertheless, Globe's request for relief was denied. Before Globe appealed to the full court, the rape trial proceeded and the defendant was acquitted.

Nine months after the conclusion of the criminal trial, the Supreme Judicial Court issued its judgment, dismissing Globe's appeal. Although the court held that the case was rendered moot by completion of the trial, it nevertheless stated that it would proceed to the merits, because the issues raised by Globe were "significant and troublesome, and . . . 'capable of repetition yet evading review.' " *Globe Newspaper Co. v. Superior Court,* 379 Mass. 846, 848, 401 N.E. 2d 360, 362 (1980), quoting *Southern Pacific Terminal Co. v. ICC,* 219 U.S. 498, 515 (1911). As a statutory matter, the court agreed with Globe that §16A did not require the exclusion of the press from the entire criminal trial. The provision was designed, the court determined, "to encourage young victims of sexual offenses to come forward; once they have come forward, the statute is designed to preserve their ability to testify by protecting them from undue psychological harm at trial." 379 Mass., at 860, 401 N.E. 2d, at 369. Relying on these twin purposes, the court concluded that §16A required the closure of sex-offense trials only during the testimony of minor victims; during other portions of such trials, closure was "a matter within the judge's sound discretion." *Id.*, at 864, 401 N.E. 2d, at 371. The court did not pass on Globe's contentions that it had a right to attend the entire criminal trial under the First and Sixth Amendments, noting that it would await this Court's decision—then pending—in *Richmond Newspapers, Inc. v. Virginia,* 448 U.S. 555 (1980).

Globe then appealed to this Court. Following our decision in *Richmond Newspapers,* we vacated the judgment of the Supreme Judicial Court, and remanded the case for further consideration in light of that decision. *Globe Newspaper Co. v. Superior Court,* 449 U.S. 894 (1980).

On remand, the Supreme Judicial Court, adhering to its earlier construction of §16A, considered whether our decision in

Richmond Newspapers required the invalidation of the mandatory closure rule of §16A. 383 Mass. 838, 423 N.E. 2d 773 (1981). In analyzing the First Amendment issue, the court recognized that there is "an unbroken tradition of openness" in criminal trials. *Id.,* at 845, 423 N.E. 2d, at 778. But the court discerned "at least one notable exception" to this tradition: "In cases involving sexual assaults, portions of trials have been closed to some segments of the public, even when the victim was an adult." *Id.,* at 846, 423 N.E. at 778. The court also emphasized that §16A's mandatory closure rule furthered "genuine State interests," which the court had identified in its earlier decision as underlying the statutory provision. These interests, the court stated, "would be defeated if a case-by-case determination were used." at 848, 423 N.E. 2d, at 779. While acknowledging that the mandatory closure requirement results in a "temporary diminution" of "the public's knowledge about these trials," the court did not think "that *Richmond Newspapers* require[d] the invalidation of the requirement, given the statute's narrow scope in an area of traditional sensitivity to the needs of victims." at 851, 423 N.E. 2d, at 781. The court accordingly dismissed Globe's appeal.

Globe again sought review in this Court. We noted probable jurisdiction. 454 U.S. 1051 (1981). For the reasons that follow, we reverse, and hold that the mandatory closure rule contained in §16A violates the First Amendment.

II

In this Court, Globe challenges that portion of the trial court's order, approved by the Supreme Judicial Court of Massachusetts, that holds that §16A requires, under all circumstances, the exclusion of the press and general public during the testimony of a minor victim in a sex-offense trial. Because the entire order expired with the completion of the rape trial at which the defendant was acquitted, we must consider at the outset whether a live controversy remains. Under Art. III, §2, of the Constitution, our jurisdiction extends only to actual cases or controversies. *Nebraska Press Assn. v. Stuart,* 427 U.S. 539, 546 (1976). "The Court has recognized, however, that jurisdiction is not necessarily defeated simply because the order attacked has expired, if the underlying dispute between the parties is one `capable of repetition, yet evading review.'" *Ibid.,* quoting *Southern Pacific Terminal Co. v. ICC,* 219 U.S., at 515.

The controversy between the parties in this case is indeed "capable of repetition, yet evading review." It can reasonably be assumed that Globe, as the publisher of a newspaper serving the Boston metropolitan area, will someday be subjected to another order relying on §16A's mandatory closure rule. See *Gannett Co. v. DePasquale*, 443 U.S. 368, 377–378 (1979); *Richmond Newspapers, Inc., v. Virginia*, 448 U.S., at 563 (plurality opinion). And because criminal trials are typically of "short duration," *ibid.*, such an order will likely "evade review, or at least considered plenary review in this Court." *Nebraska Press Assn. v. Stuart*, supra, at 547. We therefore conclude that the controversy before us is not moot within the meaning of Art. III, and turn to the merits.

III

A

The Court's recent decision in *Richmond Newspapers* firmly established for the first time that the press and general public have a constitutional right of access to criminal trials. Although there was no opinion of the Court in that case, seven Justices recognized that this right of access is embodied in the First Amendment, and applied to the States through the Fourteenth Amendment. 448 U.S. at 558–581 (plurality opinion); *id.*, at 584–598 (Brennan, J. concurring in judgment); *id.*, at 598–601 (Stewart, J., concurring in judgment); *id.*, at 601–604 (Blackmun, J., concurring in judgment).

Of course, this right of access to criminal trials is not explicitly mentioned in terms in the First Amendment. But we have long eschewed any "narrow, literal conception" of the Amendment's terms, *NAACP v. Button*, 371 U.S. 415, 430 (1963), for the Framers were concerned with broad principles, and wrote against a background of shared values and practices. The First Amendment is thus broad enough to encompass those rights that, while not unambiguously enumerated in the very terms of the Amendment, are nonetheless necessary to the enjoyment of other First Amendment rights. . . .

Two features of the criminal justice system, emphasized in the various opinions in *Richmond Newspapers*, together serve to explain why a right of access to criminal trials in particular is properly afforded protection by the First Amendment. First, the criminal trial historically has been open to the press and general public. "[A]t the time when our organic laws were adopted, criminal trials both here and in England had long been presumptively open." *Richmond Newspapers, Inc., v. Virginia,* supra, at 569 (plurality opinion). And since that time, the presumption of openness has remained secure. Indeed, at the time of this Court's decision in *In re Oliver,* 333 U.S. 257 (1948), the presumption was so solidly grounded that the Court was "unable to find a single instance of a criminal trial conducted in camera in any federal, state, or municipal court during the history of this country." *Id.,* at 266 (footnote omitted). This uniform rule of openness has been viewed as significant in constitutional terms not only "because the Constitution carries the gloss of history," but also because "a tradition of accessibility implies the favorable judgment of experience." *Richmond Newspapers, Inc., v. Virginia,* supra, at 589 (Brennan, J., concurring in judgment).

Second, the right of access to criminal trials plays a particularly significant role in the functioning of the judicial process and the government as a whole. Public scrutiny of a criminal trial enhances the quality and safeguards the integrity of the factfinding process, with benefits to both the defendant and to society as a whole. Moreover, public access to the criminal trial fosters an appearance of fairness, thereby heightening public respect for the judicial process. And in the broadest terms, public access to criminal trials permits the public to participate in and serve as a check upon the judicial process—an essential component in our structure of self-government. In sum, the institutional value of the open criminal trial is recognized in both logic and experience.

B

Although the right of access to criminal trials is of constitutional stature, it is not absolute. . . . But the circumstances under which the press and public can be barred from a criminal trial are limited; the State's justification in denying access must be a weighty one. Where, as in the present case, the State attempts to deny the right of access in order to inhibit the disclosure of sensitive information, it must be shown that the denial is necessitated by a compelling governmental interest, and is narrowly tailored to serve that interest. . . . We now consider the state interests advanced to support Massachusetts' mandatory rule barring press and public access to criminal sex-offense trials during the testimony of minor victims.

IV

The state interests asserted to support §16A, though articulated in various ways, are reducible to two: the protection of minor victims of sex crimes from further trauma and embarrassment; and the encouragement of such victims to come forward and testify in a truthful and credible manner. We consider these interests in turn.

We agree with appellee that the first interest—safeguarding the physical and psychological well-being of a minor—is a compelling one. But as compelling as that interest is, it does not justify a mandatory closure rule, for it is clear that the circumstances of the particular case may affect the significance of the interest. A trial court can determine on a case-by-case basis whether closure is necessary to protect the welfare of a minor victim. Among the factors to be weighed are the minor victim's age, psychological maturity and understanding, the nature of the crime, the desires of the victim, and the interests of parents and relatives. Section 16A, in contrast, requires closure even if the victim does not seek the exclusion of the press and general public, and would not suffer injury by their presence. In the case before us, for example, the names of the minor victims were already in the public record, and the record indicates that the victims may have been willing to testify despite the presence of the press. If the trial court had been permitted to exercise its discretion, closure might well have been deemed unnecessary. In short, §16A cannot be viewed as a narrowly tailored means of accommodating the State's asserted interest: That interest could be served just as well by requiring the trial court to determine on a case-by-case basis whether the State's legitimate concern for the well-being of the minor victim necessitates closure. Such an approach ensures that the constitutional right of the press and public to gain access to criminal trials will not be restricted except where necessary to protect the State's interest.

Nor can §16A be justified on the basis of the Commonwealth's second asserted interest—the encouragement of minor victims of sex crimes to come forward and provide accurate testimony. The Commonwealth has offered no empirical support for the claim that the rule of automatic closure contained in §16A will lead to an increase in the number of minor sex victims coming forward and cooperating with state authorities. Not only is the claim speculative in empirical terms, but it is also open to serious question as a matter of logic and common sense. Although §16A bars the press and general public from the courtroom during the testimony of minor sex victims, the press is not denied access to the transcript, court personnel, or any other possible source that could provide an account of the minor victim's testimony. Thus §16A cannot prevent the press from publicizing the substance of a minor victim's testimony, as well as his or her identity. If the Commonwealth's interest in encouraging minor victims to come forward depends on keeping such matters secret, §16A hardly advances that interest in an effective manner. And even if §16A effectively advanced the State's interest, it is doubtful that the interest would be sufficient to overcome the constitutional attack, for that same interest could be relied on to support an array of mandatory closure rules designed to encourage victims to come forward: Surely it cannot be suggested that minor victims of sex crimes are the only crime victims who because of publicity attendant to criminal trials, are reluctant to come forward and testify. The State's argument based on this interest therefore proves too much, and runs contrary to the very foundation of the right of access recognized in *Richmond Newspapers:* namely, "that a presumption of openness inheres in the very nature of a criminal trial under our system of justice." 448 U.S., at 573 (plurality opinion).

V

For the foregoing reasons, we hold that §16A, as construed by the Massachusetts Supreme Judicial Court, violates the First Amendment to the Constitution. Accordingly, the judgment of the Massachusetts Supreme Judicial Court is Reversed.

Chief Justice Burger, with whom Justice Rehnquist joins, dissenting.

Historically our society has gone to great lengths to protect minors charged with crime, particularly by prohibiting the release of the names of offenders, barring the press and public from juvenile proceedings, and sealing the records of those proceedings. Yet today the Court holds unconstitutional a state statute designed to protect not the accused, but the minor victims of sex crimes. In doing so, it advances a disturbing paradox. Although states are permitted, for example, to mandate the closure of all proceedings in order to protect a 17-year-old charged with rape, they are not permitted to require the closing of part of criminal proceedings in order to protect an innocent child who has been raped or otherwise sexually abused.

The Court has tried to make its holding a narrow one by not disturbing the authority of state legislatures to enact more narrowly drawn statutes giving trial judges the discretion to exclude the public and the press from the courtroom during the minor victim's testimony. . . . I also do not read the Court's opinion as foreclosing a state statute which mandates closure except in cases where the victim agrees to testify in open court. But the Court's decision is nevertheless a gross invasion of state authority and a state's duty to protect its citizens—in this case minor victims of crime. I cannot agree with the Court's expansive interpretation of our decision in *Richmond Newspapers, Inc. v. Virginia*, 448 U.S. 555 (1980), or its cavalier rejection of the serious interests supporting Massachusetts' mandatory closure rule. Accordingly, I dissent. . . .

Justice Stevens, dissenting.

The duration of a criminal trial generally is shorter than the time it takes for this Court's jurisdiction to be invoked and our judgment on the merits to be announced. As a result, our power to review pretrial or midtrial orders implicating the freedom of the press has rested on the exception to the mootness doctrine for orders "capable of repetition, yet evading review." See *Richmond Newspapers, Inc. v. Virginia*, 448 U.S. 555. . . .

Today the Court expands that exception in order to pass on the constitutionality of a statute that, as presently construed, has never been applied in a live controversy. In this case, unlike the three cases cited above, the governing state law was materially changed after the trial court's order had expired by its own terms. There consequently is no possibility "that the same complaining party will be subject to the same action again." *Gannett Co. v. DePasquale*, supra, at 377 (quoting *Weinstein v. Bradford*, 423 U.S. 147, 149).

The fact that the Massachusetts Supreme Judicial Court narrowly construed—and then upheld in the abstract—the state statute that the trial court had read to mandate the closure of the entire trial bears on our review function in other respects. We have only recently recognized the First Amendment right of access to newsworthy matter. . . . In developing constitutional jurisprudence, there is a special importance in deciding cases on

concrete facts. . . . Only in specific controversies can the Court
decide how this right of access to criminal trials can be accommodated with other societal interests, such as the protection of
victims or defendants. The advisory opinion the Court an-
nounces today shed virtually no light on how such rights
should be accommodated.

The question of whether the Court should entertain a facial
attack on a statute that bears on the right of access cannot be
answered simply by noting that the right has its source in the
First Amendment. . . . For the right of access is plainly not coex-
tensive with the right of expression that was vindicated in *Nebraska Press Assn., supra.* Because statutes that bear on this right
of access do not deter protected activity in the way that other
laws sometimes interfere with the right of expression, we
should follow the norm of reviewing these statutes as applied
rather than on their face.

It is not clear when, if ever, the Court will need to confront
the question whether a mandatory partial-closure statute is unconstitutional. If the order hypothesized by the Supreme Judicial Court, instead of the trial court's order, had actually been
entered in this case, and if the press had been given prompt access to a transcript of the testimony of the minor victims, appellant might not even have appealed. At the very least the press,
the prosecutor, and defense counsel would have argued the
constitutionality of the partial-closure order in the context of the
facts relevant to such an order, and a different controversy
would have been framed for appellate review. . . .

The Court does not hold that on this record a closure order
limited to the testimony of the minor victims would have been
unconstitutional. Rather, the Court holds only that if ever such
an order is entered, it must be supported by adequate findings.
Normally, if the constitutional deficiency is the absence of findings to support a trial order, the Court would either remand for
factfinding, or examine the record itself, before deciding
whether the order measured up to constitutional standards. The
infeasibility of this course of action—since no such order was
entered in this case and since the order that was entered has expired—further demonstrates that the Court's comment on the
First Amendment issues implicated by the Massachusetts
statute is advisory, hypothetical, and, at best, premature.

I would dismiss the appeal.

Idaho v. Wright

497 U.S. 805

This case requires us to decide whether the admission at trial of certain hearsay statements made by a child declarant to an examining pediatrician violates a defendant's rights under the Confrontation Clause of the Sixth Amendment.

I

Respondent Laura Lee Wright was jointly charged with Robert L. Giles of two counts of lewd conduct with a minor under 16, in violation of Idaho Code §18-1508 (1987). The alleged victims were respondent's two daughters, one of whom was $5^{1}\!/_{2}$ and the other $2^{1}\!/_{2}$ years old at the time the crimes were charged.

Respondent and her ex-husband, Louis Wright, the father of the older daughter, had reached an informal agreement whereby each parent would have custody of the older daughter for six consecutive months. The allegations surfaced in November 1986 when the older daughter told Cynthia Goodman, Louis Wright's female companion, that Giles had had sexual intercourse with her while respondent held her down and covered her mouth, . . . and that she had seen respondent and Giles do the same thing to respondent's younger daughter. . . . The younger daughter was living with her parents—respondent and Giles—at the time of the alleged offenses.

Goodman reported the older daughter's disclosures to the police the next day and took the older daughter to the hospital. A medical examination of the older daughter revealed evidence of sexual abuse. One of the examining physicians was Dr. John Jambura, a pediatrician with extensive experience in child abuse cases. . . . Police and welfare officials took the younger daughter into custody that day for protection and investigation. Dr. Jambura examined her the following day and found conditions "strongly suggestive of sexual abuse with vaginal contact," occurring approximately two to three days prior to the examination. . . .

At the joint trial of respondent and Giles, the trial court conducted a voir dire examination of the younger daughter, who was three years old at the time of trial, to determine whether she was capable of testifying. . . . The court concluded, and the parties agreed, that the younger daughter was "not capable of communicating to the jury."

At issue in this case is the admission at trial of certain state-ments made by the younger daughter to Dr. Jambura in re-sponse to questions he asked regarding the alleged abuse. Over objection by respondent and Giles, the trial court permitted Dr. Jambura to testify before the jury as follows:

"Q. [By the prosecutor] Now, calling your attention then to your examination of [the younger daughter] on November 10th. What—would you describe any interview dialogue that you had with [her] at that time? Excuse me, before you get to that, would you lay a setting of where this took place and who else might have been present?

"A. This took place in my office, in my examining room, and, as I recall, I believe previous testimony I said that I recall a female attendant being present, I don't recall her identity. "I started out with basically, 'Hi, how are you,' you know, 'What did you have for breakfast this morning?' Essentially a few minutes of just sort of chitchat.

"Q. Was there any response from [the daughter] to that first—those first questions?

"A. There was. She started to carry on a very relaxed animated conversation. I then proceeded to just gently start asking ques-tions about, 'Well, how are things at home,' you know, those sorts. Gently moving into the domestic situation and then moved into four questions in particular, as I reflected in my records, 'Do you play with daddy? Does daddy play with you? Does daddy touch you with his pee-pee? Do you touch his pee-pee?' And again we then established what was meant by pee-pee, it was a generic term for genital area.

"Q. Before you get into that, what was, as best you recollect, what was her response to the question 'Do you play with daddy?'

"A. Yes, we play—I remember her making a comment about yes we play a lot and expanding on that and talking about spend-ing time with daddy.

"Q. And 'Does daddy play with you?' Was there any response?

"A. She responded to that as well, that they played together in a variety of circumstances and, you know, seemed very unaf-fected by the question.

"Q. And then what did you say and her response?

"A. When I asked her 'Does daddy touch you with his pee-pee,' she did admit to that. When I asked, 'Do you touch his pee-pee,' she did not have any response.

"Q. Excuse me. Did you notice any change in her affect or attitude in that line of questioning?

"A. Yes.

"Q. What did you observe?

"A. She would not—oh, she did not talk any further about that. She would not elucidate what exactly—what kind of touching was taking place, or how it was happening. She did, however, say that daddy does do this with me, but he does it a lot more with my sister than with me.

"Q. And how did she offer that last statement? Was that in response to a question or was that just a volunteered statement?

"A. That was a volunteered statement as I sat and waited for her to respond, again after she sort of clammed-up, and that was the next statement that she made after just allowing some silence to occur."

On cross-examination, Dr. Jambura acknowledged that a picture that he drew during his questioning of the younger daughter had been discarded. . . . Dr. Jambura also stated that although he had dictated notes to summarize the conversation, his notes were not detailed and did not record any changes in the child's affect or attitude. . . .

The trial court admitted these statements under Idaho's residual hearsay exception, which provides in relevant part:

"Rule 803. Hearsay exceptions; availability of declarant immaterial.—The following are not excluded by the hearsay rule, even though the declarant is available as a witness.

"(24) Other exceptions. A statement not specifically covered by any of the foregoing exceptions but having equivalent circumstantial guarantees of trustworthiness, if the court determines that (A) the statement is offered as evidence of a material fact; (B) the statement is more probative on the point for which it is offered than any other evidence which the proponent can procure through reasonable efforts; and (C) the general purposes of these rules and the interests of justice will best be served by admission of the statement into evidence." Idaho Rule Evid. 803(24).

Respondent and Giles were each convicted of two counts of lewd conduct with a minor under 16 and sentenced to 20 years' imprisonment. Each appealed only from the conviction involving the younger daughter. Giles contended that the trial court erred in admitting Dr. Jambura's testimony under Idaho's residual hearsay exception. The Idaho Supreme Court disagreed and affirmed his conviction. . . . Respondent asserted that the admission of Dr. Jambura's testimony under the residual hearsay exception nevertheless violated her rights under the Confrontation Clause. The Idaho Supreme Court agreed and reversed respondent's conviction. 116 Idaho 382, 775 P. 2d 1224 (1989).

The Supreme Court of Idaho held that the admission of the inculpatory hearsay testimony violated respondent's federal constitutional right to confrontation because the testimony did not fall within a traditional hearsay exception and was based on an interview that lacked procedural safeguards. . . . The court found Dr. Jambura's interview technique inadequate because "the questions and answers were not recorded on videotape for preservation and perusal by the defense at or before trial; and, blatantly leading questions were used in the interrogation." *Ibid.* The statements also lacked trustworthiness, according to the court, because "this interrogation was performed by someone with a preconceived idea of what the child should be disclosing." *Ibid.* Noting that expert testimony and child psychology texts indicated that children are susceptible to suggestion and are therefore likely to be misled by leading questions, the court found that "[t]he circumstances surrounding this interview demonstrate dangers of unreliability which, because the interview was not [audio or video] recorded, can never be fully assessed." . . . The court concluded that the younger daughter's statements lacked the particularized guarantees of trustworthiness necessary to satisfy the requirements of the Confrontation Clause and that therefore the trial court erred in admitting them. . . . Because the court was not convinced, beyond a reasonable doubt, that the jury would have reached the same result had the error not occurred, the court reversed respondent's conviction on the count involving the younger daughter and remanded for a new trial. . . .

We granted certiorari, 493 U.S. 1041 (1990), and now affirm.

II

The Confrontation Clause of the Sixth Amendment, made applicable to the States through the Fourteenth Amendment, provides: "In all criminal prosecutions, the accused shall enjoy the right . . . to be confronted with the witnesses against him."

From the earliest days of our Confrontation Clause jurisprudence, we have consistently held that the Clause does not necessarily prohibit the admission of hearsay statements against a criminal defendant, even though the admission of such statements might be thought to violate the literal terms of the Clause. . . . We reaffirmed only recently that "[w]hile a literal interpretation of the Confrontation Clause could bar the use of any out-of-court statements when the declarant is unavailable, this Court has rejected that view as 'unintended and too extreme.' " . . .

Although we have recognized that hearsay rules and the Confrontation Clause are generally designed to protect similar values, we have also been careful not to equate the Confrontation Clause's prohibitions with the general rule prohibiting the admission of hearsay statements. . . . The Confrontation Clause, in other words, bars the admission of some evidence that would otherwise be admissible under an exception to the hearsay rule. . . .

In *Ohio v. Roberts,* we set forth "a general approach" for determining when incriminating statements admissible under an exception to the hearsay rule also meet the requirements of the Confrontation Clause. 448 U.S., at 65. We noted that the Confrontation Clause "operates in two separate ways to restrict the range of admissible hearsay." *Ibid.* "First, in conformance with the Framers' preference for face-to-face accusation, the Sixth Amendment establishes a rule of necessity. In the usual case . . . , the prosecution must either produce, or demonstrate the unavailability of, the declarant whose statement it wishes to use against the defendant." *Ibid.* (citations omitted). Second, once a witness is shown to be unavailable, "his statement is admissible only if it bears adequate `indicia of reliability.' Reliability can be inferred without more in a case where the evidence falls within a firmly rooted hearsay exception. In other cases, the evidence must be excluded, at least absent a showing of particularized guarantee of trustworthiness." . . .

Applying the *Roberts* approach to this case, we first note that this case does not raise the question whether, before a child's out-of-court statements are admitted, the Confrontation Clause requires the prosecution to show that a child witness is unavailable at trial—and, if so, what that showing requires. The trial court in this case found that respondent's younger daughter was incapable of communicating with the jury, and defense counsel agreed. . . . The court below neither questioned this finding nor discussed the general requirement of unavailability. For purposes of deciding this case, we assume without deciding that, to the extent the unavailability requirement applies in this case, the younger daughter was an unavailable witness within the meaning of the Confrontation Clause.

The crux of the question presented is therefore whether the State, as the proponent of evidence presumptively barred by the hearsay rule and the Confrontation Clause, has carried its burden of proving that the younger daughter's incriminating statements to Dr. Jambura bore sufficient indicia of reliability to withstand scrutiny under the Clause. The court below held that, although the trial court had properly admitted the statements under the State's residual hearsay exception, the statements were "fraught with the dangers of unreliability which the Confrontation Clause is designed to highlight and obviate.". . . The State asserts that the court below erected too stringent a standard for admitting the statements and that the statements were, under the totality of the circumstances, sufficiently reliable for Confrontation Clause purposes. . . .

We note at the outset that Idaho's residual hearsay exception, Idaho Rule Evid. 803(24), under which the challenged statements were admitted, App. 113–115, is not a firmly rooted hearsay exception for Confrontation Clause purposes. . . .

Although we agree with the court below that the Confrontation Clause bars the admission of the younger daughter's hearsay statements, we reject the apparently dispositive weight placed by that court on the lack of procedural safeguards at the interview. Out-of-court statements made by children regarding sexual abuse arise in a wide variety of circumstances, and we do not believe the Constitution imposes a fixed set of procedural prerequisites to the admission of such statements at trial. The procedural requirements identified by the court below, to the extent regarded as conditions precedent to the admission of child hearsay statements in child sexual abuse cases, may in many instances be inappropriate or unnecessary to a determination whether a given statement is sufficiently trustworthy for Confrontation Clauses purposes. See, e.g., *Nelson v. Farrey*, 874 F. 2d 1222, 1229 (CA7 1989) (videotape requirement not feasible, especially where defendant had not yet been criminally charged), cert. denied, 493 U.S. 1042 (1990); J. Myers, Child Witness Law and Practice §4.6, pp. 129–134 (1987) (use of leading questions with children, when appropriate, does not necessarily render responses untrustworthy). Although the procedural guidelines propounded by the court below may well enhance the reliability of out-of-court statements of children regarding sexual abuse, we decline to read into the Confrontation Clause a preconceived and artificial litmus test for the procedural propriety of professional interviews in which children make hearsay statements against a defendant. . . .

The state and federal courts have identified a number of factors that we think properly relate to whether hearsay statements made by a child witness in child sexual abuse cases are reliable. . . . Although these cases . . . involve the application of various hearsay exceptions to statements of child declarants, we think the factors identified also apply to whether such statements bear "particularized guarantees of trustworthiness" under the Confrontation Clause. These factors are, of course, not exclusive, and courts have considerable leeway in their consideration of appropriate factors. We therefore decline to endorse a mechanical test for determining "particularized guarantees of trustworthiness" under the Clause. Rather, the unifying principle is that these factors relate to whether the child declarant was particularly likely to be telling the truth when the statement was made.

As our discussion above suggests, we are unpersuaded by the State's contention that evidence corroborating the truth of a hearsay statement may properly support a finding that the statement bears "particularized guarantees of trustworthiness." To be admissible under the Confrontation Clause, hearsay evidence used to convict a defendant must possess indicia of reliability by virtue of its inherent trustworthiness, not by reference to other evidence at trial. . . .

In short, the use of corroborating evidence to support a hearsay statement's "particularized guarantees of trustworthiness" would permit admission of a presumptively unreliable statement by bootstrapping on the trustworthiness of other evidence at trial, a result we think at odds with the requirement that hearsay evidence admitted under the Confrontation Clause be so trustworthy that cross-examination of the declarant would be of marginal utility. . . .

Finally, we reject respondent's contention that the younger daughter's out-of-court statements in this case are *per se* unreliable, or at least presumptively unreliable, on the ground that the trial court found the younger daughter incompetent to testify at trial. First, respondent's contention rests upon a questionable reading of the record in this case. The trial court found only that the younger daughter was "not capable of communicating to the jury." App. 39. Although Idaho law provides that a child witness may not testify if he "appear[s] incapable of receiving just impressions of the facts respecting which they are examined, or of relating them truly," Idaho Code §9-202 (Supp. 1989); Idaho Rule Evid. 601(a), the trial court in this case made no such findings. Indeed, the more reasonable inference is that, by ruling that the statements were admissible under Idaho's residual hearsay exception, the trial court implicitly found that the younger daughter, at the time she made the statements, was capable of receiving just impressions of the facts and of relating them truly. . . . In addition, we have in any event held that the Confrontation Clause does not erect a per se rule barring the admission of prior statements of a declarant who is unable to communicate to the jury at the time of trial. . . . Although such inability might be relevant to whether the earlier hearsay statement possessed particularized guarantees of trustworthiness, a *per se* rule of exclusion would not only frustrate the truthseeking purpose of the Confrontation Clause, but would also hinder States in their own "enlightened development in the law of evidence," *Evans*, 400 U.S., at 95 (Harlan, J., concurring in result).

III

The trial court in this case, in ruling that the Confrontation Clause did not prohibit admission of the younger daughter's hearsay statements, relied on the following factors:
"In this case, of course, there is physical evidence to corroborate that sexual abuse occurred. It also would seem to be the case that there is no motive to make up a story of this nature in a child of these years. We're not talking about a pubescent youth who may fantasize. The nature of the statements themselves as to sexual abuse are such that they fall outside the general believability that a child could make them up or would make them up. This is simply not the type of statement, I believe, that one would expect a child to fabricate.
"We come then to the identification itself. Are there any indicia of reliability as to identification? From the doctor's testimony it appears that the injuries testified to occurred at the time that the victim was in the custody of the Defendants. The [older daughter] has testified as to identification of [the] perpetrators. Those—the identification of the perpetrators in this case are persons well known to the [younger daughter]. This is not a case in which a child is called upon to identify a stranger or a person with whom they would have no knowledge of their

identity or ability to recollect and recall. Those factors are sufficient indicia of reliability to permit the admission of the statements." App. 115.

Of the factors the trial court found relevant, only two relate to circumstances surrounding the making of the statements: whether the child had a motive to "make up a story of this nature," and whether, given the child's age, the statements are of the type "that one would expect a child to fabricate." *Ibid.* The other factors on which the trial court relied, however, such as the presence of physical evidence of abuse, the opportunity of respondent to commit the offense, and the older daughter's corroborating identification, relate instead to whether other evidence existed to corroborate the truth of the statement. These factors, as we have discussed, are irrelevant to a showing of the "particularized guarantees of trustworthiness" necessary for admission of hearsay statements under the Confrontation Clause.

We think the Supreme Court of Idaho properly focused on the presumptive unreliability of the out-of-court statements and on the suggestive manner in which Dr. Jambura conducted the interview. Viewing the totality of the circumstances surrounding the younger daughter's responses to Dr. Jambura's questions, we find no special reason for supposing that the incriminating statements were particularly trustworthy. The younger daughter's last statement regarding the abuse of the older daughter, however, presents a closer question. According to Dr. Jambura, the younger daughter "volunteered" that statement "after she sort of clammed-up." *Id.,* at 123. Although the spontaneity of the statement and the change in demeanor suggest that the younger daughter was telling the truth when she made the statement, we note that it is possible that "[i]f there is evidence of prior interrogation, prompting, or manipulation by adults, spontaneity may be an inaccurate indicator of trustworthiness." *Robinson,* 153 Ariz., at 201, 735 P. 2d, at 811. Moreover, the statement was not made under circumstances of reliability comparable to those required, for example, for the admission of excited utterances or statements made for purposes of medical diagnosis or treatment. Given the presumption of inadmissibility accorded accusatory hearsay statements not admitted pursuant to a firmly rooted hearsay exception, *Lee,* 476 U.S., at 543, we agree with the court below that the State has failed to show that the younger daughter's incriminating statements to the pediatrician possessed sufficient "particularized guarantees of trustworthiness" under the Confrontation Clause to overcome that presumption.

The State does not challenge the Idaho Supreme Court's conclusion that the Confrontation Clause error in this case was not harmless beyond a reasonable doubt, and we see no reason to revisit the issue. We therefore agree with that court that respondent's conviction involving the younger daughter must be reversed and the case remanded for further proceedings. Accordingly, the judgment of the Supreme Court of Idaho is affirmed.

Justice Kennedy, with whom the Chief Justice, Justice White, and Justice Blackmun join, dissenting.

The issue is whether the Sixth Amendment right of confrontation is violated when statements from a child who is unavailable to testify at trial are admitted under a hearsay exception against a defendant who stands accused of abusing her. The Court today holds that it is not, provided that the child's statements bear "particularized guarantees of trustworthiness." *Ohio v. Roberts,* 448 U.S. 56, 66 (1980). I agree. My disagreement is with the rule the Court invents to control this inquiry and with the Court's ultimate determination that the statements in question here must be inadmissible as violative of the Confrontation Clause.

Given the principle, for cases involving hearsay statements that do not come within one of the traditional hearsay exceptions, that admissibility depends upon finding particular guarantees of trustworthiness in each case, it is difficult to state rules of general application. I believe the Court recognizes this. The majority errs, in my view, by adopting a rule that corroboration of the statement by other evidence is an impermissible part of the trustworthiness inquiry. The Court's apparent ruling is that corroborating evidence may not be considered in whole or in part for this purpose. This limitation, at least on a facial interpretation of the Court's analytic categories, is a new creation by the Court; it likely will prove unworkable and does not even square with the examples of reliability indicators the Court itself invokes; and it is contrary to our own precedents.

I see no constitutional justification for this decision to prescind corroborating evidence from consideration of the question whether a child's statements are reliable. It is a matter of common sense for most people that one of the best ways to determine whether what someone says is trustworthy is to see if it is corroborated by other evidence. In the context of child abuse, for example, if part of the child's hearsay statement is that the assailant tied her wrists or had a scar on his lower abdomen, and there is physical evidence or testimony to corroborate the child's statement, evidence which the child could not have fabricated, we are more likely to believe that what the child says is true. Conversely, one can imagine a situation in which a child makes a statement which is spontaneous or is otherwise made under circumstances indicating that it is reliable, but which also contains undisputed factual inaccuracies so great that the credibility of the child's statements is substantially undermined. Under the Court's analysis, the statement would satisfy the requirements of the Confrontation Clause despite substantial doubt about its reliability. Nothing in the law of evidence or the law of the Confrontation Clause countenances such a result; on the contrary, most federal courts have looked to the existence of corroborating evidence or the lack thereof to determine the reliability of hearsay statements not coming within one of the traditional hearsay exceptions. . . . Specifically with reference to hearsay statements by children, a review of the cases has led a leading commentator on child witness law to conclude flatly: "If the content of an out-of-court statement is supported or corroborated by other evidence, the reliability of the hearsay is strengthened." J. Myers, Child Witness Law and Practice §5.37, p. 364 (1987). The Court's apparent misgivings about the weight to be given corroborating evidence, see *ante*, at 824, may or may not be correct, but those misgivings do not justify wholesale elimination of this evidence from consideration, in derogation of an overwhelming judicial and legislative consensus to the contrary. States are of course free, as a matter of state law, to demand corroboration of an unavailable child declarant's statements as well as other indicia of reliability before allowing the statements to be admitted into evidence. Until today, however, no similar distinction could be found in our precedents interpreting the Confrontation Clause. If anything, the many state statutes requiring corroboration of a child declarant's statements emphasize the relevance, not the irrelevance, of corroborating evidence to the determination whether an unavailable child witness' statements bear particularized guarantees of trustworthiness, which is the ultimate inquiry under the Confrontation Clause. In sum, whatever doubt the Court has with the weight to be given the corroborating evidence found in this case is no justification for rejecting the considered wisdom of virtually the entire legal community that corroborating evidence is relevant to reliability and trustworthiness.

Far from rejecting this commonsense proposition, the very cases relied upon by the Court today embrace it. . . .

The Court today suggests that the presence of corroborating evidence goes more to the issue whether the admission of the hearsay statements was harmless error than whether the statements themselves were reliable and therefore admissible. . . . Once again, in the context of interlocking confessions, our previous cases have been unequivocal in rejecting this suggestion:

"Quite obviously, what the `interlocking' nature of the codefendant's confession pertains to is not its harmfulness but rather its reliability: If it confirms essentially the same facts as the defendant's own confession it is more likely to be true." *Cruz v. New York*, 481 U.S. 186, 192 (1987) (emphasis in original).

. . . In short, corroboration has been an essential element in our past hearsay cases, and there is no justification for a categorical refusal to consider it here.

Our Fourth Amendment cases are also premised upon the idea that corroboration is a legitimate indicator of reliability. We have long held that corroboration is an essential element in determining whether police may act on the basis of an informant's tip, for the simple reason that "because an informant is shown to be right about some things, he is probably right about other facts that he has alleged." *Alabama v. White*, 496 U.S. 325, 331 (1990). . . .

The Court does not offer any justification for barring the consideration of corroborating evidence, other than the suggestion that corroborating evidence does not bolster the "inherent trustworthiness" of the statements. . . . But for purposes of determining the reliability of the statements, I can discern no difference between the factors that the Court believes indicate "inherent trustworthiness" and those, like corroborating evidence, that apparently do not. Even the factors endorsed by the Court will involve consideration of the very evidence the Court purports to exclude from the reliability analysis. The Court notes that one test of reliability is whether the child "use[d] . . . terminology unexpected of a child of similar age." *Ante*, at 821. But making this determination requires consideration of the child's vocabulary skills and past opportunity, or lack thereof, to learn the terminology at issue. And, when all of the extrinsic circumstances of a case are considered, it may be shown that use of a particular word or vocabulary in fact supports the inference of prolonged contact with the defendant, who was known to use the vocabulary in question. As a further example, the Court notes that motive to fabricate is an index of reliability. *Ibid.* But if the suspect charges that a third person concocted a false case against him and coached the child, surely it is relevant to show that the third person had no contact with the child or no opportunity to suggest false testimony. Given the contradictions inherent in the Court's test when measured against its own examples, I expect its holding will soon prove to be as unworkable as it is illogical.

The short of the matter is that both the circumstances existing at the time the child makes the statements and the existence of corroborating evidence indicate, to a greater or lesser degree, whether the statements are reliable. If the Court means to suggest that the circumstances surrounding the making of a statement are the best indicators of reliability, I doubt this is so in every instance. And, if it were true in a particular case, that does not warrant ignoring other indicators of reliability such as corroborating evidence, absent some other reason for excluding it. If anything, I should think that corroborating evidence in the form of testimony or physical evidence, apart from the narrow circumstances in which the statement was made, would be a preferred means of determining a statement's reliability for purposes of the Confrontation Clause, for the simple reason that, unlike other indicators of trustworthiness, corroborating evidence can be addressed by the defendant and assessed by the trial court in an objective and critical way.

In this case, the younger daughter's statements are corroborated in at least four respects: (1) physical evidence that she was the victim of sexual abuse; (2) evidence that she had been in the custody of the suspect at the time the injuries occurred; (3) testimony of the older daughter that their father abused the younger daughter, thus corroborating the younger daughter's statement; and (4) the testimony of the older daughter that she herself was abused by their father, thus corroborating the younger daughter's statement that her sister had also been abused. These facts, coupled with the circumstances surrounding the making of the statements acknowledged by the Court as suggesting that the statements are reliable, give rise to a legitimate argument that admission of the statements did not violate the Confrontation Clause. Because the Idaho Supreme Court did not consider these factors, I would vacate its judgment reversing respondent's conviction and remand for it to consider in the first instance whether the child's statements bore "particularized guarantees of trustworthiness" under the analysis set forth in this separate opinion.

For these reasons, I respectfully dissent.

References

Butler, Sandra. 1985. *Conspiracy of Silence: The Trauma of Incest*. New York: Bantam.

Committee for Children. 1993. *Child Abuse and Neglect*. Seattle, WA: Committee for Children.

Courtois, Christine. 1988. *Healing the Incest Wound: Adult Survivors in Therapy*. New York: W. W. Norton.

Finkelhor, David, Gerald T. Hotaling, I. A. Lewis, and Christine Smith. 1990. "Sexual Abuse in a National Survey of Adult Men and Women: Prevalence, Characteristics, and Risk Factors." *Child Abuse and Neglect* 14: 19–28.

Finkelhor, David, Linda Williams, and Nanci Burns. 1989. *Nursery Crimes: Sexual Abuse in Day Care*. Newbury Park, CA: Sage.

Fromuth, Mary Ellen, and Barry R. Burkhart. 1987. "Childhood Sexual Victimization among College Men: Definitional and Methodological Issues." *Violence and Victims* 2, 4: 241–253.

Grayson, Joann, ed. 1989. "Sexually Victimized Boys." *Virginia Child Protection Newsletter* 29.

Johnson, Robert L., and Diane K. Shrier. 1985. "Sexual Victimization of Boys: Experience at an Adolescent Medical Clinic." *Journal of Adolescent Health Care* 6, 5: 372–376.

Kinsey, Alfred C., Wardell B. Pomeroy, Clyde E. Martin, and Paul H. Gebhard. 1953. *Sexual Behavior in the Human Female*. Philadelphia: W. B. Saunders.

Langan, Patrick A., and Caroline Wolf Harlow. 1994. "Child Rape Victims, 1992." Crime Data Brief. Washington, DC: U.S. Department of Justice, Bureau of Justice Statistics.

McCurdy, Karen, and Deborah Daro. 1994. *Current Trends in Child Abuse Reporting and Fatalities: The Results of the 1993 Annual Fifty State Survey*. Chicago: National Committee for the Prevention of Child Abuse.

NCCAN (National Center on Child Abuse and Neglect). 1981. *Study Findings: National Study of the Incidence and Severity of Child Abuse and Neglect*. Washington, DC: U.S. Department of Health and Human Services.

Rogers, C., and J. Thomas. 1984. "Sexual Victimization of Children in the U.S.A.: Patterns and Trends." *Clinical Proceedings* 40: 211–221.

Russell, Diana E. 1986. *The Secret Trauma: Incest in the Lives of Girls and Women.* New York: Basic Books.

Sedlak, A. J. 1987. *Study of National Incidence and Prevalence of Child Abuse and Neglect Final Report.* Prepared for the National Center on Child Abuse and Neglect. Washington, DC: Westat, Inc.

U.S. Department of Justice. 1989. "Stranger Abduction Homicides of Children." *Juvenile Justice Bulletin.*

———. 1990. *National Incidence Studies on Missing, Abducted, Runaway, and Thrownaway Children in America.* Washington, DC: U.S. Department of Justice.

Wyatt, Gail E. 1985. "The Sexual Abuse of Afro-American and White American Women in Childhood." *Child Abuse and Neglect* 9: 507–519.

Directory of Organizations

5

This chapter describes organizations, listed alphabetically, that work in a variety of ways with children who have been sexually abused or with the abusers themselves. They may be research oriented, prevention oriented, or service oriented. These organizations represent the types of services offered by programs throughout the country; this is by no means an inclusive list of all organizations dealing with childhood sexual abuse.

Adults Molested as Children United
P.O. Box 952
San Jose, CA 95108
(408) 453-7616

As one component of the Parents United program (see separate entry) of the Giarretto Institute, this self-help program was founded in 1981 to help adults who were sexually abused as children. The program goals include reevaluating and developing values, confronting the perpetrator, stopping self-destructive behavior, showing members how to make choices in their lives, becoming active by living in the present, learning self-awareness and self-help skills, forming new kinds of relationships, and helping members to feel good about themselves. The emphasis in the open group meetings is on self-help and support by allowing members to tell their stories and receive feedback. Professionals at each meeting help redirect negative feelings and behavior toward positive and constructive activities.

American Bar Association (ABA)
Center on Children and the Law
1800 M Street, NW
Washington, DC 20036
(202) 331-2250
Fax: (202) 331-2225

The Center was founded in 1978 by the ABA Young Lawyers Division to improve children's quality of life by improving laws, policies, and judicial procedures concerning children; conducting research and disseminating results; enhancing skills of legal professionals; educating and assisting nonattorneys in understanding child-related law; and increasing public awareness. Areas of expertise include child abuse and neglect, including child sexual abuse and exploitation, child welfare and child protective service system enhancement, foster care, termination of parental rights, parental substance abuse, child custody, and parental kidnapping. Working with child welfare agencies to develop curricula and training materials, the Center offers training programs in advanced trial skills for child welfare agency attorneys, interstate child support enforcement, improving attorney/caseworker teamwork, reducing delays in termination of parental rights cases, legal training for child welfare caseworkers, and a judicial legal training curriculum on drugs, alcohol and families. Statewide policy studies are conducted to help states update child welfare laws and procedures.

Publications: Child Welfare Law Reporter, a 16-page monthly legal information service that contains case law abstracts on a variety of topics, including child sexual abuse and exploitation; *The Prosecution of Child Sexual and Physical Abuse Cases: Final Research Report*, containing the results of a three-year study of prosecutor's offices; *Child Sexual Abuse Judicial Education Manual*, for judges and other professionals, providing training units on multidisciplinary issues, a bibliography, listings of experts in the fields of law, medicine, and social science and of major conferences and training programs related to multidisciplinary issues involving sexual abusers and victims, and reprints of materials; *Judicial Primer on Child Sexual Abuse Cases; and Child Maltreatment: A Summary and Analysis of Criminal Statutes.*

American Humane Association
Children's Division
63 Inverness Drive E.
Englewood, CO 80112-5117
(303) 792-9900; (800) 227-5242
Fax: (303) 792-5333

The American Humane Association was founded in 1877 and is the only national organization working to protect both children and animals from abuse, neglect, cruelty, and exploitation. Their Children's Division works to break the cycle of abuse through training, risk assessment, research, and policy development programs initiated to provide effective child protective systems. Through their child advocacy efforts, they work to influence better laws and public policy. They offer continuing education programs and set program standards and program evaluation methods that have improved the quality of care and services. They sponsor national conferences and regional workshops and offer a variety of publications.

They also operate the National Resource Center on Child Abuse and Neglect. This center provides current information about the causes and effects of child abuse and neglect, including child sexual abuse; they advocate for national standards, improved child welfare policies, and federal and state legislation important to the support of children and their families. The center provides resource materials for professionals, advocates, legislators, and the general public and various programs provide community awareness.

Publications: Protecting Children and Animals: Agenda for a Non-Violent Future and *A Child Sexual Abuse Curriculum for Social Workers.* Posters, informative brochures, and resource packets are also available.

**American Professional Society on the
Abuse of Children, Inc. (APSAC)**
407 South Dearborn
Suite 1300
Chicago, IL 60605
(312) 554-0166
Fax: (312) 554-0919

The American Professional Society on the Abuse of Children is an interdisciplinary society of professionals working with abused and neglected children and their families. Their mission is to improve society's response to abused and neglected children through the promotion of effective interdisciplinary approaches to identifying, intervening in, treating, and preventing abuse and neglect. Members include psychologists, social workers, attorneys, physicians, nurses, law enforcement personnel, child protection workers, administrators, researchers, and members of the allied professions. Several task forces usually are working on guidelines for professionals in the field; task forces currently are working on guidelines in the areas of medical evaluation of physical and sexual abuse, treatment of sexually abused children, and the use of anatomically detailed dolls. APSAC works to encourage research in all areas of child abuse and neglect, to further interdisciplinary professional education, to develop national guidelines for professionals in the field, to improve coordination among professionals, and to provide guidance, support, and encouragement to professionals.

Augusta Child Advocacy Center, Inc.
1834 Fenwick Street
Augusta, GA 30904
(706) 738-7863

Founded in 1986, the Augusta Child Advocacy Center is a nonprofit organization dedicated to combatting the physical and sexual abuse of children. It represents the efforts of concerned professionals who have worked together to redesign the system of child abuse investigation and response so that the focus is on the child and his or her family. The Center's Task Force on Child Abuse is composed of members from the Department of Family and Children's Services, Rape Crisis Services, the Richmond County Sheriff's Department, the Augusta Police Department, the district attorney's office, the Juvenile Court, Community Mental Health, University Hospital Pediatrics, and the Richmond County School Board. Their Child Advocate Program helps prepare families for court appearances and ensures that the child has a videotaped interview concerning the abuse, eliminating the trauma to the child of multiple interviews. Their Sexual Abuse Treatment Program offers individual and group counseling and a support program for the nonoffending family member. They offer educational programs and activities on prevention, detection, and treatment of child abuse through a resource library and speakers' bureau and mentoring of teenage mothers using volunteers in the My Sister/My Friend Program. Their Court Appointed Special Advocate (CASA) Program provides trained community volunteers, appointed by a judge, to speak on behalf of the child who has been removed from his or her home and involved in a court proceeding. They are currently working on a video to help prepare children for court appearances. They are a member of the National Network of Children's Advocacy Centers.

Chicago Child Abuse Resource Center
La Rabida Children's Hospital and Research Center
East 65th Street at Lake Michigan
Chicago, IL 60649
(312) 363-6700

The Chicago Child Abuse Resource Center was established at La Rabida Children's Hospital in 1977 to address the complex needs of abused and neglected children and the needs of those who care for them. The program provides a wide variety of services devoted to assuring the physical and psychosocial well-being of children who have experienced sexual abuse, physical abuse, neglect, and fetal abuse. Inpatient and outpatient treatment for sexually abused children is provided by a multidisciplinary team and includes expert interviewing by special team members through the Victim Sensitive Interview Project. Other services provided include counseling for the child and his or her family; a special medical and psychosocial clinic serving sexually abused children; information, education and training programs for professionals and community groups; consultation services for health care professionals, social service agencies, schools, and law enforcement agencies; and a special clinic, the Discovery Clinic, helping children in situations where sexual abuse is a possibility, but where no definitive statements concerning sexual abuse have been made. This clinic offers a medical examination of the child, a diagnostic assessment, a psychosocial assessment of the family, a feedback session for the family, and referral services if requested. The program is a member of the National Network of Children's Advocacy Centers.

Child Abuse Services Team (CAST)
Orangewood Children's Home
401 City Drive South, 2nd Floor
Orange, CA 92668
(714) 935-6390

The Child Abuse Services Team Task Force was organized in 1987 to develop a multidisciplinary team program for conducting child sexual abuse investigations. Their primary mission is to decrease the trauma children experience during the investigation phase. After police and/or social workers determine sexual abuse allegations, the child is brought to CAST to obtain support throughout the investigation process (e.g., interviews, medical exams) using an on-site child advocate who provides structured play and emotional support. An interview is conducted by a child interview specialist who includes both protective custody and criminal aspects in the interview. Professionals on the team then determine protective custody needs, criminal prosecution potential, court advocacy for the child, and crisis intervention therapy. The goal is for these services to help reduce the trauma that children are often exposed to when they are involved in an abuse investigation; the Center also enables social services, police, the district attorney, medical personnel, and therapists to collaborate on all investigations in which they participate. Opportunities for multidisciplinary training are offered to enhance each professional's knowledge in this field; specific training includes interview training and education in cross-cultural, medical, and legal issues.

Child Advocacy Center
560 Delaware Avenue
Buffalo, NY 14202
(716) 886-KIDS

The Child Advocacy Center uses a multidisciplinary approach in its program to provide sexually abused children and their families with a child-friendly environment to help them feel warm, safe, and supported. Services include child and family interviews, investigation of the sexual abuse allegation, medical services, mental health treatment, case management, victim advocacy, family support, prosecution if warranted and desired, training for professionals, and community education. The Center is dedicated to multidisciplinary cooperation among all agencies involved in the intervention and prevention of sexual abuse of children. Their goals are to prevent trauma to the child that is often caused by multiple contacts and interviews with community professionals; to provide the family with necessary services and assist them in regaining maximum function; to maintain open communication and case coordination with all involved agencies; to coordinate and track investigative, prosecutorial, and treatment efforts through careful case management; to obtain information for improved prosecution of cases; to provide training to enhance professional skills needed to respond effectively to child sexual abuse cases; and to increase community awareness and understanding of child sexual abuse.

Child and Family Advocacy Center (CFAC)
401 South Second Street
Elkhart, IN 46515
(219) 522-6089
Fax: (219) 522-0465

The Child and Family Advocacy Center was formed to provide leadership and coordination of services to children who have allegedly been abused, both physically and sexually. The Center's goal is to provide leadership and coordination services to agencies to create a multidisciplinary, standardized response to child abuse investigations, to improve treatment of children and their families, and to provide more effective primary and secondary prevention. Law enforcement or child protective service teams conduct integrated forensic interviews to gather evidence for criminal and civil proceedings. They have developed and implemented countywide standardized protocols regarding child abuse investigations, polygraph procedures, protective custody strategies, and the collection of physical evidence. A follow-up meeting with the family is conducted at intervals of one month, three months, and six months to ensure that the child and family are receiving all necessary services. CFAC is a member of the National Network of Children's Advocacy Centers.

Child Sexual Abuse Treatment Program
The Giarretto Institute
232 E. Gish Road, First Floor
San Jose, CA 95112
(408) 453-7616
Fax: (408) 453-9064

Founded in 1971, the Child Sexual Abuse Treatment Program (CSATP) has provided in-depth professional treatment and guided self- help services to over 20,000 sexually abused children and their families. It is the first program to provide integrated professional and self-help services. Its parent organization, the Giarretto Institute, is a nonprofit licensed psychology clinic specializing in the treatment of child sexual abuse. CSATP offers individual, family, and group therapy to children and their families as well as guided self-help support. The program's goals are to encourage positive changes within the family in order to ensure the safety and well-being of the child. Program personnel focus on stopping the abuse and preventing its reoccurrence, alleviating the child's feelings of guilt and anger, developing high self-esteem by encouraging the development of healthy family relationships, and teaching parents positive and effective parenting and communication skills. Intensive workshops and one-day basic and advanced seminars are offered to professionals who work in the field of child sexual abuse, including mental health professionals, child protective services workers, probation officers, attorneys, police, judges, medical professionals, and educators. Programs supported include Adults Molested as Children United, Parents United, and Daughters and Sons United (see separate listings).

Child Welfare League of America
440 First Street, NW
Suite 310
Washington, DC 20001
(202) 638-2952
Fax: (202) 638-4004

The Child Welfare League focuses on improving care and services for abused, neglected, or dependent children, youth, and their families. The League provides consultation services, conducts research, maintains a library and information services, develops standards for child welfare practice, and administers special projects.

Publications: Child Welfare: Journal of Policy, Practice, and Program presents articles for child welfare professionals; *What Only a Mother Can Tell You about Child Sexual Abuse* provides tips to parents whose children have been sexually abused, as told by a mother whose own child was sexually abused; and *Confronting Child Sexual Abuse*, a video training series for professionals involved in providing services to children who have been sexually abused.

Childhelp USA
6463 Independence Avenue
Woodland Hills, CA 91367
(818) 347-7280

Childhelp USA is one of the largest nonprofit organizations focusing on the prevention and treatment of child abuse and neglect, including child sexual abuse. They have offices in Los Angeles, Washington, D.C., and Knoxville, Tennessee, and they also operate the Village of Childhelp in Beaumont, California, and the Alice C. Tyler Village of Childhelp East in Culpeper, Virginia, as well as the Childhelp IOF Foresters National Child Abuse Hotline (800-4-A-CHILD), which includes 62,000 local service organizations. Children at both Childhelp Villages receive psychological therapy, speech therapy, recreational therapy, play therapy, and art therapy and participate in ranch activities, sports programs, and a chapel program. The villages offer parenting classes and family therapy for abusive parents. They also operate the Survivors of Childhood Abuse and Prevention Program, which helps adults stop the cycle of abuse and work out their feelings about their own abuse. Community resources are encouraged and provided, including a speakers' bureau, parenting resources, and public information programs.

Publications: Child Abuse and You. . . , a pamphlet describing many types of child abuse, including childhood sexual abuse.

Children's Advocacy and Treatment Center
322 NW F Street
Grants Pass, OR 97526
(503) 474-KIDS

The Children's Advocacy and Treatment Center offers a sanctuary and resource for children, promoting a homelike atmosphere to provide the sexually abused child with a feeling of safety and security. The center's goal is to prevent the child from being re-victimized by coordinating the child's community, legal, and treatment needs, thus assuring that the child's care and well-being is the first priority of all team members. Treatment facilities are provided that are equipped with special therapy rooms and office space that help make the child feel accepted, warm, and secure. All sexually abused children in the area are taken into the center; investigative interviews are conducted by a trained team of law enforcement and social work personnel. Videotapes of interviews are made to minimize the need for multiple interviews. A Court-Appointed Special Advocate (CASA) program is offered that provides a specially trained volunteer appointed by a judge to represent the best interests of abused children in court and to ensure continuity in all judicial proceedings. These volunteers are trained to help develop a plan to provide permanency for a child; they conduct a complete investigation of the case by interviewing all involved parties and then submit a report to the court that includes an independent recommendation as to what services are in the best interest of the child. They help ensure that the case is kept active and that the child understands the court system; they also monitor the treatment plan set up by the court.

Children's Advocacy Center
4000 Chestnut Street
Philadelphia, PA 19104
(215) 387-9500
Fax: (215) 387-9513

The Philadelphia area has many separate agencies that provide medical, legal, and social services to children who have been physically and sexually abused; the Children's Advocacy Center helps coordinate all of these services. It acts to prevent further trauma to the child and to ensure that each child receives all of the services he or she requires. A warm, homelike environment is provided to enhance the child's feelings of safety and security. The program encourages and receives coordination and cooperation from the city's legal, social, governmental, medical, and community groups. Services offered include joint law enforcement/child protection service interviews, medical referrals, mental health evaluations, legal referrals, specialized victim services, multidisciplinary training, support groups, community services, an information resource center, and crisis intervention. The Center is a member of the National Network of Children's Advocacy Centers.

Children's Advocacy Center of Arizona
1115 West McDowell
Phoenix, AZ 85007
(602) 257-8952
Fax: (602) 257-4409

The Children's Advocacy Center of Arizona is a nonprofit organization dedicated to providing services to children who are sexually and severely physically abused and to their nonoffending family members. The Center also provides services to children who have been traumatized by witnessing a violent crime. Designed to meet the needs of children for warmth, support, and protection, the Center offers forensic interviews, counseling services, and education programs. Services are coordinated with local law enforcement, social service, mental health, education, and other relevant agencies. Public education programs include a parent empowerment program that is designed to help empower nonoffending parents to take a more active role in providing assistance for their children after sexual abuse has been disclosed.

Children's Advocacy Center of Hamilton County
909 Vine Street
P.O. Box 6186
Chattanooga, TN 37401-6186
(615) 266-6918
Fax: (615) 265-0620

The Children's Advocacy Center of Hamilton County is a private, nonprofit organization that coordinates services provided to children and their families in the crisis period following a report of physical or sexual abuse. During the investigation, children are able to tell their stories to caring adults in a child-friendly environment. The professionals and volunteers working with the Center staff include representatives from law enforcement, the Department of Human Services, juvenile court, the district attorney's office, the medical profession, and mental health and counseling services. Children and their family members are encouraged to feel safe in a secure environment; law enforcement personnel receive critical and comprehensive information for prosecution, if necessary; all agencies participate in open communication and cooperation; and the community as a whole benefits from a variety of educational and prevention programs. The Center is a member of the National Network of Children's Advocacy Centers.

Children's Advocacy Center of Maui
1773-A Wili Pa Loop
Wailuku, HI 96793
(808) 244-1024

The Children's Advocacy Center of Maui offers a warm place for children who have been physically or sexually abused to be interviewed about reports of abuse, especially sexual abuse. Using trained interviewers and video recordings, the Center is able to avoid multiple interviews of children. Cooperating organizations include the Department of Human Services' Child Welfare

Services, the Maui Police Department, Sex Abuse Interventions, Inc., the Office of the Prosecuting Attorney, Victim Witness, Department of the Attorney General, and the Friends of the Children's Advocacy Center. The Friends of the Children's Advocacy Center is a nonprofit corporation organized to support the abused children of the county. It includes community and business people helping to develop supportive programs and in-kind assistance for children and families dealing with physical and sexual abuse. Some of the Center's programs include a family emergency fund to help parents get to the Center and other service agencies; temporary child care while the parent looks for work; food and other items that will help the family get back on its feet; a medical emergency fund for counseling and medical treatment; distribution of donated goods and services; training for social workers, police interviewers, and medical personnel; and a special occasion fund that provides money for children who have been removed from their homes to participate in normal school and after-school activities. They are a member of the National Network of Children's Advocacy Centers.

Children's Advocacy Center of Sullivan County
P.O. Box 867
Blountville, TN 37617
(615) 323-3914

The Children's Advocacy Center of Sullivan County is a cooperative effort among agencies throughout Sullivan County to respond effectively to child abuse, particularly child sexual abuse. Whenever possible, abused children are directed to the center, where specially trained professionals conduct interviews and assessments and provide crisis intervention for the children and their families. By providing a nonthreatening environment, the Center hopes to reduce the emotional trauma the children and their families often experience in these situations. Their immediate intervention offers support to the family, attempts to keep the family together, and if necessary, increases the chances of prosecution. The goal is for children who go through the Center to feel safer and less confused and to have greater physical and legal protection; The Center hopes families will find it easier to return to a normal life, law enforcement personnel will receive more comprehensive information, social services and treatment personnel will enjoy greater communication and cooperation, and children will be less likely to fall through the cracks. The Center is a member of the National Network of Children's Advocacy Centers.

Children's Advocacy Center of the Bluegrass, Inc.
183 Walton Avenue
Lexington, KY 40508-2315
(606) 225-KIDS

The Children's Advocacy Center of the Bluegrass provides services to sexually abused children and their families, works to improve the community's response to child sexual abuse, and helps encourage and facilitate the coordination of professional services to children and their families in one location during the intervention process. The program's goal is to lessen the trauma experienced by a sexually abused child as the case moves through the criminal justice system, primarily by bringing professionals to the child in a homelike setting. A multidisciplinary intervention system is offered that includes police, prosecutors, social workers, therapists, educators, and medical personnel in a single location. Interviews are conducted in age-appropriate rooms emphasizing the child's comfort; a minimal number of interviews are conducted, and proper evidence collection is emphasized. The multidisciplinary team serves as the child's and family's special companion through the legal process, coordinates community services, answers questions about the status of the case, and assists in obtaining victim compensation. The program is a member of the National Network of Children's Advocacy Centers.

Collin County Children's Advocacy Center
1316 E. 14th Street
Plano, TX 75074
(214) 516-0814

The Junior League of Plano formed a Children's Advocacy Center Task Force in 1990 to help develop a united effort in combating and treating childhood sexual abuse. The Collin County Children's Advocacy Center opened in 1992 as the result of this task force. It is a nonprofit organization and community partnership formed to minimize the trauma a sexually abused child faces when seeking treatment. Using a multidisciplinary approach, the Center is designed to provide each child with a friendly, nonthreatening, homelike environment that offers support and protection. Components of the program include a neutral facility with trained interview staff, case review, joint investigation/interviews, coordinated referral for medical examination and evaluation, referrals for counseling and therapy, case tracking, victim advocate and support services, training for professionals in related fields, and community education. The goal is for participating children and families to experience reduced trauma and receive prompt and ongoing treatment tailored to specific individual needs. The Center holds offenders accountable for their actions and hopes to empower nonoffending parents to protect their children. Additional understanding of and respect for all professionals is encouraged, more effective decisions may be reached through the sharing of professional expertise, and more specialized training is available for professionals.

Committee for Children
2203 Airport Way South
Suite 500
Seattle, WA 98134
(800) 634-4449; Seattle area: (206) 343-1223
Fax: (206) 343-1445

Founded in 1979, the Committee for Children is a nonprofit organization providing educational materials, original research, training, and community education for the prevention of child abuse and youth violence. They offer a client support line for people who are in the process of implementing their programs, a preview library, and research assistance and publish *Prevention Update*, a newsletter.

Publications: Talking About Touching™, a curriculum to help children from preschool through high school avoid becoming victims of sexual abuse, and *Yes You Can Say No*, a video that teaches assertiveness and reporting skills.

Corner House
Interagency Child Abuse Evaluation Center
2502 10th Avenue South
Minneapolis, MN 55404
(612) 872-6225
Fax: (612) 872-1230

Corner House is a partnership of public and private agencies providing a safe and welcoming environment to children who have been sexually abused. Agencies involved in providing services include Hennepin County Children and Family Service, Hennepin County Attorney, Minneapolis Police Department, Minneapolis Children's Medical Center, suburban police jurisdictions in Hennepin County, and the Hennepin County Medical

Center. Their purpose is to improve the assessment and investigation of child sexual abuse, by emphasizing the needs of sexually abused children, facilitating coordination of services, and sharing the knowledge, skills, and expertise of all professionals involved in child sexual abuse prevention and treatment. Videotaped interviews are conducted by professionals sensitive to the dynamics of child sexual abuse. A medical team conducts non-emergency physical examinations in a friendly homelike environment. A case team reviews cases and makes recommendations for treatment. The interagency team meets monthly to discuss issues of concern to the coordination of services. The partnership's training and resource center offers an interviewer training course for police officers, child protection workers, and assistant county attorneys. Additional training courses include advanced forensic interview training, preassessment training, videotaped interview assessment, and on-site interview training.

Publications: A workbook, *Interviewing Children Reliably and Credibly,* contains information on the art and science of an interview, dynamics of sexual abuse, the "child first" doctrine, the interview process, essential skills and tools, cultural competency, and making a determination.

CURE-SORT
P.O. Box 7782
Baltimore, MD 21221-0782

CURE-SORT (Citizens United for the Rehabilitation of Errants—Sex Offenders Restored through Treatment) was formally organized in 1975 and became a national organization in 1985. Members from throughout the United States wish to see a more meaningful and healing approach to the issue of sex offenses. CURE-SORT's mission is to use productive and positive energies throughout the community to reduce the incidence of sexual abuse and to help establish alternatives to incarceration; to use community resources to promote the rehabilitation of sex offenders; to encourage community involvement to help rehabilitate the victim, the family, and the offender; and to lobby against proposed bills in the U.S. Congress that are considered to be detrimental to the rehabilitation of sex offenders. The program encourages the development of effective community-based sex offender rehabilitation programs, the voluntary participation of offenders in rehabilitation programs, review of the records of currently incarcerated sex offenders to determine how many would be amenable to treatment, publication of information concerning the costs and benefits to the community of the use of rehabilitation, and the constructive coverage of the issues relating to sex offenders by the media.

Dallas Children's Advocacy Center
3611 Swiss Avenue
Dallas, TX 75204
(214) 818-2600
Fax: (214) 823-4819

The Dallas Children's Advocacy Center offers a coordinated, multidisciplinary intervention system to treat children who have been sexually or physically abused, involving police, prosecutors, child protective workers, therapists, and medical personnel working together as a team in a single location. The goal of the team is to minimize the trauma to a child, provide immediate and long-term treatment and other services, and ensure that all cases are properly identified. Interviews are conducted in an age-appropriate room, emphasizing the child's comfort, minimizing the number of interviews the child must endure, and ensuring the proper collection of evidence. The Center offers a variety of therapeutic services, including individual and family counseling, crisis intervention, court accompaniment, consultation with the child's school, and assistance in obtaining victim compensation. Services also are provided to nonoffending family members whose interests are also the best interests of the child. Medical examinations are coordinated through the Center. Multidisciplinary training is offered to professionals and community education is provided on ways to recognize abuse and the requirements and methods of reporting child abuse. A database is maintained to track information on each child, ensure timely services, and gather information for further research.

Daughters and Sons United
P.O. Box 952
San Jose, CA 95108
(408) 280-5055

Daughters and Sons United is the children's component of Parents United (see separate entry). This program closely coordinates their activities with the Child Sexual Abuse Treatment Program of the Giarretto Institute and is available at approximately 90 local

Parents United chapters across the nation. Local programs can help alleviate the trauma each sexually abused child experiences by providing intensive emotional support during the initial crisis, help for the child to understand his or her feelings, and assurance to the child that he or she is not alone (that other children have also been sexually abused). Chapters aim to promote personal growth and communication skills, to help alleviate any guilt the child feels, to prevent future self-abusive behavior, to prevent future dysfunctional patterns in relationships, and to break the multigenerational pattern of abuse. Members meet regularly under the guidance of professionals who lead discussions on topics that are relevant to members' physical and emotional well-being. They may also participate in community education programs.

False Memory Syndrome Foundation
3401 Market Street
Suite 130
Philadelphia, PA 19104
(215) 387-1865
(800) 568-8882
Fax: (215) 387-1917

The purpose of the False Memory Syndrome Foundation is to examine the reasons why and how this syndrome occurs, to prevent new cases, to help the victims, and to help reconcile and reunite all family members. In order to achieve these goals, the Foundation works with professionals to publicize the nature and prevalence of this syndrome, to provide access to counseling, to promote and sponsor scientific and medical research into the causes of this syndrome, and to help determine reliable methods to distinguish between true cases of sexual abuse and those created by false memories. Information on causes, current research, and legal rights also is provided.

Four Corners Child Advocacy Center
140 N. Linden
Cortez, CO 81321
(970) 565-8155

The Four Corners Child Advocacy Center is a private, nonprofit organization dedicated to the well-being of sexually and physically abused children. It is a grassroots community and professional response to over 300 cases of physical and sexual abuse reported locally each year. The Center's goal is to minimize the emotional trauma to children and their families during the investigation and prosecution of child abuse. They operate a home where the goal is to create a safe, nurturing, and child-friendly atmosphere. A trained volunteer victim advocate provides emotional support as well as information and guidance. Agencies, professionals, and therapists come to see the child at the Center for investigative interviews, medical exams, pretrial preparation, and therapy. Services can be coordinated to provide the best, most effective treatment possible. The Center also offers community education and prevention programs, an information clearinghouse, and training programs for professionals and lay persons in the area. Improvement of the regional response to abuse is achieved through coordination of federal, tribal, state, and local efforts. The Center is a member of the National Network of Children's Advocacy Centers.

Garth House
Mickey Mehaffy Children's Advocacy Program
1895 McFadden
Beaumont, TX 77701
(409) 838-9084
Fax: (409) 838-9106

The Garth House, a nonprofit program started in 1991, attempts to provide an environment that reflects the physical and emotional atmosphere of a home rather than the atmosphere of a clinic or an institution. Children who have been sexually or physically abused are referred to Garth House by law enforcement officials and child protective services personnel. Professionals provide their services to the children in one location, preventing the child from being shuttled around from police headquarters, to Child Protective Services offices, to physicians, and then to mental health professionals. Each interview is videotaped and made available to all agencies involved in the provision of services. The videotape can be used by law enforcement personnel and the district attorney's office in criminal or civil proceedings. Weekly meetings are held and all agencies involved participate in reviewing cases. Staff members also maintain a data file in order to provide comprehensive statistical information about sexual and physical abuse.

Incest Survivors Anonymous
World Service Office

P.O. Box 17245
Long Beach, CA 90807-7245
(310) 428-5599

Founded in 1980 by an incest survivor, Incest Survivors Anonymous is a 12-step program that aims to help incest survivors and their family members, spouses, and friends recover from their experiences. They have adapted the Twelve Steps and Twelve Traditions from Alcoholics Anonymous to help people who have experienced incest. While the format of their group meetings may vary, they often choose a topic relating to incest and talk freely about their feelings, experiences, and memories; in their meetings, members seek understanding, acceptance, forgiveness, and serenity. Goals of the program are to recognize the negative behavior patterns and programming that many people who have been sexually abused have developed in childhood, often in response to fear, and to develop a new way of life, with peace of mind and understanding.

Incest Survivors Resource Network
International (ISRNI)
P.O. Box 7375
Las Cruces, NM 88006-7375
(505) 521-4260
Fax: (505) 521-3723

In 1983 at the New York City Friends Meeting House, the Incest Survivors Resource Network International was founded as an educational resource for both national and international community and professional organizations. It is operated as a religious group focusing on world peace witness by survivors of incest interested in the relationship between unresolved traumatic stress and violence in the world. ISRNI encourages communication and cooperation between professionals and self-help organizations. It operates the first national helpline answered by survivors of incest. It cosponsors several conferences, including the National Forum on Victim Rights, with the National Organization for Victim Assistance.

(C. Henry) Kempe National Center
for the Prevention and Treatment
of Child Abuse and Neglect
University of Colorado Health Sciences Center
Department of Pediatrics

1205 Oneida Street
Denver, CO 80220-2944
(303) 321-3963
Fax: (303) 329-3523

The Center was opened in 1972 to provide a clinically based resource for training, consultation, program development and education, and research in all forms of child abuse and neglect. The Center is committed to multidisciplinary approaches to improving the recognition, treatment, and prevention of all forms of abuse and neglect. Several programs have been instituted to help children and their families, including Therapeutic Preschool, the Family Evaluation Team, the Child Advocacy and Protection Team, the Community Caring Project, the Perpetration Prevention Project, the National Child Abuse and Neglect Clinical Resource Center, and the Prevention Research Center for Family and Child Health.

Publications: Child Abuse and Neglect: The International Journal, which encompasses all areas of child abuse and neglect. The Center's publications catalog also offers a variety of books and other resources on child sexual abuse.

Kids First, Inc.
110 South Pool Street
P.O. Box 23
Elizabeth City, NC 27906
(919) 338-5658; (919) 331-1653

Kids First, established in 1992, offers advocacy and support services to child victims of sexual and physical abuse, including child and family counseling, forensic medical examinations, a Kids in Court school to help prepare child witnesses for their upcoming court appearances, community education programs, and training programs for professionals who work with sexually and physically abused children and their families. The program offers a multidisciplinary team approach; team members include representatives from departments of social services, law enforcement, sheriff's departments, the district attorney's office, and the medical community; adult probation personnel, court counselors, public school system personnel, and guardian ad litem program members; and representatives from local and state governments, juvenile services divisions, child abuse hotlines, and mental health services. Once a case is reported to the center, the director assigns a primary team that is responsible for coordinating a comprehensive plan to help the child and his or her family. The program is a member of the National Network of Children's Advocacy Centers.

King County Sexual Assault Resource Center
P.O. Box 300
Renton, WA 98057
(206) 226-5062

Originally founded as King County Rape Relief, this resource center is a nonprofit organization providing services to women, children, and men who have been sexually victimized. The staff's goal is to help all clients make the transition from victim to survivor. Individual counseling is provided for children who have been sexually abused, and the families of these children receive family therapy and support. The Center's philosophy is that education is the key to preventing and eventually eliminating sexual assault, and they offer a wide variety of educational and training programs to educators, service providers, professionals, and the community. Their advocacy staff offer crisis intervention and confidential support and information 24 hours a day, medical information, legal information, advocacy, court accompaniment, and forensic medical examinations for children that are coordinated through the County Health Department. Training workshops are provided on topics such as ending sexual violence, striving for empowerment (an education support group model for teenage girls), chemical dependency and sexual assault (based on the premise that many children who are sexually abused grow up to have problems with alcohol and drugs), and related risks: child abuse, family violence, and chemical dependency.

Publications: He Told Me Not To Tell, a booklet on how to talk with children about sexual abuse, *A Frog Talks More about Touching*, a script for a series of skits for children in kindergarten through grade six about good touches and bad touches, and a booklet, *Helping Your Child To Be Safe.*

Lake County Children's Advocacy Center
323 N. West Street
Waukegan, IL 60085
(708) 360-6870

The Lake County Children's Advocacy Center was founded as a result of a 1985 task force on child sexual abuse. The Center is a cooperative effort between the Illinois Department of Children and Family Services, the Lake County Sheriff's Police, the Waukegan Police Department, the State's Attorney's Office, and local law enforcement agencies and employs a multidisciplinary treatment concept to help victims of child sexual abuse. The Center's multidisciplinary and single interview approach is designed to reduce the trauma children often face when being subjected to multiple, independent interviews. The goal is to implement a strong social and legal support structure to minimize trauma and stress to the child, using a highly trained staff to conduct sensitive and thorough investigations. Crisis intervention and court advocacy for children and their families are provided by a social worker. A speaker's bureau is available to interested organizations and groups.

LaPorte County Child Abuse Prevention Council
7451 W. Johnson Rd.
Michigan City, IN 46360
(219) 874-0007

The LaPorte County Child Abuse Prevention Council was founded in 1989 as a nonprofit organization dedicated to increasing community awareness of child abuse and neglect and coordinating services for these children and their families. They provide community education through a speaker's bureau as well as information and referral services. Family programs include a parent education program, a school body-safety program, and parent support groups. The Council plans to meet family needs through survivors' groups, people against child abuse groups, and an annual survivors' days workshop. Professionals in the field of child abuse receive training, consultation services through a child abuse advisory team, and legislative advocacy. The Council also operates Dunebrook, a multidisciplinary child abuse prevention care center designed to offer a warm, safe place in which children can be interviewed and other services can be coordinated.

Midwest Children's Resource Center
Fort Road Medical Building, Suite 200
360 Sherman Street
St. Paul, MN 55102
(612) 220-6750
Fax: (612) 220-6770

The Midwest Children's Resource Center is a regional resource center for children, professionals, and programs in diagnosing, treating, and preventing child abuse. The Center provides diagnosis, treatment, and consultation services for sexually, physically, and emotionally abused children. It is the only site in Minnesota for comprehensive multidisciplinary training in the area of child abuse; over 1,000 law enforcement personnel, child protection workers, county attorneys, medical professionals, and mental health professionals are trained each year. The Suspected Child Abuse and Neglect (SCAN) Program was initiated in 1992 to provide 24-hour coordination of services for abused children; this program integrates hospital and community agency services, with the goals of encouraging cooperation among all agencies and easing the trauma to children and their families.

**National Center for Missing
and Exploited Children**
2101 Wilson Boulevard, Suite 550
Arlington, VA 22201-3052
(703) 235-3900
Hotline: (800) THE-LOST [(800) 843-5678]
Fax: (703) 235-4067

The National Center was mandated by the U.S. Congress in 1984 and in 1990 merged with the Adam Walsh Child Resource Center. Since 1984, it has handled almost 700,000 calls through its toll-free hotline for reporting information on missing or exploited children. The Center offers a staff of case managers who are former law enforcement and social service professionals. Services provided include instructions on how to conduct an investigation into the whereabouts of the missing or exploited child, national distribution of the child's photo, and legal and technical assistance. The case enhancement and information analysis unit helps local law enforcement agencies by providing useful, up-to-date information about the child. Project ALERT (America's Law Enforcement Retiree Team) offers free, on-site support to state and local police in missing or exploited child cases. The Center also receives tips on people who participate in child pornography. It offers educational programs to children, teachers, parents, health care professionals, and law enforcement personnel. The legal staff offers information to attorneys, families and legislators.

Publications: Child Molesters: A Behavioral Analysis, Child Sex Rings: A Behavioral Analysis, Children Traumatized in Sex Rings, and *Family Abduction.* Brochures include topics such as child protection, tips to help prevent sexual exploitation of children, rules for safety, and the Just in Case . . . Series that offers advice on finding professional help for children who have been sexually assaulted, advice on choosing day care and preventing the exploitation or sexual abuse of children, what to do if your child is sexually abused or exploited, and other related topics.

National Center on Child Abuse
and Neglect (NCCAN)
National Clearinghouse on
Child Abuse and Neglect Information
U.S. Department of Health and Human Services
P.O. Box 1182
Washington, DC 20013
(703) 385-7565; (800) 394-3366
Fax: (703) 385-3206

The National Center on Child Abuse and Neglect was established in 1974 by the Child Abuse Prevention and Treatment Act (Public Law 93-247) as the primary federal agency charged with helping states and communities address the problems of child maltreatment. NCCAN oversees all federal child abuse and neglect efforts and allocates child maltreatment funds appropriated by Congress. They are responsible for conducting research on the causes, prevention, and treatment of child abuse and neglect; collecting, analyzing, and disseminating information to professionals concerned with child abuse and neglect; increasing public awareness of the problems of child maltreatment; and assisting states and communities in developing programs related to the prevention, identification, and treatment of child abuse and neglect.

NCCAN operates a clearinghouse that collects, stores, organizes, and disseminates information on all aspects of child maltreatment. They provide services and products in a variety of areas to organizations, researchers, and the general public. Manuals, reports, directories, catalogs, literature reviews, annotated bibliographies, and fact sheets are available through the clearinghouse. For a fee, the clearinghouse information specialists provide custom searches of the child abuse and neglect database.

Publications: Child Sexual Abuse: Intervention and Treatment Issues, a manual designed for all professionals working in the field of child sexual abuse; *Child Sexual Abuse*, a review of the current literature on child sexual abuse; and annotated bibliographies on interviewing techniques used with sexual abuse victims, male victims of sexual abuse, prevention, treatment for victims, and treatment for perpetrators.

National Child Abuse Defense
and Resource Center (NCADRC)
P.O. Box 638
Holland, OH 43528
(419) 865-0513
Fax: (419) 865-0526

A nonprofit organization, the National Child Abuse Defense and Resource Center was founded to offer help to people who have been falsely accused of some form of child abuse, including sexual abuse. The program's goals are to provide information to professionals, organizations, and government units; to ensure that due process, constitutional rights, human rights, and family concerns are considered when people are reported for abuse; to reduce public hysteria over child sexual abuse; to ensure that those implementing child abuse law and policy are properly trained and qualified; to help formulate laws and policies that define child abuse and specify investigative procedures; and to provide information and emotional support to all people falsely accused of sexual abuse. They operate an extensive library of research materials, legal case law, and articles. All of the staff are volunteers; they provide general information and may offer limited advice on steps people can take when they are falsely accused. They can recommend attorneys and other experts in the field.

Publications: Guilty Until Proven Innocent: A Manual for Surviving False Allegations of Child Abuse, by Kimberly Hart, the current executive director of NCADRC, and *Making Monsters,* by Richard Ofshe and Ethan Waters, which discusses false memories, psychotherapy, and sexual hysteria. These are samples of available publications.

National Committee to Prevent Child Abuse
332 South Michigan Avenue
Suite 1600
Chicago, IL 60604
(312) 663-3520

This organization is a volunteer-based organization dedicated to involving all concerned citizens in actions to prevent child abuse in all its forms, including physical abuse, emotional maltreatment, neglect, and sexual abuse. Activities include prevention programs, public awareness, education and training, research, and advocacy.

Publications: A Look at Child Sexual Abuse by Jon Conte, which reviews current information; *Sexual Victimization of Children*, which explains the various forms of sexual exploitation of children, characteristics of molesters, and behavioral characteristics of children who have been molested; *Basic Facts About Child Sexual Abuse*; *Talking About Sexual Abuse*, a guide for parents; *What Every Kid Should Know About Sexual Abuse*; and *You Don't Have to Molest That Child*, which speaks directly to molesters and potential molesters.

**National Council of Juvenile
and Family Court Judges**
P.O. Box 8970
Reno, NV 89507
(702) 784-6012
Fax: (702) 784-6628

The National Council of Juvenile and Family Court Judges provides direction on juvenile and family law to the nation's juvenile and family jurists. It offers continuing education to judges, referees, probation officers, social workers, law enforcement personnel, and other juvenile justice professionals. It stays abreast of the changing areas of the law in such areas as child abuse and neglect, crack babies, foster care, custody issues, school violence, gangs, and serious juvenile crime. It offers programs addressing current topics in these areas.

Publications: Child Sexual Abuse: Improving the System's Response, which discusses the nature of the problem, detection, intervention, adjudication, and disposition; *Intrafamilial Child Sexual Abuse Intervention: The Impact of Juvenile Court Hearings and Felony Trial Diversions* and *Public Sentiment toward Innovative Child Sexual Abuse Intervention Strategies: Consensus and Conflict,* two monographs on child sexual abuse; and audio tapes on treatment techniques in child sexual abuse, sibling incest, and the team approach to treating sexual abuse.

**National Institute for the Study,
Prevention and Treatment of Sexual Trauma**
104 E. Biddle Street
Baltimore, MD 21202
(410) 539-1661

The Institute was first established in 1980 as a sexual disorders clinic at the Johns Hopkins Hospital in order to provide high quality clinical care. In 1991, the Institute became a private clinic providing care to clients with a variety of sexual disorders, including exhibitionism, voyeurism, and pedophilia, and to victims of sexual trauma, including children who have been sexually traumatized. This program also focuses on learning more about the prevention of these disorders by encouraging scholarly research and teaching. Services provided include comprehensive psychiatric and forensic evaluations and consultations; individual, group, and family therapy; pharmacotherapy; and educational seminars for professionals and the lay public. Referrals are accepted by phone or by mail from patients, medical professionals, social service professionals, or legal professionals.

National Network of Children's Advocacy Centers
106 Lincoln Street
Huntsville, AL 35801
(205) 533-5437

The National Network of Children's Advocacy Centers is a nonprofit organization comprising members and affiliates whose mission is to provide technical assistance, training, and networking opportunities to help communities establish and maintain Children's Advocacy Centers. The Centers' goals are to provide quality services for helping victims of child abuse, particularly child sexual abuse. The Network was formed in 1988 as a response to the proliferation of facility-based child abuse programs and because of the demand from grassroots organizations for help and guidance. Children's Advocacy Centers coordinate the activity of all involved public and private agencies with the goal of facilitating meaningful intervention by the agencies and minimizing revictimization through repetitious interviews and examinations. The Network has established minimum standards set by the Network board that are viewed as crucial to successful intervention in child abuse cases. These minimum standards must be achieved by all programs accepted for full membership. Member agencies must be private, nonprofit or government based; have a safe separate space with assigned personnel designated for investigation and coordination of abuse cases; have an interdisciplinary coordinated systems approach to the investigation of reports; have an interdisciplinary case review process; have a comprehensive tracking system with information from each participating agency; and have interdisciplinary specialized training for all professionals involved in child sexual abuse cases. As of this writing, there are 70 member sites.

National Resource Center on Child Sexual Abuse
107 Lincoln Street
Huntsville, AL 35801
(205) 534-6868; (800) 543-7006

The National Resource Center on Child Sexual Abuse is funded by the National Center on Child Abuse and Neglect, U.S. Department of Health and Human Services, and is operated by the National Children's Advocacy Center. The Center provides technical support to all professionals who work with sexually abused children and their families, including social workers, law enforcement investigators, medical personnel, therapists, researchers, administrators, prosecutors, teachers, judges, and volunteers. Each request for information is handled by a specially trained staff member, with extensive files, databases of experts and programs, and a reference library available to assist them. The Center also maintains contacts with organizations and professionals in all disciplines that deal with sexually abused children throughout the country. Local and state information is available through their State Contact Centers. They work closely with the National Resource Center on Child Abuse and Neglect and the Clearinghouse on Child Abuse and Neglect Information. The Center convenes think tank sessions, gatherings of experts who examine various aspects of a single topic, and Research Consensus Groups, working groups of leading researchers who identify consistent findings among research studies on a single topic, meet regularly. In addition to their toll-free information service, they offer training and technical assistance services, and a variety of publications are available either free of charge or for a small fee. The Center's goals are to provide information, training, and technical assistance to all professionals who work with sexually abused children and their families, to help connect research and practice, to promote interagency as well as multidisciplinary cooperation and coordination, to identify and disseminate valuable resources, to support all professionals in the field of child sexual abuse, and to be a center of leadership and excellence.

Northern Kentucky Children's Advocacy Center
103 Landmark Drive, Suite 200
Bellevue, KY 41073
(606) 572-3456

The Northern Kentucky Children's Advocacy Center of the St. Luke's Hospitals is dedicated to providing a child-friendly environment for the prevention, evaluation, and treatment of child sexual abuse. Services offered include interviewing services, multidisciplinary case reviews, counseling and support groups for children and their families, a comprehensive tracking system, community education, training programs for professionals, and medical examinations. The Center coordinates the community's response to child sexual abuse under one roof with the goal of preventing the revictimization of children by eliminating the need for multiple interviews and visits to several agencies.

Parents Anonymous (PA)
The National Organization
675 West Foothill Boulevard, Suite 220
Claremont, CA 91711
(909) 621-6184
Fax: (909) 625-6304

Parents Anonymous was founded in 1970 as a national parent self-help program to prevent child abuse and neglect, with specialized groups for children. The national organization provides leadership and support to state and local organizations, which offer over 2,100 groups for parents and children; these groups are offered free of charge to families. Their programs include parent support groups, parent education workshops, home visitation services, stressline (stress hotline) services, advocacy, and public awareness activities. All of these programs are based on seven guiding principles: mutual assistance, empowerment, support, ownership, caring, nonviolence, and anonymity and confidentiality. PA designs and helps implement new programs, develops curricula and materials, conducts workshops and conferences, provides professional consultation services, encourages public awareness activities, conducts and encourages research, and provides information and referral services to parents, professionals, and the general public.

Parents United
P.O. Box 952
San Jose, CA 95108
(408) 453-7616

Parents United is a self-help organization dedicated to assisting parents, children, and others concerned with child sexual abuse.

It began under the direction of Hank Giarretto and is one of the best-known national organizations representing the interests of sexually abused children and their families. It has two associated programs: Daughters and Sons United and Adults Molested as Children United (see separate entries). Members may include offenders, spouses of offenders, children who have been sexually abused, adults molested as children and others, including siblings, step-parents, parents, and spouses. The organization works closely with law enforcement, social services, the judicial system, and other professional agencies. The goal is to help individuals who have been sexually abused explore the factors that might have contributed to the abuse and work through the damage the abuse caused. Community education is also an important part of the program.

Pueblo Child Advocacy Center
301 West 13th Street
Pueblo, CO 81003
(719) 583-6332

The Pueblo Child Advocacy Center is a nonprofit organization established in 1986 to break the cycle of sexual and physical child abuse through intervention and prevention services. The Center works closely with other local agencies to coordinate services provided to children and their families; these agencies include police and sheriff's departments, social services personnel, the district attorney's office, mental health professionals, health department personnel, and medical personnel. At the center, children are interviewed, medically examined, provided with therapy and sometimes prepared for court proceedings. The program is one of the original six child advocacy centers developed in the country and is a nationally recognized model program. The Center offers a setting designed to be warm and nurturing in which investigations, medical examinations, crisis intervention, victim assistance, and treatment services are provided. Interagency problem solving, open communication, and professional skills development are encouraged and facilitated by the program, which also encourages community commitment to preventing the physical and sexual abuse of children. The Center is a member of the National Network of Children's Advocacy Centers.

The Safer Society
P.O. Box 340
Brandon, VT 05733-0340

(802) 247-3132 (general inquiries and orders)
(802) 247-5141 (information and referrals)

A nonprofit organization, the Safer Society offers research, advocacy, and referral services for the prevention and treatment of sexual abuse throughout the country. They maintain a computerized database of agencies, institutions, and individuals who provide specialized assessment and treatment services for juvenile and adult sex offenders; a computer file containing those programs that treat abused children is also maintained. Referrals are made for individuals, programs, professionals, and family members to specialized treatment programs throughout the country. The Society conducts specialized training institutes, which are intensive three-day educational workshops, on issues of current importance in the field of sexual abuse prevention and treatment. Consultation services are provided to states and counties to help plan and set up comprehensive treatment programs.

Publications: Shining Through: Pulling It Together After Sexual Abuse by Mindy Loiselle and Leslie Bailey Wright, a workbook for young women who have been sexually abused; *Female Adolescent Sexual Abusers* by Marcia T. Turner and Tracey N. Turner, an exploratory study of mothers who molest their daughters; guided workbooks for adult sex offenders; *Women and Men Who Sexually Abuse Children* by Craig Allen, a comparative study of female and male abusers; and *Adults Molested as Children* by Euan Bear, a manual for adults beginning to remember and face being abused as children.

St. Clair Children's Advocacy Center
The Children's Place
P.O. Box 632
18200 Alabama Highway 174
Pell City, AL 35125
(205) 338-8847

The St. Clair Children's Advocacy Center offers programs to children who have been physically or sexually abused and to their families. It offers a forum for agency representatives and professionals who work with abused children to coordinate their work to assist the children and their families. Before the Advocacy Center was organized, child abuse victims would undergo multiple interviews to satisfy the needs of the Department of Human Resources, law enforcement officials, the district attorney, and providers of mental health counseling services. Their program, the Children's Place, replaces this system with a united approach, offering a nonthreatening environment where children who are believed to be sexually or severely physically abused and their nonoffending family members can go for interviews, evaluation, intervention, evidence gathering, and counseling. The Center strives to provide the child with a warm, nonthreatening environment and someone to talk to about his or her problem. The program also provides training and education for professionals. They are a member of the National Network of Children's Advocacy Centers.

St. Luke's Regional Medical Center
Children At Risk Evaluation Services (CARES) Program
Idaho Professional Building
125 E. Idaho Street
Boise, ID 83712
(208) 386-3063

The Children At Risk Evaluation Services Program was founded in 1989 in response to the need for a neutral, centralized service for the assessment and evaluation of children who are alleged victims of sexual abuse. It provides a comprehensive evaluation of the alleged abuse by using videotaped interviews conducted by specially trained registered nurses and audiotaped physical examinations, conducted by a physician or a pediatric nurse practitioner. The program seeks to minimize the trauma to which children who are alleged to be victims of sexual abuse are exposed. The program provides a sensitive, professional, and caring environment; expert and comprehensive evaluation; a cooperative effort with community agencies; a safe, controlled, and confidential setting for patients and their families; and a quick response to referrals made to help protect and meet the needs of children.

Salt Lake County Children's Justice Center
257 11th Avenue
Salt Lake City, UT 84103
(801) 355-0781
Fax: (801) 355-3578

The Children's Justice Center offers a homelike facility to provide services to children who have been sexually or physically abused. It offers a child-friendly environment, designed to make children feel safe and comfortable. A multidisciplinary team coordinates the interview process, assesses the need for support services, and reviews police investigation results, child protection issues, medical concerns, treatment issues, and prosecution concerns. The program offers a comprehensive child and family interview process, audiotaped and videotaped interviews, counseling and treatment referrals, victim-witness support services, community education, professional training, support and information services for parents, case staffings, and assistance and coordination on difficult cases. They also screen cases for prosecution and monitor case progress.

Sexual Abuse Investigative Team (SAINT)
3444 East Bonanza Road
Las Vegas, NV 89101
(702) 455-5371
Fax: (702) 455-5592

The SAINT program uses a multidisciplinary approach in dealing with sexual abuse of children to reduce the trauma to child victims. Members of the multidisciplinary team include law enforcement personnel, the district attorney, child protective services personnel, medical personnel, and mental health counselors. The program provides a nonthreatening, child-friendly location for interviews and medical examinations, reduces the number of interviewers who question the child, conducts forensically complete medical examinations, and provides crisis intervention, assessment, and referral for long-term therapy. They have a comfortable, nonthreatening interview room with a one-way mirror that allows for observation of the interviews by appropriate professionals; audio and videotaping equipment is also available. Forensic medical examinations are conducted in a brightly decorated room by specially trained medical practitioners, in an effort to reduce the trauma sexually abused children experience when examined in a cold, institutional setting. Therapeutic assistance is provided to the children and their families.

Southwest Center for Abuse
Recovery and Education
6200 N. Central Expressway, Suite 209
Dallas, TX 75206
(214) 373-6607

Founded in 1982 as the Incest Recovery Association, the Southwest Center for Abuse Recovery and Education (Southwest

CARE) is a nonprofit organization with a focus on helping those affected by incest and child sexual abuse. Their three service areas include incest recovery services, child sexual abuse education services, and child sexual abuse professional training services. The adolescent clinical treatment program offers intake assessment, group therapy, and individual therapy. Through their education services group, they provide public education, including an information and referral service, a national conference for survivors of incest, and speakers who travel to schools, community colleges, churches, and civic organizations to talk about incest. The professional training group offers workshops on treatment for a variety of professionals, consultation services, and agency in-service (continuing education) workshops.

Publications: Several brochures on incest, including *The Long-Term Negative Effects on the Adult Victim of Childhood Incest*, *When the Silence Is Broken*, and *Men Have Been Victims Too*.

Stop It Now!
P.O. Box 495
Haydenville, MA 01039
(413) 268-3096

This program is concerned with ending the sexual abuse of children through the use of public advocacy. It was founded on the principle that our society has the ability to challenge unwanted human behaviors and to change them through intelligent use of the media. While they believe that children should be warned and trained to prevent their own sexual abuse, this program's focus is to put the burden of stopping the sexual abuse of children on the shoulders of adults. They also believe that because most experts agree that a large proportion of sex abusers can and will stop their harmful behavior if they are reached and are provided with good treatment programs, society must hold them responsible for their criminal behavior and expect them to change. Their Reach Out program works to stop abuse by challenging offenders to stop their abuse and seek treatment, helping to identify potential abusers and encouraging them to seek help, empowering family and friends to confront the abuser, and creating a social climate in this country that will not tolerate the sexual abuse of children. They use op-ed articles, a speakers' bureau, talk shows, television and radio public service announcements, magazine articles, and slogans to educate the public about childhood sexual abuse.

Stuart House
Santa Monica Hospital
1336 Sixteenth Street
Santa Monica, CA 90404
(310) 319-4248

Stuart House was established in 1988 by the Santa Monica Rape Treatment Center and several public agencies to reduce the trauma and ensure effective treatment to children who have been sexually abused. It is located in a house designed with the needs of children in mind. Cases are managed by a skilled, multidisciplinary team that includes a deputy district attorney, a law enforcement investigator, a representative from the Department of Children's Services, and a child advocate. This team follows procedures designed to eliminate repetitive interviews and ensure that evidence is properly collected. The child advocate coordinates services to the child and the family, introduces the child to the other team members, and is always available to answer questions from the child or the family. Therapeutic services include individual, family, and group therapy; crisis intervention; court accompaniment; consultation with the child's school; and assistance in receiving victim compensation. Training for professionals and community education programs are also offered.

Survivors of Incest Anonymous
P.O. Box 21817
Baltimore, MD 21222-6817
(410) 433-2365

Survivors of Incest Anonymous is a 12-step program organized to help incest survivors and their family members, spouses, and friends recover from their incest experiences. They have taken the Twelve Steps and Twelve Traditions from Alcoholics Anonymous and adapted them to incest. In their meetings, they seek understanding, acceptance, forgiveness, and serenity. They strive to recognize the negative behavior patterns they developed in childhood in order to survive their experiences, and develop a new, more positive way of life.

Women Against Rape
Child Watch
P.O. Box 346
Collingswood, NJ 08108
(609) 858-7800; (800) 491-WATCH

One component of the Women Against Rape program is Child Watch, a program to help victims of incest and molestation. Services include a 24-hour hotline; counseling; rap sessions on incest; escort to police stations, hospitals, and courts; junior and senior high school programs; and a volunteer training program.

Publications: Incest/Molestation: Prevention Through Education, a brochure that discusses characteristics of high risk families, reasons why family members may know about but not do anything about incest, and ways to prevent the occurrence of incest and child molestation.

VOICES in Action
P.O. Box 148309
Chicago, IL 60614
(800) 7-VOICE-8; (312) 327-1500

VOICES (Victims of Incest Can Emerge Survivors) is a nonprofit organization founded in 1980 as a self-help group providing support for victims of incest and child sexual abuse. The program's goals are to help victims of incest and child sexual abuse become survivors and to educate the public in the area of child sexual abuse, its prevalence and impact, and ways to prevent it. VOICES serves as a clearinghouse for the gathering and disseminating of information regarding incest, works to help victims find support in their efforts to move from victim to survivor, fosters programs that reflect the needs of incest victims, generates public-awareness activities and educational programs, facilitates research in the field of child sexual abuse, and offers programs to make the public aware of the importance of prevention and education.

Women Incested Needing
Group Support (WINGS)
WINGS Foundation, Inc.
8007 West Colfax Avenue
CS#27, Box 129
Lakewood, CO 80215
(303) 238-8660; (800) 373-8671

Women Incested Needing Group Support is a nonprofit organization founded in 1982 by survivors of incest. The group is dedicated to helping women tackle the issue of sexual abuse and start the healing process. It is a peer support group whose goal is to foster a confidential and caring environment in which members can share experiences and learn from each other. WINGS offers a clearinghouse for information on psychotherapists specializing in treating sexual abuse, weekly support group meetings, a sexual abuse handbook, organized social and recreational activities, a speakers' bureau, and assistance in starting WINGS groups in local areas.

Print Resources 6

This chapter contains descriptions of recently published books, handbooks, manuals, journal articles, and training guides on childhood sexual abuse. Because so many books and journal articles have been published recently on the topic of child sexual abuse, this chapter contains a representative sample on various topics within this field; by no means is it a comprehensive listing of the current literature in the field.

Books

Adams, Caren, and Jennifer Fay. *Helping Your Child Recover from Sexual Abuse.* Seattle: University of Washington Press, 1987. 160 pp. ISBN 0-295-96806-0.

Adams and Fay, both counselors at King County Rape Relief in Renton, Washington, have written this book for parents on how to talk about sexual abuse with a child who has been sexually abused. They provide information on how to survive the trauma, how to promote healing as the child gets older, how to protect the child from additional abuse, and how to survive and grow beyond the hurt that parents experience. It is in essence a guidebook, set up with information for parents on the left-hand page and things to say to a child and activities for the child on the right-hand page. Topics covered include how to respond when the child first tells his or her parents about the abuse, how to deal with the legal system and with the responses of other family members and friends, what reactions to expect from children after they have been sexually abused, how to rebuild the child's self-esteem, how to deal with the sexuality issues that usually arise, how to protect the child from being abused again, and how to move on from the abuse experience. This book offers practical guidance for parents in an easy-to-read format, presenting information on each stage that a child usually goes through after having been sexually abused.

Bass, Ellen, and Laura Davis. *The Courage to Heal: A Guide for Survivors of Child Sexual Abuse.* 3d ed. New York: Harper-Perennial, 1994. 605 pp. Resource guide, index. ISBN 0-06-095066-8.

When Ellen Bass and Laura Davis wrote this book, first published in 1988, little information was available about the sexual abuse of children and no real support was available for survivors as adults. Few therapists knew much about sexual abuse and there were even fewer support groups available for adult survivors. Bass and Davis wrote the book "to offer survivors practical, empowering first-hand information and to provide respectful, compassionate guidance through the healing process" (p. 13). Initially the book was not considered controversial; however, in 1992 a highly publicized backlash materialized, accusing survivors of concocting false memories of sexual abuse as children and condemning them for destroying their families. Many people believed that *The Courage to Heal* had played a major role in damaging survivors, therapists, and families by creating false memories. The third edition changes some of the language that was particularly criticized, deletes dated information, and clarifies information in other sections. For example, in the chapter on choosing a therapist, the authors state: "If you feel your therapist is pressuring you to say you were abused, you're seeing the wrong therapist. No one can tell you whether or not you were abused. You are the expert in your own life" (p. 325). They added these comments in reaction to the widespread belief that many therapists were suggesting to clients that they were abused as children, when they really had not been abused; many people believed that the authors in the first edition of this book had suggested that clients should believe their therapists no matter what they said.

The book is an excellent resource for information related to sexual abuse. Topics covered include recognizing the damage that the sexual abuse has done, learning how to cope, deciding to heal, remembering the abuse, telling someone about the abuse, understanding that it was not the victim's fault, grieving, mourning, anger, disclosure, and forgiveness. The authors discuss how to change past patterns with regard to feelings, intimacy, sex, children, parenting, and counseling. Several stories of survivors are presented to help the reader understand that other women have been sexually abused, that they are not alone, and that they can heal. They address the backlash against survivors of childhood sexual abuse. They also offer 55 pages of resources for survivors, including organizations, print material, and videos. These are broken down into several categories, including international, national, and regional organizations; outdoor programs for survivors; religious concerns; abuse by helping professionals, including therapists and clergy members; sadistic ritual abuse; multiple personalities; male survivors; healing music and games; women of color; older women; disabled women; lesbians; and writing and drawing as healing tools.

Berendzen, Richard, and Laura Palmer. *Come Here: A Man Overcomes the Tragic Aftermath of Childhood Sexual Abuse.* New York: Villard Books, 1993. 307 pp. Bibliography. ISBN 0-679-41777-X.

As a child, Richard Berendzen was sexually abused by his mother, a woman whose mental health was questionable. He never knew whether his mother would be lucid and motherly or violent and abusive. Until she was committed to a state mental institution when he was a teenager, he learned to go through life at home with a protective shield around him, showing no emotion, hoping that he would survive. He went off to school first at Southern Methodist University and then Massachusetts Institute of Technology to study physics and astronomy, to become the best through hard work and education. After earning his Ph.D. from Harvard University he and his wife moved to Boston, where he taught at Boston University. He moved on to the American University in Washington, D.C., becoming its president in 1979. Berendzen served as president until he was asked to resign in 1991 after making several indecent telephone calls to day-care centers implying that he might be engaging in sexual activity with his children and waiting for reactions. He enrolled in the Sexual Disorders Clinic at the Johns Hopkins Hospital in Baltimore, run by Dr. Fred Berlin. In this book he emotionally and vividly describes his life, the sexual abuse he endured, the treatment he underwent to understand the reasons why he made those telephone calls, and how he and his family put their lives back together. He emphasizes his belief that he never would have revealed the abuse to anyone, that no matter what he was told, he would never have had the courage to talk about sexual abuse. He believed that he was responsible for understanding and resolving it himself and thought that by immersing himself in work and family activities he would be able to leave the experience behind. In his work following treatment, he talks with many groups to help them understand child sexual abuse and why he and other victims are reluctant to talk about their own experiences.

Berrick, Jill, and Neil Gilbert. *With the Best of Intentions: The Child Sexual Abuse Prevention Movement.* New York: Guilford Press, 1991. 210 pp. References. ISBN 0-89862-564-5.

The number of child sexual abuse prevention programs developed for parents and school systems has grown tremendously in the past several years. This book examines the design, purpose, and consequences of programs to prevent child sexual abuse designed for students from preschool through the third grade. The social movement advocating empowerment of the child as a way of preventing abuse is discussed. The designs of several curricula developed for large-scale prevention activities in schools and a comparative analysis of these programs are presented. Ways children learn most effectively about protecting themselves and preventing abuse are suggested, parents' and teachers' thoughts on prevention programs are included, and prevention policies are examined.

Berry, Jason. *Lead Us Not into Temptation: Catholic Priests and the Sexual Abuse of Children.* New York: Doubleday, 1992. 407 pp. Index. ISBN 0-385-42436-1.

Beginning with the story of sexual abuse of altar boys by a priest in a Louisiana parish, Berry follows the unfolding story with a journalist's curiosity and an expectant father's horror. He describes the physical and emotional trauma to the boys and their families and the indifference of the Catholic hierarchy to the families' pain. Berry goes on to discuss the history of celibacy in the church and the number of priests leaving the church to marry, the church's ban on birth control, and the number of homosexuals in the priesthood. He is quick to point out that research has shown that contrary to widely held beliefs, the rate of child molestation among homosexuals is no higher than that among heterosexuals. He presents an evaluation of therapy as a means of treating pedophiles and analyzes the political dynamics of celibacy. He paints a picture of cover-ups and of threats by the church to sue newspapers that publish stories about priests who have molested children, and he describes the actions the church takes to protect the priests at the expense of the victims, while the victims are often made to feel guilty about damaging the church by going public with their stories. He writes with hope that in the future, as attitudes change, the church will fully accept responsibility for sexual abuse of children by clergy and help its clergy to become healthy and responsible.

Besharov, Douglas J., ed. *Protecting Children from Abuse and Neglect: Policy and Practice.* Springfield, IL: Charles C. Thomas, 1988. 490 pp. References. ISBN 0-398-05428-2.

Besharov wrote this book for policymakers and practitioners to provide a comprehensive review of the effort to protect children from all types of neglect and abuse, including sexual abuse. Chapters include discussions of child abuse reporting laws, the growth of child protection efforts, the lack of protection for the unborn child, past efforts to encourage permanency planning for children in foster care, the legal response to the abuse of children in out-of-home care, legal approaches to solving problems in child welfare systems through impact legislation, the prevention of child abuse, and child abuse and neglect reporting and investigation with a focus on policy guidelines concerning the role of protection agencies, parental rights, and case disposition. Problems caused by the overly ambitious expectations of child protection agencies are evaluated. A comparative study of state laws concerning reporting, investigation, court procedures, and criminal sanctions is included in an appendix.

Boyle, Patrick. *Scout's Honor: Sexual Abuse in America's Most Trusted Institution.* Rocklin, CA: Prima Publishing, 1994. 397 pp. Bibliography, index. ISBN 1-55958-365-7.

As a journalist for the *Washington Times*, Patrick Boyle spent two years gathering information for a series of articles of sexual abuse in the Boy Scouts organization and then quit his job to concentrate his energies full time on this book. He contacted dozens of molesters, and eight former Scout leaders who sexually abused Scouts agreed to be interviewed and have their stories included in the book. One of them, Carl Bittenbender, provides the central role, in part because he was able to move from one area to another and continue to molest boys without anyone reporting him to the Boy Scouts' central organization; the reader is amazed and appalled at how easy it was for Carl to constantly join different Scout groups and find new boys to molest. He wanted his story told, after initial objections, in order to help parents and other adults understand how molesters think and work and how parents can protect their children from abusers. Boyle describes how Carl and other molesters were able to join the Scouts and how easy it was to find suitable boys and isolate them from others. He demonstrates how many of the molesters were able to take several boys on camping trips, with no other adults present, and molest them in their own tents. Some molesters were able to entice the boys to their homes. Boyle reveals the existence of confidential files held at Scout headquarters that provide information on molesters within the organization and what was done, or not done, with this information. The steps that the organization has taken to combat the sexual abuse of boys are described, including videos the Scouts have produced, changes in the Scout handbooks that discuss sexual abuse, and rules that have been instituted to protect Scouts.

Crewdson, John. *By Silence Betrayed: Sexual Abuse of Children in America.* New York: Harper and Row, 1988. 267 pp. Index. ISBN 0-06-097203-3.

When he was the day metropolitan editor for the *Chicago Tribune,* Crewdson became aware of child abuse and child abusers after seeing the incredible response to an article in his paper about the 1984 ABC-TV movie *Something about Amelia.* He followed up his interest in childhood sexual abuse by attending the Third National Conference on the Sexual Victimization of Children in Washington, D.C., later in 1984. Subsequently he was assigned to Los Angeles as the *Tribune's* correspondent there, and he spent over one year writing about the sexual abuse of children. In this book, he explores all facets of child sexual abuse, including attempts to estimate the number of children sexually abused; who these children are; the kinds of people who are abusers; the judicial system and how it works, both for and against, the children; the difficulty of determining whether or not a child is telling the truth; various approaches to treating abusers, either by putting them in jail or diverting them into some type of treatment program; and the growth in popularity of all types of prevention programs. He also discusses the McMartin case, in which staff members at a prominent preschool in Manhattan Beach, California, were accused of sexually abusing several of the children enrolled. Crewdson carefully explains many of the prominent issues about childhood sexual abuse and helps provide a clear and realistic understanding of this problem.

Crowley, Patricia. *Not My Child: A Mother Confronts Her Child's Sexual Abuse.* New York: Doubleday, 1990. 309 pp. ISBN 0-385-26098-9.

Patricia Crowley, a pseudonym used to protect her family, recounts the story of child sexual abuse at the Wee Care Day Nursery in Maplewood, New Jersey. A successful editor at a major metropolitan newspaper, Crowley enjoyed a fulfilling family life and career. She had a live-in housekeeper to help take care of their four children, Caroline, seven years old; Hannah, five years old; Ellen, two years old; and Robert, five months old. She and her husband sent Hannah to the Wee Care Day Nursery two days a week so that she could be exposed to and learn to interact with other children her age. In this compelling book, she describes the acts of sexual abuse committed by one of the teachers at Wee Care, Margaret Kelly Michaels. Michaels's lawyers argued that the parents were on a witch hunt, that none of the abuse happened, and that the children just made it all up at the urging of their parents. Crowley describes the effects of the abuse on her child, the other children, and their families. By the time Michaels was found guilty on 115 of 131 counts against her, several of the families were no longer together and the effects on the children were still evident and profound.

Dziech, Billie Wright, and Charles B. Schudson. *On Trial: America's Courts and Their Treatment of Sexually Abused Children.* 2d ed. Boston: Beacon Press, 1991. 240 pp. Bibliography. ISBN 0-8070-0415-4.

The role of the courts in the treatment of sexually abused children has been examined recently by many in the field of child sexual abuse. In this book, the authors explore the issues involved in the legal profession's treatment of child victims. The extent of the problem of sexual abuse, the attitudes of society toward the victim and the trauma experienced by the victim, and the trauma created by the legal system are explored. American legal history and the inconsistent treatment of children and sex crimes are examined. Parent-child relationships, the different ways in which children respond to abuse, and current child development issues are discussed. The author offers questions that an adult might typically ask a child testifying in a case of sexual abuse. An example of a child sexual abuse case offers the reader a look at how the criminal justice system works and its weaknesses in child sexual abuse cases. Other topics considered include competency and hearsay rules, using videotaped testimony of children, using closed-circuit television with the child so he or she does not have to appear in front of the defendant, and the best use of expert testimony. Changes to the criminal justice system are suggested to help improve the handling of child sexual abuse cases, recent decisions and trends in the ways the court system treats children are presented, and national and state resources are listed.

Faller, Kathleen C. *Understanding Child Sexual Maltreatment.* Newbury Park, CA: Sage Publications, 1990. 251 pp. References. ISBN 0-8039-3842-X.

A resource for mental health professionals, this book defines sexual abuse, describes a victim-centered approach to treating children who have been sexually abused, and offers information on the prevalence, incidence, and major indicators of sexual abuse. Using relevant examples, the author defines sexual abuse, describes the various types of sexually abusive relationships, and offers theories on the reasons why people sexually abuse children. Mental health professionals are helped in their attempts to work with other agencies by descriptions of the roles of other professionals, including protective services, police, lawyers, and courts, in working with sexually abused children and their families. Advice is given on testifying in court in cases of sexual abuse. Guidelines are offered to help determine the severity of the abuse, the effects of the abuse, the treatment prognosis, and whether or not to remove the victim from the home in which the abuse occurred.

Finkelhor, David, Linda M. Williams, and Nanci Burns. *Nursery Crimes: Sexual Abuse in Day Care.* Newbury Park, CA: Sage Publications, 1988. 272 pp. References. ISBN 0-8039-3400-9.

Finkelhor and his associates conducted a two-year national investigation of child sexual abuse in day care centers. They examined a wide range of questions in relation to well-known cases of such as well as cases that received little or no publicity. Centers included in the study were those that cared for children younger than seven years old and that offered care to more than six children. The question of whether or not day-care centers place children at high risk for child sexual abuse is discussed. Perpetrators are described, along with the characteristics of child victims, the dynamics of sexual abuse, the processes of detecting and disclosing abuse and of working with children after the abuse has occurred, characteristics of day-care centers, and the professional response to reports of child sexual abuse. The authors assure parents that day-care centers do not place their children at a sufficiently higher risk for sexual abuse to warrant avoidance of day care and that increased parental involvement in the day-care center activities and an understanding and sensitivity to their children can help in preventing sexual abuse.

Finkelhor, David, with Sharon Araji, Larry Baron, Angela Browne, Stefanie D. Peters, and Gail E. Wyatt. *A Sourcebook on Child Sexual Abuse.* Newbury Park, CA: Sage Publications, 1986. 276 pp. References, index. ISBN 0-8039-2748-5.

David Finkelhor and his associates have reviewed ten years of research, both published and unpublished, in the area of child sexual abuse, from the mid-1970s to the mid-1980s. They compare the findings of these research studies with those of previous years, when little research was done concerning child sexual abuse. They analyze the quality of the research conducted and the problems associated with interpretation of the data. Prevalence of sexual abuse is discussed, along with the problems involved in defining child sexual abuse and measuring its occurrence. The major factors that place children at high risk for sexual abuse are discussed. Theories concerning child molesters are presented; while much of this information is somewhat dated, this is the first book to pull together much of the information on this subject. Issues related to recidivism are presented, including the fact that studies on recidivism usually include only those offenders who have been arrested and convicted of a sexual abuse crime, whereas most offenders are never arrested, convicted, or sent to prison. Initial and long-term effects of child sexual abuse are discussed. Issues of methodology are presented and discussed. Finally, the prevention of child sexual abuse is examined, including types of programs and ways of evaluating the success of these programs.

Fredrickson, Renee. *Repressed Memories: A Journey to Recovery from Sexual Abuse.* New York: Simon & Schuster, 1992. 240 pp. Index. ISBN 0-671-76716-X.

Several experts in the field believe that children repress some or all of the memories related to any sexual abuse experiences they have. Based on her clinical experience, Dr. Fredrickson believes that adults can heal the pain of their earlier experiences of sexual abuse as children only when they are able to recover these memories. In this book, she explains how memories are repressed, what the warning signs are for repressed memories, why recovery of all memories is so important to the physical and emotional health of the person, and how to recover repressed memories and begin the healing process. Each chapter ends with a section called "Empowering Yourself," which is designed to help readers apply what they have read to their own lives.

Friess, Donna L. *Cry the Darkness: One Woman's Triumph over the Tragedy of Incest.* Deerfield Beach, FL: Health Communications, Inc., 1993. 280 pp. ISBN 1-55874-258-1.

Friess, a professor of communications, was sexually abused by her father from the time she was six years old. In this book, she relives her childhood and tells about her discovery that she was not the only one he had ever sexually abused. Friess describes how she created a wonderful life for her own family despite the forces that shaped her childhood. Then, faced with the fear that her father could soon be molesting his young granddaughter, her niece, she debates whether or not to turn him into the authorities. She describes the fear that engulfs her as she confides to her husband what happened to her as a child. With his strong and loving support and the support of other family members and friends, she and her half-sister decide to end his abuse. They turn him into the authorities and he is arrested. She describes the experiences of her family as the court proceedings drag on. He is finally convicted on several counts and sentenced to the maximum allowed in California, 12 years and 9 months in prison. Because of this case, "California state law was changed to include menace and duress as grounds for rape charges. . . . Never again will a judge be able to discard rape charges because they were based only on threats to the victim." (p. 277).

Gardner, Richard A. *Sex Abuse Hysteria: Salem Witch Trials Revisited.* Cresskill, NJ: Creative Therapeutics, 1991. 156 pp. References, index. ISBN 0-933812-22-1.

Gardner wrote this book, based on his experience in child custody litigation for over 25 years, to help people understand the growth of accusations of sexual abuse in divorce and custody proceedings in recent years. Although some of the accusations are true, he has seen such accusations used as a weapon for seeking revenge on a hated spouse, with no basis in fact. This book describes the basic problem, the psychological and social factors that have led many people to use this technique to harm others. It provides detailed information on the normal fantasies of childhood, sex abuse prevention programs, the ubiquity of environmental sexual stimuli, the parental contribution, the validators of sexual abuse, the children involved, the role of physicians, prosecutors, judges, lawyers, and therapists, and society's role in false accusations of child sexual abuse.

Gilbert, Neil, J. D. Berrick, N. L. LeProhn, and N. Nyman. *Protecting Young Children from Sexual Abuse: Does Preschool Training Work?* Lexington, MA: Lexington Books, 1989. 160 pp. References. ISBN 0-669-20103-0.

This book, based on a study conducted under a grant from the National Center on Child Abuse and Neglect, analyzes existing child sexual abuse prevention programs. Topics considered include the various types of prevention programs and suggestions for improving them, various ways of presenting information to children so that they can comprehend it, and an evaluation of California's child abuse prevention services.

Goldstein, Eleanor. *Confabulations: Creating False Memories, Destroying Families.* Boca Raton, FL: SIRS Books, 1992. 335 pp. ISBN 0-89777-1443-3.

Many people in therapy believe that they were sexually abused as children even though they have no current, conscious memory of the sexual abuse, and they come to believe that this abuse is the source of their current problems. Goldstein believes that this has created mass hysteria, that more and more people are coming to believe that they were sexually abused as children; this belief is destroying families, although little evidence exists to corroborate these findings. She offers the reader several families' stories, in which one member went for counseling to find the cause of a certain problem, either a marriage problem, an eating disorder, an inexplicable illness, or some other problem, and came out with a diagnosis of childhood sexual abuse even though he or she has no memory of any abuse and no evidence that such abuse occurred. Other chapters offer the views of therapists; a discussion of *The Courage to Heal,* a book by Ellen Bass and Laura Davis that has stirred a great deal of controversy over the issue of repressed memories; a discussion of the new age movement and its impact on false memories; feminism; and satanism.

Goodman, Gail S., and Bette L. Bottoms, eds. *Child Victims, Child Witnesses: Understanding and Improving Testimony.* New York: Guilford Press, 1993. 328 pp. References. ISBN 0-89862-789-3.

Goodman and Bottoms present the current findings of research into the area of child witnesses in court hearings and address psychological and legal issues. Topics include a description of the development of children's memory, the importance and characteristics of autobiographical memory, children's ability to provide credible testimony, the potential use of verbal and physical cues in improving children's memory of events, and the use of anatomically correct dolls. Suggestions are made for conducting interviews with children who have allegedly been sexually abused. The problems that children encounter when they testify in court are explained and attempts to minimize the differences between the demands of the legal system and children's ability to testify are discussed. Other chapters include a review of the research concerning children's ability to tell the truth, jurors' perceptions of children's ability to tell the truth, mock jurors' perceptions of children as witnesses, the impact of intervention in child sexual abuse cases, children's testimony within the context of the British legal system, perceptions of child sexual abuse victims, and additional research on the subject of children as witnesses.

Gray, Ellen B. *Unequal Justice: The Prosecution of Child Sexual Abuse.* New York: Free Press, 1993. 256 pp. Bibliography. ISBN 0-02-912663-0.

Prosecuting cases of child sexual abuse has always been difficult, and many prosecutors shy away from these cases. When the only witness is the child who has allegedly been abused, building a case against an alleged perpetrator is time-consuming and often impossible. This book, based on a study conducted by the National Council of Jewish Women Center for the Child, reviews the results of this study, which tracked cases of child sexual abuse through the criminal justice system in eight different jurisdictions throughout the United States for one year, from September 1987 through August 1988. The demographics, the system set up for interagency referrals, and the legal methods used in each jurisdiction selected are presented. The victims, offenders, and cases are described, along with a discussion of the relevant factors, such as the age of the child, the relationship of the alleged perpetrator to the child, the type of case, any medical evidence present, and the criminal history and race of the alleged perpetrator. The importance of procedural reforms, the examination of the child to determine his or her competency as a witness, the child's testimony and the decision-making processes of the jurors as well as their attitudes toward the child and the alleged offender and toward the trial in general are discussed. Study findings related to expert testimony and the credibility of child witnesses are also presented. The study revealed that over 90 percent of the cases presented to prosecutors in these jurisdictions did not go to trial, that African-American defendants are treated more harshly than other defendants, that child witnesses do not often benefit from procedural reforms, and that expert witnesses were not overly biased toward children.

Hagans, Kathryn B., and Joyce Case. *When Your Child Has Been Molested: A Parent's Guide to Healing and Recovery.* Lexington, MA: Lexington Books, 1988. 163 pp. Glossary, index. ISBN 0-669-17980-9.

In this book, Hagans, director of a sexual abuse treatment program, and Case, a freelance writer, provide parents with a practical guide to help them survive the traumatic experience of a sexual molestation. They show parents what they will encounter from the moment their child admits (or that they suspect) that he or she has been sexually abused. Topics discussed include facts about sexual abuse and abusers, parental reactions, why it is so important to report the abuse to the proper authorities, believing the child, what to say to the child, behavior patterns indicating possible sexual abuse, the types of professionals who can provide help to the child and the family, how to help the investigators, how to help the child cope, dealing with the normal parental feelings of guilt, what to say to other family members and to friends, what court proceedings are like, how to communicate with other family members to help heal any breakdowns, and what to do when the abuse is incest. The authors provide what they call "reality checks" throughout the book to help family members understand that they are not alone in their experiences with sexual abuse.

Hawkins, Paula. *Children at Risk: My Fight against Child Abuse—A Personal Story and a Public Plea.* Bethesda, MD: Adler and Adler, 1986. 191 pp. ISBN 0-917561-18-X.

Senator Paula Hawkins was sexually abused as a child by a neighbor, who had also abused other children while they were at his house. He was never convicted, primarily because of the testimony of his wife, who claimed that she was always around when the children were playing at her house, and she would have known if her husband was abusing the children. No one believed Hawkins and the other children who also testified. Hawkins discussed the effects of abuse on the child, legislation to help child victims, missing children, sexual exploitation, the scope of the problem of child sexual abuse, indicators of sexual abuse, and what parents can do to prevent it.

Hechler, David. *The Battle and the Backlash: The Child Sexual Abuse War.* Lexington, MA: Lexington Books, 1988. 376 pp. Notes, index. ISBN 0-669-14097-X.

Hechler sees many issues in the field of child sexual abuse that stir strong emotional responses and form battle lines between the believers and the skeptics: the denial and trivialization of child sexual abuse, the problems involved in prosecuting offenders, the legal rights of defendants, the role of expert witnesses, false accusations in cases of divorce and custody, the role of the therapist, and the role of the media. He is concerned about the raging debate between those who believe that children would never lie about something so serious as sexual abuse and those who believe that children are fully capable of being brainwashed by investigators and other influential people in their lives. Chapters focus on the battle for acceptance; the role of denial as a coping mechanism; case studies; the role of the courts; the backlash; and the role of the experts in this field. Appendixes offer statements from an incest survivor, a spokesman for the North American Man/Boy Love Association (NAMBLA), a therapist working with offenders, a detective, and a defense attorney.

Hillman, Donald, and Janice Solek-Tefft. *Spiders and Flies: Help for Parents and Teachers of Sexually Abused Children.* Lexington, MA: Lexington Books, 1988. 199 pp. Bibliography, index. ISBN 0-669-17982-5.

Hillman and Solek-Tefft provide parents, teachers, and counselors with a set of skills that they can use when they believe that a child has been sexually abused. They offer a summary of ideas for use with all children to discover current or past abuse and to prevent future abuse. Information about childhood sexual abuse is provided, including statistics, common myths about sexual abuse, normal sexual development, types of abusive encounters, factors that affect the severity of abuse, short-term and long-term effects of abuse, the importance of believing the children, when not to believe children, general problems, the role of the family, characteristics of the incestuous family, victims and perpetrators, the legal process, the dynamics of sexual abuse, prevention, counseling, and frequently asked questions about sexual abuse.

Hoorwitz, Aaron N. *The Clinical Detective: Techniques in the Evaluation of Sexual Abuse.* New York: W. W. Norton and Co., 1992. 303 pp. ISBN 0-393-70124-7.

Written for the mental health professional working with victims of sexual abuse, this book consists primarily of a series of dialogues between a supervisor and clinician and between a clinician and a child. This format offers valuable insight for the clinician into how to interview an alleged victim. Other chapters provide basic information on people who should be interviewed and broad topics that should be addressed in these interviews, the various steps in a typical interview, techniques used for encouraging an interviewee to provide details of the experience and provide good descriptions of the abuse, the ways in which an interviewer can influence the information received, and how information is organized and evaluated.

Horton, Anne L., B. L. Johnson, L. M. Roundy, and D. Williams, eds. *The Incest Perpetrator: A Family Member No One Wants to Treat.* Newbury Park, CA: Sage Publications, 1990. 292 pp. ISBN 0-8039-3391-6.

The treatment of perpetrators of incest, especially fathers, has been a controversial topic among many treatment professionals; many believe that these offenders are harder for them to deal with than with any other type of offender. Because the treatment of incest offenders has not been a high priority for many treatment professionals, the editors of this volume believe that a review of incest and its perpetrators is important. The book includes the opinions of researchers in many fields. Topics discussed are the nature and characteristics of incest perpetrators, how society deals with them, and a variety of treatment issues.

Society's traditional view of incest offenders is examined, and an alternative view to the common one that incest offenders act out nonsexual desires is presented. Policy issues in the treatment of offenders are examined, along with differences between biological fathers and nonbiological fathers, adolescent and female perpetrators, and sexual addiction. The authors discuss ways to identify offenders, use of community resources, issues for clinical intervention, current treatment providers, self-help programs, and issues of confidentiality. Guidelines for treating incest offenders and their families are presented. Appendixes include a resource directory and a description of an incest perpetrator project.

Hunter, Howard. *Man and Child: An Insight into Child Sexual Abuse by a Convicted Molester, with a Comprehensive Resource Guide.* Jefferson, SC: McFarland and Co., 1991. 248 pp. References. ISBN 0-89950-528-7.

Written by a convicted child molester, this book provides readers with an overview of childhood sexual abuse and motivates them to help prevent such abuse. Chapters offer a series of questions and answers about many aspects of childhood sexual abuse, including types of sexual offenses against children, characteristics of victims and offenders, treatment options for offenders, the importance of reporting alleged child sexual abuse to the proper authorities, factors that may contribute to sexually abusive behavior, incidence and prevalence, prevention, and the role that pornography and alcohol play in the sexual abuse of children. Parents are provided with information that helps them understand how a molester may operate, how to identify molesters, how to recognize signs of sexual abuse, and how to talk with the child about sexual abuse. The inconsistency of laws relating to child sexual abuse and conflicts among professionals in many areas of childhood sexual abuse are discussed.

Hunter, Mic. *Abused Boys: The Neglected Victims of Sexual Abuse.* New York: Columbine, 1990. 340 pp. Index, bibliography. ISBN 0-449-90629-9.

Mic Hunter is a psychologist, chemical dependency counselor, and expert in the area of the treatment of male victims of childhood sexual abuse. He decided to write this book after he started working with men who had been sexually abused as children and found few resources available. In this book, he discusses the frequency of sexual abuse of boys, factors affecting the impact of childhood sexual abuse, areas of one's life that are affected by the sexual abuse, and recovery issues. At the end of each chapter, he asks several questions to help readers identify their thoughts and emotions. He also includes moving stories written by men recovering from sexual abuse and their partners. Hunter also discusses factors to consider when choosing a therapist and what a person can say to someone who has been sexually abused. The final chapter offers a list of organizations involved in issues related to sexual abuse and reading material relevant to this topic.

Huskey, Alice. *Stolen Childhood: What You Need To Know about Sexual Abuse.* Downers Grove, IL: InterVarsity Press, 1990. 181 pp. References. ISBN 0-8308-1216-4.

The many aspects of childhood sexual abuse from a Christian perspective, including psychological, parental, and spiritual aspects, are presented in this book. The author describes the indicators of child sexual abuse, including sexual knowledge that is inappropriate for the child's age, the child's confession, changes in the child's grades in school, a sudden fear of a certain person known to the child or of certain situations, antisocial behavior, physical pain experienced by the child, and self-mutilating behavior. Abusers are described as unable to maintain role boundaries and as having addictive personalities, sexual compulsion, poor parental role models, and a desire to remain isolated.

Kempe, Ruth S., and C. Henry Kempe. *The Common Secret: Sexual Abuse of Children and Adolescents.* New York: W. H. Freeman and Co., 1984. 284 pp. References, index. ISBN 0-7167-1625-9.

Ruth and Henry Kempe, long known for their work with abused and neglected children, wrote this book to help readers—students, nurses, physicians, teachers, ministers, priests, lawyers, legislators, and the general public—understand the extent of child sexual abuse and the major issues surrounding it. Chapters provide information on definitions and incidence, extrafamilial sexual abuse, incest, legal aspects, comprehensive first aid after childhood sexual abuse, evaluation and treatment of extrafamilial sexual abuse, evaluation and treatment of incest, the effects of abuse on children and adolescents, and ways to prevent child sexual abuse. Appendixes provide information on a model criminal diversion program, forms for evaluation and case records, and educational materials on child sexual abuse. The authors have included examples from case histories throughout the book.

Lew, Mike. *Victims No Longer: Men Recovering from Incest and Other Sexual Child Abuse.* New York: Harper & Row, 1988. 326 pp. Index. ISBN 0-06-097300-5.

Written as a handbook for men recovering from childhood incest and other types of sexual abuse and for the people who care about these men, Lew wanted to "provide as much information as possible to as many people as possible about a subject that seems to be ignored as often as possible" (p. 3). He also wanted to provide a framework in which healing can take place, show people that recovery is possible, start people thinking about and discussing childhood sexual abuse, and share some of the experiences of men in recovery to help others just starting on that road. Chapters include a discussion of the myths and realities of incest, messages about masculinity that often make it difficult for men to admit that they were sexually abused as children, men and feelings, sexuality and homosexuality, strategies for survival, forgetting, denying, distancing, pretending, numbing, self-image, self-esteem, telling the secret, relationships and the importance of social support, individual and group counseling, forgiving and forgetting, and moving on. A list of resources is provided.

Loftus, Elizabeth, and Katherine Ketcham. *The Myth of Repressed Memory: False Memories and Allegations of Sexual Abuse.* New York: St. Martin's Press, 1994. 290 pp. References, index. ISBN 0-312-11454-0.

Elizabeth Loftus, a psychologist and expert on memory and how it works, and Katherine Ketcham, author and researcher, have written this book about repressed memories following trauma, specifically childhood sexual abuse. They interviewed hundreds of therapists, psychologists, psychiatrists, sociologists, criminologists, lawyers, law enforcement personnel, and those who have "recovered" memories of abuse and those they have accused of sexually abusing them as children. They offer actual stories of women who, with the help of therapists, have recovered repressed memories of sexual abuse and provide the poignant reactions of these women and their family members to these allegations of abuse. Loftus is skeptical of most of these recovered memories; she believes that many of these alleged victims are actually victims of therapists encouraged to believe that their patients' problems are caused by repressed memories of childhood sexual abuse. However, Loftus is quick to recognize the difficulties in this area: "I do not want to see a return of those days, not so very long ago, when a victim's cries for help went unheard and accusations of sexual abuse were automatically dismissed as fantasy or wish-fulfillment. . . . Nor can I automatically accept the idea that significant numbers of fanatical therapists are carelessly implanting memories in their clients' vulnerable minds" (p. 32). Loftus discusses the lack of scientific evidence that points to the existence and reliability of repressed memories. She shows the human tragedy evident throughout the search for repressed memories and so-called healing that can be accomplished once these memories are recovered. She presents a balanced, thoughtful, and easily understood analysis of how memory works and how easy it is for many people to believe in repressed memories as the answer to their problems.

Manshel, Lisa. *Nap Time.* New York: William Morrow and Company, 1990. 364 pp. ISBN 0-688-08763-9.

Lisa Manshel reports on a case of sexual abuse at the Wee Care Day Nursery, a suburban day-care center in Maplewood, New Jersey. After attending the trial of Margaret Kelly Michaels, the defendant in the case, daily and conducting extensive interviews with social workers, prosecutors, defense attorneys, investigators, parents, researchers, teachers, child psychologists, members of the press, and several trial witnesses, she has written a compelling story about how sexual abuse can occur at a day-care center and what happens when allegations of sexual abuse are made. Manshel describes the trial, providing stark and shocking parts of the testimony provided by the children and their parents. The children's testimony and the rest of the prosecution's case, as well as the testimony of expert witnesses presented by the defense along with Michaels's own testimony, are summarized. Michaels was found guilty on 115 of 131 counts against her and was sentenced to 47 years in prison, without the possibility of parole for 14 years.

Marshall, William L., D. R. Laws, and Howard E. Barbaree, eds. *Handbook of Sexual Assault: Issues, Theories, and Treatment of the Offender.* New York: Plenum Press, 1990. 405 pp. References. ISBN 0-306-43272-2.

This is an excellent resource book on sexual assault; it provides a comprehensive review and discussion of theories of sexual assault as well as assessment and treatment of offenders. Chapters provide information on the nature and extent of sexual assault, development of taxonomic models, the use of sexual assault as an expression of power and control, social and cultural factors, the role of cognition, a feminist perspective, a review of recent studies on incestuous fathers, an integrated theory of the etiology of sexual offending behavior, modification of sexual preferences, ways to enhance therapeutic progress, the outcome of comprehensive cognitive-behavioral treatment programs, and future directions for research in this field.

Matsakis, Aphrodite. *When the Bough Breaks.* Oakland, CA: New Harbinger Publications, 1991. 258 pp. ISBN 1-879237-01-6.

Based on her personal experience with sexual abuse as well as over 15 years of clinical experience working with children who were sexually abused, Dr. Matsakis has written this book to help those affected by sexual abuse, specifically parents. She discusses the normal feelings that parents have in response to finding that their child has been sexually abused and provides specific information about child sexual abuse—its characteristics, prevalence, common symptoms, and psychological consequences. Matsakis compares the emotional stages that parents of a sexually abused child go through to the five stages that Elizabeth Kubler-Ross identified related to death and dying: denial, anger, bargaining, depression, and acceptance. Disclosure of the abuse, including who and when to tell, and how to deal with the reactions of others are included. The healing process, including the use of therapy, therapeutic goals, types of therapy, and guidelines for choosing a therapist help a parent understand and deal with ways to help a child recover from this experience. Matsakis discusses ways of coping with phobias and anxieties, truancy and other problems in school, depression, and nightmares and other sleep disorders, as well as types of helpful medication. She also covers feelings of suicide and the decision to hospitalize a child.

Mayer, Robert S. *Satan's Children: Case Studies in Multiple Personality.* New York: G. P. Putnam's Sons, 1991. 267 pp. ISBN 0-399-13627-4.

Mayer, a nationally recognized expert in multiple personality disorder (MPD), discusses several cases of MPD, helping to define what MPD is and the relationship between MPD and findings of satanic ritual abuse. Despite the beliefs of many colleagues and supervisors who claimed that many people diagnosed with MPD were just faking these personalities as a way of resisting treatment and playing with the therapist, Dr. Mayer pursued his belief that MPD did exist in many of his clients and was a valid diagnosis. He believes that many people with MPD were physically or sexually abused as children and developed different personalities to help deal with the trauma of abuse. In this book, Mayer relates the stories of several of his MPD clients who told haunting stories of being involved in ritual abuse committed by followers of satanic cults. These clients did not represent the majority of his clients, but Mayer believes that their stories must be told, that society must understand the horrors that these people have been through.

Miller, Alice. *Thou Shalt Not Be Aware: Society's Betrayal of the Child.* Translated by Hildegarde and Hunter Hannum. New York: Meridian, 1986. 329 pp. Bibliography. ISBN 0-452-00929-4.

Dr. Miller, in this ground-breaking book, presents her premise that sexually abused children have obeyed the dictum "Thou shalt not be aware," believing that they are to blame for what happens to them. Miller argues that therapists have harmed those they have treated by trying to make them fit neatly into popular psychological theories, instead of listening to and learning from them. She argues that therapists must start listening to the children, identify with them, to understand them. Therapists must become advocates for their clients instead of representing current societal theories and values. They must not spare the parents at any cost, but must understand the ways in which sexuality can be used to control or have power over those weaker in society.

Mones, Paul. *When a Child Kills: Abused Children Who Kill Their Parents.* New York: Pocket Books, 1991. 361 pp. ISBN 0-671-67421-8.

Paul Mones is an attorney and children's rights advocate who defends abused children who are accused of killing their parents. He tells the stories of eight of those children in this book. He reviews the literature on child abuse, showing how these cases confront society with the contradictions and confusion about our ideas of the roles of parents and children and our attitudes toward family violence. These stories show us how the legal system deals with these cases and what happens to the friends and family members involved; in many cases, it fails to protect the children and, ultimately, the parents and other family members.

Child abuse and other forms of family violence take a devastating toll on families and on society, and Mones provides an inside look at what happens to some of these families.

O'Connell, Michael A., E. Leberg, and C. R. Donaldson. *Working with Sex Offenders: Guidelines for Therapist Selection.* Newbury Park, CA: Sage Publications, 1990. 131 pp. References. ISBN 0-8039-3754-7.

This book is written for judges, prosecuting attorneys, child protection services workers, and probation and parole officers to help them in referring sex offenders for evaluation and treatment and for therapists to help in deciding whether or not to treat a sexual offender. Topics include behavioral characteristics of sex offenders and their victims, the components necessary for evaluating and treating these offenders, qualifications that therapists who treat offenders should have, and a discussion of the social context in which treatment occurs. Treatment issues, including controls, defenses, deviant sexual arousal, and cognitive distortions, are examined, along with methods used in therapeutic treatment, the effectiveness of various types of treatment, and decisions to reunite offenders with their families.

O'Donohue, William, and James H. Geer, eds. *The Sexual Abuse of Children.* Hillsdale, NJ: Lawrence Erlbaum Associates, 1992. Vol. 1: *Theory and Research,* 0-8058-0339-4; Vol. 2: *Clinical Issues,* ISBN 0-8058-0954-6.

This two-volume work contains a wealth of information on child sexual abuse. The first volume focuses on epidemiology, sexual abuse from a developmental perspective, sexuality and sexual abuse of mentally retarded persons, a feminist view of child sexual abuse, legal issues, and definitional and ethical issues. Volume 2 focuses on more practical issues such as primary prevention strategies, individual and group treatment of abused children, the various types of behavioral treatment for both victims and offenders, adolescent sex offenders, the role of the medical professional in detecting child sexual abuse, and ways of assessing the credibility of child sexual abuse allegations.

Poston, Carol, and Karen Lison. *Reclaiming Our Lives: Hope for Adult Survivors of Incest.* Boston: Little, Brown and Company, 1989. 280 pp. References, index. ISBN 0-316-71472-0.

Poston, an incest survivor, and Lison, a therapist specializing in treating incest victims, have written this book to help survivors take back their lives. They intersperse throughout the book the stories of many women who survived incest as children. Ways that children survive incest include psychological escapes, such as developing multiple personalities, dissociating from the experience as it occurs, and failing to recall the experience through localized or selective amnesia; physical escapes, such as running away from home as soon as they are able; mind games, usually a combination of psychological and physical escapes, including accepting bribes, making deals with the abuser, or using any other means to convince themselves that they indeed have some power in this situation. The issue of sexuality is discussed, from the survivors' feelings of being sex objects to the difficulty of participating in or understanding a positive, healthy sexual relationship with another person. Entering therapy and dealing with feelings of shame, sadness, anger, rage, fear, and guilt are often difficult things to do, but the authors talk positively about the benefits of therapy and the healing process in general. They offer 26 ways, as an A to Z list, to help victims get through the recovery process and reclaim their lives.

Rush, Florence. *The Best Kept Secret: Sexual Abuse of Children.* New York: McGraw-Hill, 1980. 226 pp. References, index. ISBN 0-8306-3907-1.

In this classic on child sexual abuse, Rush counters the common beliefs about the sexual abuse of children that were held prior to the 1980s, including the belief that children usually were not seriously harmed by sexual abuse and that they were often the instigators of the abuse. She provides a detailed historical analysis of child sexual abuse throughout history, including both Christian and Judaic traditions concerning children as well as early Greek actions toward children, child marriage in India. and growing up in Victorian England. The ways in which law, religion, media attitudes, and psychological theories have contributed to the victimization of children are explored. Sexual abuse of boys, more common than many people once believed, is discussed. Child prostitution and child pornography are also examined.

Ryan, Gail D., and Sandy L. Lane, eds. *Juvenile Sexual Offending: Causes, Consequences, and Correction.* Lexington, MA: Lexington Books, 1991. 438 pp. References. ISBN 0-669-19464-6.

Designed to help clinicians and graduate students understand the causes, consequences, and correction strategies for juvenile sexual offenders, this book focuses primarily on child sexual abuse; rape and other deviant sexual behaviors are treated separately when differences exist in theory and practice between these behaviors and child sexual abuse. The extent of the problem is explored, a history of juvenile sexual offenders is provided, and a rationale for intervening and treating these offenders is offered. Other chapters include a presentation of etiologic theories; a developmental perspective, offering a examination of sexuality, deviancy, and the role of sexuality in juvenile sexual offending; a discussion of the consequences of sexual offending; legal and therapeutic responses; types of treatment; prevention strategies; and the effects on the clinician of working with juvenile sexual offenders.

Sakheim, David K., and Susan E. Devine, eds. *Out of Darkness: Exploring Satanism and Ritual Abuse.* New York: Lexington Books, 1992. 316 pp. Index. ISBN 0-02-927651-9.

Interest in satanic ritual abuse and allegations of children being sexually abused in situations involving some type of ritual abuse have grown in the past several years. Sakheim and Devine believe that therapists must have current and reliable information in order to successfully treat victims of this type of sexual abuse. Chapters provide an overview of the history of satanic religions, satanic beliefs and practices, alternative hypotheses regarding claims of satanic cult activity, child forensic evaluations and claims of ritual abuse, a law enforcement perspective, psychological testing and ritual abuse, the experiences of five families, a theory of psychological adaptation to severe trauma, diagnosis and treatment of children and their families, recognition and treatment of survivors, and the major issues in working therapeutically with individuals who have been exposed to severe trauma.

Schetky, Diane H., and Arthur H. Green. *Child Sexual Abuse: A Handbook for Health Care and Legal Professionals.* New York: Brunner-Mazel, 1988. 248 pp. References. ISBN 0-87630-495-1.

This comprehensive textbook is written for health care and legal professionals who participate in the evaluation of alleged child sexual abuse cases. Topics discussed include a historical perspective of the sexual abuse of children, child sexual abuse in the context of normal psychosexual development, current literature on the subject, conducting clinical and medical evaluations, problems resulting from false accusations of abuse, sibling abuse, male victims of sexual abuse, abuse of children in institutional settings, child pornography, child prostitution, assessing and treating the male sexual offender, the child as a witness in legal proceedings, the role of the clinician as an expert witness in legal proceedings, and the treatment and prevention of child sexual abuse. A list of educational materials for prevention, treatment, and training activities is included.

Sgroi, Suzanne M. *Vulnerable Populations: Sexual Abuse Treatment for Children, Adult Survivors, Offenders, and Persons with Mental Retardation.* Vol. 2. Lexington, MA: Lexington Books, 1989. 448 pp. References. ISBN 0-669-20942-2.

Sgroi examines treatment programs for both victims and perpetrators. Guidelines are presented for using play therapy with sexually abused children, treatment of children in a psychiatric inpatient unit is explored, and providing cyclic time-limited group therapy for adolescent girls who were sexually abused is discussed. Other chapters present information on treating adolescent male victims, the stages of recovery, peer group therapy for adult survivors, effects on the spirituality of adult survivors, a description of a private program in Maryland offering treatment services to a variety of offenders, sexual offender behaviors, and a community-based treatment program for sexual offenders who abuse children. A teaching guide and curriculum for training mentally retarded adults on ways to avoid sexual abuse is provided.

Spiegel, Lawrence D. *A Question of Innocence: A True Story of False Accusation.* Parsippany, NJ: Unicorn Publishing Company, 1986. 276 pp. Afterword by Douglas Besharov. ISBN 088101-055-3QQ.

Lawrence Spiegel, a psychology professor and therapist in private practice at the time this story takes place, recounts the story of his bitter divorce and the custody battle over his daughter, Jessica. Refusing to allow him to see Jessica, his ex-wife charged him with molesting her. Spiegel describes the battles in court, his own emotional distress, the failure of the legal system to protect him and his daughter, and the financial burden for anyone falsely accused of sexual abuse. The jury founds Spiegel not guilty; most people involved believe that these charges were his ex-wife's way of getting even with him. For over two years, while the case made its way through the legal system, Spiegel was not able to see or talk with his daughter. After this trial, he was required by law to return to Family Court if he wanted to reinstate his parental rights; the Family Court judge entered an order for joint legal custody, liberal visitation, and the reinstatement of full parental rights. In the final chapters, Spiegel answers the questions many people have about how a situation like this can occur, how people can file false allegations of sexual abuse, how the social services departments and legal system get caught up in these lies, and what people can do when faced with this type of situation.

Terr, Lenore. *Unchained Memories: True Stories of Traumatic Memories, Lost and Found.* New York: Basic Books, 1994. 282 pp. Notes, index. ISBN 0-465-08823-6.

Considered one of the foremost experts on trauma and memory, Lenore Terr is a clinical professor of psychiatry at the Langely Porter Psychiatric Institute of the University of California in San Francisco. This book is a collection of stories about people who have recalled traumatic memories from their childhoods, including memories of sexual abuse by a parent or other trusted adult. Terr describes how memory works, how trauma experienced as a child can be forgotten, and how these memories may return. The story of Eileen Franklin Lipsker, who one day while watching her daughter play recovered memories of her father murdering her best friend when she and her friend were about eight years old, is described. Explanations are provided about how she could remember these events years after they had occurred. Terr presents information about memory and trauma similar to her testimony as a witness for the prosecution in the case against Eileen's father. In another case of dissociation, Terr describes how people are able to distance themselves from a place or situation that is highly emotional or traumatic. Marilyn Van Derbur Atler's story is told, how she separated herself into a day child and night child, how she was able to deal with the sexual abuse by her father at night by becoming an entirely different child during the day. She went on to become Miss America in 1958 and finally revealed the abuse. Other stories of traumatic experiences children have experienced and forgotten, or repressed, are presented along with evidence that these stories are indeed true. Terr concedes that not all stories of repressed memories are true, that some may be fabricated, possibly with the help of others, including therapists, but she contends that memories can indeed be repressed and that stories of repressed memories must be examined individually to determine their validity.

Tower, Cynthia Crosson. *Secret Scars: A Guide for Survivors of Child Sexual Abuse.* New York: Viking, 1988. 207 pp. Bibliography, index. ISBN 0-670-82214-0.

A social worker in protective services with a doctorate in counseling psychology, Tower began to realize over a period of 20 years that child sexual abuse was often overlooked and the symptoms attributed to other conditions, making those who had been sexually abused as children even more reluctant to admit the abuse. Tower provides a definition of sexual abuse, discusses feelings that people who have been sexually abused as children can identify with, helping them understand the basis of these feelings and what can be done to help recover from the abuse experience. The differing emotions and reactions that women and men experience as a result of abuse are highlighted. The types of people who abuse children are identified as well as their motivations. Reasons why some people experience multiple victimizations, that is, become victims over and over again, are described. Tower discusses therapy extensively. Ways to survive the abuse experience and how to tell the children of survivors about their experience are also presented.

Trepper, Jerry S., and Mary Jo Barrett. *Systemic Treatment of Incest: A Therapeutic Handbook.* New York: Brunner-Mazel, 1989. 277 pp. References. ISBN 0-87630-560-5.

Using a multiple systems model, this book focuses on treatment issues concerning families affected by incest. Information on incest is presented and causal models, including the perpetrator-victim, family systems, ecosystemic, and multiple-systems models, are discussed. The multiple-systems model is described in detail to help therapists realize the importance of understanding the ways that the offending parent starts and continues the abuse as well as the ways that society, the dysfunctional interaction among all family members, and other factors also may contribute. Pretreatment planning, clinical assessment, and methods of denial are presented. Treatment techniques, such as family, individual, group, and sibling therapy, are discussed in detail.

Wiehe, Vernon R. *Sibling Abuse: Hidden Physical, Emotional, and Sexual Trauma.* Lexington, MA: Lexington Books, 1990. 187 pp. Notes, index. ISBN 0-669-24362-0.

Wiehe wrote this book to bring the subject of sibling abuse, which most people believe is not widespread, to public attention. Professionals and students are the primary audience for this book. Chapters provide information on physical abuse, emotional abuse, sexual abuse, parental reactions to sibling abuse, understanding sibling abuse, effects of abuse on the victim, ways to distinguish abusive behavior from normal behavior, and preventing abuse. Throughout the book, Wiehe allows children who have been abused by their siblings a chance to tell their own stories.

Wright, Lawrence. *Remembering Satan: A Case of Recovered Memory and the Shattering of an American Family.* New York: Alfred A. Knopf, 1994. 207 pp. ISBN 0-679-43155-1.

Wright, a staff writer for the *New Yorker,* describes the terrifying story of a family caught up in a case of repressed memories of child sexual abuse. Paul Ingram, who appeared happily married with five children, was charged with childhood sexual abuse by his two daughters, aged 18 and 22, who claimed to have recovered repressed memories of the abuse. Their stories of what occurred in their home became more bizarre as time passed. Ingram, a deputy sheriff in Olympia when he was accused, was taken in for questioning and, when he claimed that he had no memory of any such abuse, was told that perhaps he was in denial and that once he admitted that the abuse had occurred, his memory would return. Over the next weeks, he did indeed "remember" many cases in which he abused his daughters. Eventually his wife and two sons also started "remembering" instances of abuse. They implicated many people, and as stories of ritual abuse, satanism, and other unnatural occurrences became more commonplace, experts in the field of memory, personnel from the FBI, and others were called in to help understand this case. In the end, Ingram came to believe that his "memories" were false, that in fact he had not abused his daughters, but his guilty plea could not be retracted and he was sentenced to 20 years in prison. Wright poignantly tells Ingram's story and provides insight into the conflicting information on repressed memories.

Yapko, Michael D. *Suggestions of Abuse: True and False Memories of Childhood Sexual Trauma.* New York: Simon & Schuster, 1994. 271 pp. Bibliography, index. ISBN 0-671-87431-4.

A clinical psychologist who has worked with abused children and their families for almost 20 years and a recognized expert in the areas of suggestibility, memory, and clinical applications of hypnosis, Michael Yapko has become increasingly concerned with the number of sexual abuse cases being "discovered" through work with repressed memories. In this book, he examines the growing number of people, mostly women, who through the use of hypnosis and other therapeutic techniques have recovered memories of sexual abuse. He believes therapists are actively or passively encouraging clients to identify themselves as victims of sexual abuse when there is no credible evidence that they indeed have been so abused, based on rather questionable use of a checklist of symptoms often associated with sexual abuse. Yapko believes that these symptoms are so common that they are often found in some combination in many people; they could point to a number of problems besides sexual abuse. He strongly believes that many of these people are destroying their own lives and the lives of their families on the basis of rather inconclusive evidence. Yapko describes how memory works, how it is selective, how memories can be redefined, and what is known about repression of memories of trauma. He shows how therapists, who are often seen as authority figures, can influence clients to accept suggestions of prior abuse. He helps readers understand how to deal with abuse or accusations of abuse within a family. The role of the therapist and how to choose a therapist are also discussed.

Journal Articles and Monographs

Albers, E. **"Child Sexual Abuse Programs: Recommendations for Refinement and Study."** *Child and Adolescent Social Work Journal* 8, 2 (April 1991): 117–125.

Many school systems throughout the country have implemented some type of child sexual abuse prevention program; many of these programs have not been evaluated for their effectiveness. The author presents a review and summary of research results on and evaluations of child sexual abuse prevention programs. Studies conducted since 1986 have shown that children do have increased knowledge about sexual abuse after being exposed to prevention programs, children who participate in programs that actively involve the children in learning retain more information than children involved in programs incorporating only passive learning methods, children may forget information they have learned within one month following the program, and most children do not exhibit negative effects from programs teaching them about sexual abuse. The author analyzes evaluation designs of many prevention programs and suggests issues for researchers to consider when devising new research studies.

Berkowitz, Carol D., Donald C. Bross, David L. Chadwick, and Jay M. Whitworth. *Diagnostic and Treatment Guidelines on Child Sexual Abuse.* Chicago: American Medical Association, 1992.

This booklet offers guidelines for physicians who diagnose and treat cases of child sexual abuse. The ethical considerations in treating these children and the findings of behavioral studies are presented. The interviewing process, the physical exam, documenting the results of the exam, reporting requirements, and providing testimony are discussed. Physicians are encouraged to be able to identify the signs of sexual abuse, conduct a medical evaluation, protect the child, remain professional, report cases of sexual abuse to the proper authorities, and testify in court for the child if necessary.

Berliner, Lucy, and Jon R. Conte. **"The Process of Victimization: The Victim's Perspective."** *Child Abuse and Neglect* 14, 1 (1990): 29–40.

This article summarizes a study conducted by the authors to identify victimization patterns of children who have been sexually abused. The subjects, who ranged in age from 10 to 18 years, were interviewed concerning the process of becoming victims, the person who abused them, and ways that this abuse might have been prevented. The investigators identified three overlapping processes involved in becoming a victim: the relationship between the child and the abuser becomes sexualized, the sexual contact is somehow justified, and the child's cooperation in the abuse is maintained. Although researchers do not know whether or not knowledge about this victimization process will help prevent instances of child sexual abuse, the authors believe that children should be taught that no one should touch them in ways that make them uncomfortable.

Bowers, J. J. **"Therapy through Art: Facilitating Treatment of Sexual Abuse."** *Journal of Psychosocial Nursing* 30, 6 (June 1992): 15–24.

Art therapy can be a valuable tool in the treatment of children, especially very young children, who have been sexually abused. For very young, preverbal children art therapy is valuable in helping recover instances of abuse because they are able to draw pictures of what has happened to them even though they are too young to be able to conceptualize and put into words what they have experienced. Art therapy can also be used to help children overcome resistance to therapy, build trust with others, reduce tension in the therapeutic environment, and stimulate their memories. Adults can also benefit from art therapy.

Bybee, Deborah, and Carol T. Mowbray. **"Community Response to Child Sexual Abuse in Day-care Settings."** *Families in Society* 74, 5 (May 1993): 268–281.

Revelations of sexual abuse of children in day-care centers often create a passionate, angry, and confused reaction in their communities. This article describes the allegations of sexual abuse at a day-care center in a small midwestern community. Using data collected from national surveys, the authors discuss the factors that may complicate or somehow affect the public response to the allegations of sexual abuse. Some of these factors include the young age of the children, the large number of children involved as well as the large number of perpetrators, the use of severe threats and other forms of coercion to keep the children silent, the possible use of pornography or ritual abuse, the possibly conflicting desires of parents and investigators, and the increased possibility of media attention. Recommendations to help enhance the public's response are made, and include increasing parental involvement in their child's day-care center, developing ways to ensure the quality of day-care center care, educating parents and children about sexual abuse, offering treatment to all child victims, and improving the investigation capabilities of law enforcement agencies and other agencies involved in these cases.

Cohen, Judith A., and Anthony P. Mannarino. **"A Treatment Model for Sexually Abused Preschoolers."** *Journal of Interpersonal Violence* 8, 1 (March 1993): 115–131.

Treating very young children who have been sexually abused can be quite complex and difficult. The authors describe a structured, short-term treatment model for abused children between the ages of 3 and 6 years. Referred to as structured parent counseling with child psychotherapy, this model has been developed from the experiences of psychotherapists working with over 200 sexually abused preschoolers. The theoretical roots of the model, its general structure and format, and specific intervention strategies for both the child and the parents are discussed. Parents' concerns are discussed, including ambivalence about the abuse and the offender, fear that their child will be irreparably harmed, possible responses to reactions their child might have as a result of the abuse such as inappropriate behavioral patterns, and their options concerning legal proceedings. Children are taught how to protect themselves from further abuse, how to be assertive, how to tell the difference between good and bad touches, how to cope with their feelings of anxiety and fear, and how to deal with their often ambivalent feelings toward the perpetrator.

Cohn, Debra S. **"Anatomical Doll Play of Preschoolers Referred for Sexual Abuse and Those Not Referred."** *Child Abuse and Neglect* 15, 4 (1991): 455–466.

Among researchers in the field of child sexual abuse, opinions differ on the reliability of using anatomically correct dolls in determining the occurrence of child sexual abuse. This article reports the results of a study that compared 35 children who were suspected of being sexually abused with 35 children randomly selected and matched with the other children in age, sex, and race. The children were given anatomically correct dolls and allowed to play with them as they wanted. Interviewers questioned them followed the play time. Two coders, who were unaware of each child's status as a sexually abused child or a member of the control group, completed separate behavioral checklists. The researchers concluded that anatomical dolls did not lead to undue anxiety in the children, that the results of doll play must be carefully interpreted, that the dolls did not cause children to display sexual activity, and that a diagnosis of sexual abuse cannot be based solely on doll play.

Conte, Jon R., and Linda A. Fogarty. **"Sexual Abuse Prevention Programs for Children."** *Education and Urban Society* 22, 3 (May 1990): 270–284.

The authors look at two questions that should be asked when developing and evaluating programs to prevent child sexual abuse. These questions include whether all children are at equal risk for being sexually abused and whether potential abusers can be identified before they sexually abuse a child. Most prevention programs focus on teaching children about their bodies, good touches and bad touches, ways to control access to their bodies, and ways in which they can tell adults about sexual abuse. Studies have shown that children often have a difficult time understanding that they are not to blame for their abuse. Teaching children about good touches and bad touches may not be as effective as teaching children how to have control over their bodies. Future studies should consider asking children for suggestions of prevention materials and subject matter.

Conte, Jon R., Steven Wolf, and Tim Smith. **"What Sexual Offenders Tell Us about Prevention Strategies."** *Child Abuse and Neglect* 13, 2 (1989): 293–301.

This article reports the results of a study concerning sexual offenders and the prevention of child sexual abuse. The researchers interviewed 20 adult sexual offenders, asking them how they selected and recruited children for sexual activities and how they encouraged these children to stay in a relationship. These offenders claimed to have a special ability to find vulnerable children, to exploit that vulnerability and coerce the children to remain in a relationship, and they describe how they desensitize children to touch. The authors discuss the implications for prevention of childhood sexual abuse.

Doris, John. *The Suggestibility of Children's Recollections.* Washington, DC: American Psychological Association, 1991. 193 pp.

Contributions are offered from leading psychological authorities in the area of suggestibility of children's memories in this book. Chapter topics include the development of memory in children, the susceptibility of preschool children's memories, assessment of the suggestibility and testimony of witnesses to the experience being recalled, the role of stress during children's testimony, the suggestibility of children's testimony especially in cases of child sexual abuse, research findings and their application to children's testimony, studies of ways to interview child witnesses, and a suggested method to assess children's statements.

Fowler, William Edmond and William G. Wagner. **"Preference for and Comfort with Male Versus Female Counselors Among Sexually Abused Girls in Individual Treatment."** *Journal of Counseling Psychology* 40, 1 (January 1993): 65–72.

Professionals working with children who have been sexually abused are beginning to realize that some children may have difficulty feeling comfortable with and relating to a counselor or therapist who is the same sex as the person who sexually abused them. The authors studied the sexual preferences that sexually abused girls had regarding their counselors and their anticipated level of comfort with either male or female counselors. Twenty sexually abused girls between the ages of 7 and 15 completed six sessions of individual counseling from either male or female counselors; all participants preferred a female counselor when they were being psychologically evaluated. After their evaluations, girls who were treated by male counselors were more comfortable with the thought of being treated by male counselors than those girls who were treated by female counselors. The authors discuss the implications of these findings.

Gellert, George A., Michael J. Durfee, and Carol D. Berkowitz. **"Developing Guidelines for HIV Antibody Testing among Victims of Pediatric Sexual Abuse."** *Child Abuse and Neglect* 14, 1 (1990): 9–17.

This article reports the results of a study to determine the current status of guidelines for HIV antibody testing of children who have been sexually abused. Sixty-three practitioners of pediatric sexual abuse assessment, located in the five regions with the highest prevalence of HIV infection, were contacted by telephone. Each practitioner was presented with a standard set of clinical situations; the results would determine whether or not a standard protocol exists among practitioners for conducting HIV antibody testing. Based on the results of the study, the authors suggest a preliminary set of guidelines for testing for HIV antibodies in children who have been sexually abused.

Heras, P. **"Cultural Considerations in the Assessment and Treatment of Child Sexual Abuse."** *Journal of Child Sexual Abuse* 1, 3 (1992): 119–124.

Many researchers and experts in the field of childhood sexual abuse are beginning to examine the cultural factors involved in this abuse. This article examines these factors and emphasizes their importance in assessing and treating children who have been sexually abused. Some of these issues include understanding the context in which the abuse occurred, the importance of family structure and how it affects the assessment process, culture differences, and dysfunctional behaviors. The author presents case examples to illustrate the problems of treating children when they are not assessed within their cultural and social contexts.

Kelley, Susan J., R. Brant, and Jill Waterman. **"Sexual Abuse of Children in Day Care Centers."** *Child Abuse and Neglect* 17, 1 (1993): 71–89.

Since the notoriety of the McMartin Preschool and the allegations of child sexual abuse leveled against many of its staff members in the early 1980s, concern has grown regarding the prevalence of child sexual abuse in day-care centers. Clinicians studying such abuse are faced with several unique challenges; these cases typically involved more than one child victim, more than one perpetrator, and often the use of severe threatening behavior to keep the children from revealing the abuse to anyone outside the center. The authors discuss previous research results on the types of abuse perpetrated by day-care staff members; the ways that the perpetrators convince the children to keep silent about the abuse; the ways in which the abuse is finally disclosed; the effects of the abuse on both parents and children involved; the types of psychological and emotional defenses used by the children affected; and the ways memory and language abilities develop in the young child.

Kreitzer, Ilene S. **"Who Can Speak for the Child? Hearsay Exceptions in Child Sexual Abuse Cases."** *Criminal Justice Journal* 13, 2 (Spring 1992): 213–241.

The use of hearsay testimony, which deprives the defendant of the right of cross-examination, in cases of child sexual abuse is examined in this article. The author reviews traditional responses to the hearsay problem, including declarations of exception, statements made for medical diagnosis or treatment exception, and the residual or catchall exception. State and federal responses to the hearsay dilemma are discussed. The effect of the U.S. Supreme Court decision in *Idaho v. Wright* (see pp. 196–209) on the prosecution of child sexual abuse cases is examined.

Lanning, Kenneth V. *Child Sex Rings: A Behavioral Analysis.* Arlington, VA: National Center for Missing and Exploited Children, April 1992. 72 pp.

Kenneth Lanning, an FBI agent assigned to the Behavioral Science Unit at the FBI Academy in Quantico, Virginia, is an expert in the area of child sex rings and child sexual abuse in satanic cults. He has identified two major types of child sex rings: historical and multidimensional. Here he defines these two types of rings, provides a historical analysis of child sex rings, and discusses societal attitudes and historical attitudes toward child sexual abuse. Chapters include a historical overview, definitions of terms commonly used in this field, and general guidelines on investigating child sex rings. Appendixes provide information on protocols used for investigating multi-victim, multi-offender child sexual exploitation and macro-case investigation.

Marshall, William L., Robin Jones, Tony Ward, Peter Johnston, and Howard E. Barbaree. **"Treatment Outcome with Sex Offenders."** *Clinical Psychology Review* 11 (1991): 465–485.

A review of the literature on the results of treatment of sexual offenders is presented in this article. Physical types of treatment, including stereotaxic ablation of central nervous system centers, physical castration, and pharmacologic agents, and their effectiveness are described. Types of psychological treatment also are discussed, including nonbehavioral approaches, cognitive-behavioral approaches, institution-based programs, and outpatient programs. The authors conclude that not all sexual offenders can be treated successfully; they believe that cognitive-behavioral programs and programs using antiandrogens along with psychological treatment can be effective in treating these offenders. Further research is suggested in the area of identification of factors contributing to the success of treatment programs.

McCormack, Arlene, and Marialena Selvaggio. **"Screening for Pedophiles in Youth-Oriented Community Agencies."** *Social Casework* 70, 1 (January 1989): 37–42.

This article describes a screening method that may help identify pedophiles who apply for jobs in community organizations involving youth; it was developed from information on offenders from the Big Brother–Big Sister Organization of Greater Lowell, Massachusetts. Candidates who may be considered suspect are those who express a desire to work with children of a specific age; those with a history of child sexual abuse, of little contact with others as teenagers, of frequent moves, of having younger friends and/or hobbies and interests involving children only, or of being extremely active in youth issues in the community; and those who believe that children are innocent or pure.

National Center for Prosecution of Child Abuse. *Child Abuse Crimes: Child Pornography.* Alexandria, VA: National Center for Prosecution of Child Abuse, 1994.

The National Center has compiled criminal child abuse legislation arranged by state, excerpting relevant state statutes; this document concerns child pornography. Sentencing information is included in cases in which it is included in a child pornography statute. General pornography statutes are not included unless they are referred to or incorporated in a child pornography statute.

National Center for Prosecution of Child Abuse. *Child Abuse Crimes: Sexual Offenses.* Alexandria, VA: National Center for Prosecution of Child Abuse, 1994.

This document from the National Center contains excerpts from state statutes regarding sexual offenses. Sentencing information is included in cases in which it is included in a statute on sexual offenses. Statutes that specifically identify children as victims are included; statutes with no reference to children are not included.

Pallone, N. J. **"The American Bar Association and Legislatively Mandated Treatment for Sex Offenders."** *Journal of Offender Rehabilitation* 17, 1–2 (1991): 105–117.

This article provides an overview of legislation on criminal sexual psychopaths, which usually prescribes treatment while incarcerated instead of incarcerating these offenders for punishment only. The American Bar Association, along with the Group for the Advancement of Psychiatry, want this legislation repealed, believing that it has not proven effective in treating sex offenders. Examples from Canadian law, which has repealed sexual psychopath laws, demonstrate that alternative approaches may be more successful; participation in prison treatment programs is voluntary in Canada. The author discusses the major issues involved in this area, including effectiveness of treatment, recidivism rates, and the impact of relevant legislation.

Protecting Our Children. Conference Proceedings from the 8th Annual National American Indian Conference on Child Abuse and Neglect. Falls Church, VA, May 11–13, 1990. Norman: University of Oklahoma, American Indian Institute, 1990. 176 pp. References.

Topics covered in this document include community awareness campaigns, guidelines for setting up a multidisciplinary team to work with child sexual abuse cases on the reservation, the Navajo staff academic training program, the conflicting roles of school counselors in identifying and reporting child sexual abuse, activities for preventing child abuse in Native American communities, implementation of child protective services, national adoption services, ritual abuse, stress management, the Navajo Nation Indian Child Welfare Act Program, ways for working with perpetrators and adult victims of child abuse and neglect, and traditional Native American beliefs about wellness.

Rencken, R. H. *Intervention Strategies for Sexual Abuse.* Alexandria, VA: American Association for Counseling and Development, 1989. 186 pp.

A clear framework for understanding the dynamics of pedophilia and child sexual abuse is presented in this document, which focuses on implementing integrated intervention strategies for professionals who work with offenders and victims. Chapters include an overview of the problem, legal issues, the criminal justice system, and strategies for intervention in cases of sexual abuse, including treatment for victims, family members, and perpetrators. Case studies are presented of a dictatorial-possessive father, a dependent father, a pseudoadult child, pedophiles, an adolescent survivor, an adult survivor, a female perpetrator, and an isolated treatment victim. Future directions and concerns are analyzed.

Romer, S. **"Child Sexual Abuse in Custody and Visitation Disputes: Problems, Progress, and Prospects."** *Golden Gate University Law Review* 20, 2 (Fall 1990): 647–680.

Allegations of child sexual abuse are sometimes made in cases of divorce or custody and visitation hearings. This article focuses on these cases, reviewing studies of the truthfulness of these allegations. California law is emphasized along with New York cases, statutes, and procedures. Ways of validating allegations and the role of child protective services in California are examined. Methods of determining the validity of allegations and diagnostic tools used by mental health evaluators are described: they include anatomically correct dolls, the child sexual abuse accommodation syndrome characteristics, and interview techniques. Ways to use medical evidence to validate a child's testimony are explained, and the proper court location (matrimonial, dependency, or criminal court) for determining custody in child sexual abuse cases is discussed.

Rossetti, Stephen J., ed. *Slayer of the Soul: Child Sexual Abuse and the Catholic Church.* Mystic, CT: Twenty-third Publications, 1991. 215 pp.

The involvement of Catholic priests in child sexual abuse is discussed in this publication. Experts in the fields of mental health, law, pastoral theology, communications, and medicine discuss theories of pedophilia and the treatment of sexual abusers within the church and provide perspectives of both victims and offenders. Issues important to the church, including treatment of the victim and the offender and whether or not either can be cured, the responses of church officials to the public and other clergy, and the challenges that face the community, are discussed. Ways that the church and the community can provide leadership in dealing with child sexual abuse by priests are suggested. Case histories of both offending priests and the abused children are provided.

Sapp, Allen D., and M. S. Vaughn. **"Sex Offender Rehabilitation Programs in State Prisons: A Nationwide Survey."** *Journal of Offender Rehabilitation* 17, 1–2 (1991): 55–75.

While the general prison population in the United States is at an all-time high, and prisons hold more sexual offenders than ever before, many experts are beginning to examine the effectiveness of prison programs to treat sex offenders. This article describes the results of a study of 73 such programs in correctional institutions throughout the country. The variety in treatment programs and strategies used to rehabilitate prisoners is discussed. Three major strategies examined are psychotherapy, organic or biologic treatment, and behavior modification.

Manuals and Training Guides

Blanchett, Herbert A. *Communication: Group Therapists' Guide.* San Jose, CA: Giarretto Institute, 1989. References. 54 pp.

This manual is part of a series from the International Child Sexual Abuse Treatment Program at the Giarretto Institute. Blanchett has developed a series of lessons and exercises to help teach people how to communicate. Session topics include paired introductions, individual communication goals, roadblocks to communication, self-awareness experiments, experiencing difficulties in interacting with others, active listening, parent-child dialogue, negotiating style, self-disclosure, learning how to settle disputes, asking for and receiving support, assertiveness, dealing with negative feelings, disidentification (ways of dissociating oneself from one's experiences), "I" statements, and how to fight fair.

Curtis, Mary Lee. *Adult Offenders: Group Therapists' Guide.* San Jose, CA: Giarretto Institute, 1989. 35 pp.

This manual describes men's offender groups offered at the International Child Sexual Abuse Treatment Program of the Giarretto Institute and provides guidelines for organizing offender groups. Curtis discusses how incest offender groups differ from other groups, how most participants are in the group because the court has ordered them to participate, how many of them are afraid for their lives if they are sent to prison (child sexual abusers are often considered the lowest of the low by other inmates), and how many of them may have been abused themselves as children. Group issues, such as cohesiveness and expressions of negative affect, are discussed. Offender issues include family of origin, self-esteem, denial, lack of empathy, communication skills, the actual sexual abuse, feelings and body signals, chemical abuse, resistance, and responsibility. Ways to effectively use confrontation to promote growth are presented. References, a reading list for therapists and group members, and an evaluation form are also included.

Ferguson, Fay. *Parenting Course: Group Therapists' Guide.* San Jose, CA: Giarretto Institute, 1989. References. 34 pp.

This training manual is part of a series from the International Child Sexual Abuse Treatment Program of the Giarretto Institute to help improve parenting skills. Class format is emphasized in this manual in order to provide assignments, feedback, and consistent review of relevant materials to participating members. Class topics include the parenting continuum, democratic parenting, goals of misbehavior, positive relationships, positive behavior, barriers to good parenting, encouragement, reflective listening, effective communication, discipline methods, the logical consequences model, the family council, guidelines for the family council, and self-esteem. A parenting group evaluation form is included. Appendixes contain information on characteristics of authoritarian, permissive, and democratic parenting, assessing the style of parenting of each participant, and examples of handouts on encouraging your child and improving relationships.

Madden, Dorothy Ester. *Non-Offending Parent: Group Therapists' Guide.* San Jose, CA: Giarretto Institute, 1989. 22 pp.

Madden wrote this training manual primarily for those providing group therapy for the nonoffending parents of children who have been sexually abused. She discusses general problem areas that affect nonoffending parents and how therapy can help resolve these problem areas and provides parents with a sense of hope and assurance that they are not alone in their suffering, with information on sexual abuse, and with ways to help them grow, incorporating new, more positive behavior. The author describes the typical group session of women who are married to offenders, dividing goals and guidelines into those that pertain to self, to one's role as mother, and one's role as wife. A guidelines and assessment form for women's groups is included along with a bibliography.

Northwest Indian Child Welfare Association. *Our Children's Future: A Child Sexual Abuse Prevention Curriculum for Native American Head Start Programs.* Portland, OR: Northwest Indian Child Welfare Association, 1991. 296 pp.

This curriculum on prevention of child sexual abuse is designed to help Head Start programs lead the efforts to stop the cycle of abuse in Native American families. An overview of child sexual abuse prevention activities in Native American communities is presented in order to help Head Start staff members familiarize themselves with the major issues involved in administering the curriculum. Teachers are assisted in understanding background material, their roles in working to stop the cycle of abuse, and ways to effectively use the curriculum. Physical and behavioral indicators of sexual abuse, misconceptions about abuse, reporting requirements, and a format for reporting abuse to the proper authorities are provided. A guide for involving parents, nine lesson plans, and a 30-minute video are also included.

Peterson, Judith. *Adults Molested as Children: Group Therapists' Guide.* San Jose: Giarretto Institute, 1989. 35 pp.

This guide, part of the International Child Sexual Abuse Treatment Program of the Giarretto Institute, provides information to therapists on background issues, concepts, and treatment procedures and goals for programs for adults molested as children. Topics include the nature of the wound; why incest victims feel so wounded; definition of an adult molested as a child; the problem of denial; defenses used by children who are sexually abused in order to protect themselves; symptoms exhibited by adults who were sexually abused as children; and characteristics of the healing process. Treatment topics cover early treatment, the importance of trust and feeling safe, inner critics and helpers, the use of closed groups, ongoing treatment, and confronting the parents. A bibliography and group evaluation form are included.

Riley, Annie. *Human Sexuality: Group Therapists' Guide.* San Jose, CA: Giarretto Institute, 1989. 62 pp.

Riley has developed this guide, part of a series of therapists' guides from the International Child Sexual Abuse Treatment Program of the Giarretto Institute, for group treatment of incest offenders, their spouses, and adults who have been molested as children. It is intended to clarify values about sex roles and sexual behavior. Sixteen weekly modules include discussions of obstacles to talking about sex; defining what is sex; language; why people have sex; what messages each participant received at home about sexuality; what intimacy is; the intimacy-and-touching continuum; what participants do to block intimacy with their partners; anatomy, physiology, and the sexual response cycle; sex histories; turn-ons and turn-offs; messages each participant received while growing up about the opposite sex; becoming an askable parent; parents/pregnant teenager role-playing exercise; sex and aging; the prostate gland; what the advantages are of being male or female; and masturbation. Separate bibliographies for clients and for therapists are included.

Szybalski, Joanne, and Susan Setziol. *Therapy for Sexually Abused Children and Their Siblings: Group Therapists' Guide.* San Jose, CA: Giarretto Institute, 1990. 81 pp.

This manual is one of a series of group therapists' guides from the International Child Sexual Abuse Treatment Program at the Giarretto Institute. In the introduction, Eleanor E. Breslin, a licensed marriage, family, and child counselor, discusses the effects of sexual abuse on a child, including the effect of the abuse on the child's self-image, on his or her relationship with others, the child's perceptions of his or her own needs, and on how the child perceives his or her sexuality. Therapy with the child and family is also discussed as well as how to assess and evaluate the needs of sexually abused children. Szybalski discuss the role of assessment, what assessment consists of, how to assess each child's problems, and what the goals of treatment should be. Setziol presents a discussion of therapy. Other topics include sexual abuse issues; ways to facilitate the process, including children's groups and nonverbal therapy; work with parents; and case examples. An evaluation form and a bibliography are included.

Tobin, P., and S. L. Farley. *Keeping Kids Safe.* Holmes Beach, FL: Learning Publications, Inc. 1990. 154 pp.

This manual provides general information on childhood sexual abuse, including prevention, effects of incest on the child, the dynamics of sexual abuse, other related child development issues, indicators used to determine sexual abuse, and procedures for reporting abuse. A child sexual abuse prevention program, the Children's Self-Help Project, is described. Guidelines for setting up a prevention program are provided, along with detailed curricula for preschool and elementary school workshops. Suggestions are made for working effectively with school system personnel, teachers, and parents. Appendixes include a bibliography, guidelines for preparing handouts, teacher and parent follow-up exercises, sample class participation forms in both English and Spanish, and lyrics to "The Touching Song."

Victim Services Agency. *Incest Treatment: A Curriculum for Training Mental Health Professionals.* New York: Victim Services Agency, 1991. 186 pp.

This manual was developed by the Victim Services Agency for training mental health professionals in New York City on the treatment of incest. It is designed as a two-day training program, although a longer training time is encouraged. Five modules are presented, including materials introducing child sexual abuse/incest (myths and facts about child sexual abuse, spectrum of sexually abusing behavior, history of the mental health profession's response to incest, theories on why incest occurs, issues in treating sexually abused children, sociocultural considerations), key concepts for intervention (victimology, family dynamics, traumagenic dynamics, the child sexual abuse accommodation syndrome), assessment and diagnosis (signs and symptoms, assessment, posttraumatic stress disorder, interviewing skills), treatment issues, and case management and coordination. The curriculum includes several handouts on topics such as the history of the mental health response to incest, issues for the treating clinician, indicators of sexual abuse, an assessment exercise, a demonstration of role-playing exercises, and a bibliography/reading list.

Behavioral Treatment for Sex Offenders

Type: VHS
Length: 57 min.
Date: 1994
Cost: $100
Source: The Safer Society Program
            and Press
            P.O. Box 340
            Brandon, VT 05733-0340
            (802) 247-3132

Treating sexual offenders is a complex process of trying to understand and deal with the many reasons they have for sexually abusing children. William Marshall, Ph.D., is one of the foremost experts in the treatment of sexual offenders, advocating the use of behavioral treatment in these cases. In this video, he explains in a straightforward and conversational style the basic elements of four different behavioral treatment techniques: covert sensitization, masturbatory reconditioning, ammonia aversion, and olfactory aversion. Marshall defines the purpose of each type of treatment, describes in clear and simple language how each technique is implemented, discusses problems or practical drawbacks that occur with each procedure, and evaluates the existing evidence concerning the reliability of each treatment technique. He offers practical tips for clinicians who use these behavioral treatment techniques.

Believe Me

Type:	VHS
Length:	21 min.
Date:	1992
Cost:	$405; rental: $75
Source:	Coronet/MTI Film and Video
	108 Wilmot Road
	Deerfield, IL 60015
	(800) 777-2400

When children are sexually abused, they are usually scared about what has happened to them, confused about why this trusted person would do something like this to them, and hurt, either physically or emotionally or both. If and when they decide to tell someone else about the abuse, they may find that no one believes them, especially if the offender is a family member or a close friend of the family. This video was developed to help children understand that it is wrong for someone else to touch them in ways that make them uncomfortable. No matter what anyone else says, this video tells them, touches that make them uncomfortable are wrong. Even if adults tell them that everything is okay, that this will be their "special secret," that adults do this to many other children, this video lets them know that none of this behavior is right and they should report it to another adult. Whenever they are confused or scared about anything, especially bad touches, they should confide in an adult.

Beyond Surviving: Parenting the Next Generation

Type:	Audio cassette
Length:	Not available
Date:	1994
Cost:	$16.95
Source:	VOICES in Action, Inc.
	P.O. Box 148309
	Chicago, IL 60614
	(312) 327-1500

Being a survivor of childhood sexual abuse may create problems for those who have their own children, affecting the ways these parents raise their children. For other survivors, the abuse they suffered makes them better, more sensitive parents. This workshop explores the issues involved in parenting for parents who were sexually abused as children and how such parents may have an advantage in understanding their own children.

Blackbird Fly

Type:	VHS
Length:	27 min.
Date:	1990
Cost:	$375
Source:	Coronet/MTI Film and Video
	108 Wilmot Road
	Deerfield, IL 60015
	(800) 777-2400

Girls who are sexually abused by their fathers face a special set of problems. In this video, Carin Jordan, a teenager, is one such girl. Bright, talented, and ambitious, she is totally confused and upset by her father's actions. While she believes she should be loyal to her father, she knows what he does to her is wrong. With help from Miss Parker, a music teacher, and Dr. Williams, a guidance counselor, she eventually is able to understand what has happened to her, to know that she is not to blame for the abuse, and to seek help to heal from this abuse. Characters in this video are portrayed by Whoopi Goldberg, Rain Pryor, Garrett Morris, and Esther Rolle, who provide inspirational moments for viewers. They help the viewer understand the many misconceptions and emotional issues involved in sexual abuse, especially incest, including the tendency of victims to blame themselves for the abuse, to believe that they condoned the abuse by not stopping it, to believe that they should be loyal to their fathers and not reveal the abuse to others, and to believe that by revealing the abuse they will be responsible for destroying their families. The video includes a discussion guide.

Body Image: The Final Place

Type:	Audio cassette
Length:	Not available
Date:	1994
Cost:	$12.95
Source:	VOICES in Action, Inc.
	P.O. Box 148309
	Chicago, IL 60614
	(312) 327-1500

Victims of childhood sexual abuse may have low self-esteem and an unhealthy image of themselves. The importance of developing a healthy body image is the topic of this workshop, focusing on survivors of childhood sexual abuse. It presents a development model of how a person develops an image of his or her own body, focuses on the importance of body image in everyday life, and describes how a person's body image influences the process of healing from childhood sexual abuse.

Breaking Silence

Type: VHS
Length: 60 min.
Date: 1984
Cost: $250
Source: Future Educational Films
1628 Union Street
San Francisco, CA 94123
(415) 673-0304

Sexual abuse can be a devastating experience for any child to endure. In attempting to understand this type of abuse, this video offers comments from survivors of childhood sexual abuse as well as from offenders who sexually abused children. An overview of sexual abuse is provided, including statistical information about sexual abuse, reasons why people sexually abuse children, and the effects of sexual abuse on the children. Several societal factors that may influence a person who sexually abuses children are described, including being sexually abused as a child and society's general acceptance of the use of aggression by males to gain power and control over people and situations. A 1992 version is 30 minutes long and is available for $79.95.

Child Molestation: Breaking the Silence

Type: VHS
Length: 20 min.
Date: 1985
Cost: $490; rental: $75
Source: Coronet/MTI Film and Video
108 Wilmot Road
Deerfield, IL 60015
(800) 777-2400

Developed for people who supervise or spend time with children, this sensitive program provides valuable information on childhood sexual abuse. Topics covered include a description of the symptoms of sexual abuse, how to recognize these symptoms, what types of people sexually abuse children, and why some people sexually abuse children. The video suggests guidelines on how to respond to children who reveal that they have been sexually abused, and reasons why it is so important for people to report abusive situations to the appropriate authorities. Children are shown a variety of ways to protect themselves from abusive situations. This video is hosted by Michael Gross from "Family Ties" and is from the Disney Educational Film Festival.

Child Sexual Abuse: Both Sides of the Coin
Type: VHS
Length: 47 min.
Date: 1991
Cost: $149.95
Source: Varied Directions International
           69 Elm St.
           Camden, ME 04843
           (207) 236-8506
           Fax: (207) 236-4512

This video offers a sensitive and emotional view of child sexual abuse and pedophilia. It was produced by Images for Thought Productions Limited, a company that promotes positive social change by offering materials on a variety of important social issues. In this video, the life of Jim Mandelin, who experienced violent sexual abuse as a child, is presented along with that of Graham Cook, a convicted pedophile who sexually abused young boys. They describe their experiences from their earliest memories to the present, vividly and painfully showing how one of them became a violent biker and the other a pedophile. At the conclusion of the video, Jim and Graham meet and discuss, for the viewer, how they started the process of healing from their experiences, by finding the appropriate help to return them to fully functioning, productive members of society. Important topics raised by the video include the sexual abuse of young males, women who sexually abuse children, street prostitution, treatment of young sex offenders, the role of addiction in abuse, physically violent offenders, ways to protect children from becoming victims of sexual abuse, ways to recognize and help children who have been sexually abused, and the variety of difficulties encountered in trying to heal from the abusive experience. The video offers valuable information on the causes and effects of childhood sexual abuse and serves as an excellent training medium for police officers, prison guards, probation officers, social workers, therapists, students, and all professionals who provide services to children and teenagers. It can also be used as an effective treatment tool for victims of abuse, offenders, and their respective support groups to stimulate thought and discussion.

Childhood Sexual Abuse: Four Case Studies
Type: 16mm, VHS
Length: 50 min.
Date: 1977
Cost: $730, 16 mm; $99, video; rental $110
Source: Coronet/MTI Film and Video
108 Wilmot Road
Deerfield, IL 60015
(800) 777-2400

Early childhood sexual abuse can have devastating effects even in adulthood. In this video produced by Cavalcade Productions, the stories of the sexual abuse of four women when they were young are poignantly presented during a weekend workshop on sexual abuse. Each woman's story is presented as a separate and unique clinical study, allowing viewers time to discuss and analyze the various clinical techniques presented. The video is ideal as material for in-service training because of its format and content. It helps prepare workers for the emotional stress that they may experience as a result of working with people who have been sexually abused as children.

The Clinical Interview
Type: ½" and ¾" video
Length: 60 min.
Date: 1986
Cost: ½" video: $195; ¾" video: $210
Source: Coronet/MTI Film and Video
108 Wilmot Road
Deerfield, IL 60015
(800) 777-2400

For children who have to testify in a courtroom about their experiences of sexual abuse, the experience can be horrifying and threatening. Clinicians who are able to communicate with these children, helping them understand the proceedings in order to determine whether or not sexual abuse has occurred, are in high demand. This video, presented by Kee MacFarlane, who is director of the Child Sexual Abuse Diagnostic Center at the Children's Institute International, provides information to professionals working with victims of sexual abuse on effective diagnostic interviewing skills, especially interviewing with young children. The material presented teaches viewers how to identify or rule out alleged sexual abuse, translate the child's explanation of what has happened to him or her into adult language, and create a safe, nonthreatening environment in which to earn the child's trust and gather information. Differences between legal and clinical viewpoints of childhood sexual abuse are examined along with the many complex legal issues that clinicians working with victims face today. The program includes a syllabus and is an excellent training tool for new practitioners dealing with sexual abuse and young child victims, as well as experienced practitioners. This video is part of the Response: Child Sexual Abuse Series, along with *A Medical View* and *When Children Are Witnesses*.

Connections: Alcohol, Drugs and Child Abuse

Type: VHS
Length: 17 min.
Date: 1993
Cost: $350; rental: $75
Source: Coronet/MTI Film and Video
           108 Wilmot Road
           Deerfield, IL 60015
           (800) 777-2400

When parents and other child-care providers are frustrated and abuse alcohol and drugs, children in their care may be physically, emotionally, or sexually abused. This video offers information about the link between substance abuse and child abuse by providing dramatic reenactments of abusive situations. These reenactments help viewers understand the dynamics of the link between drug and alcohol abuse and child abuse. Topics discussed include the symptoms of child abuse, signs that can help in recognizing abuse, differing patterns of abuse, denial of abuse by the offender and/or other family members, suggestions for good parenting skills, and low-cost services available to families in drug- or alcohol-related crisis.

A Crime Never Forgotten

Type: VHS
Length: 23 min.
Date: 1991

Cost: $250; rental: $75
Source: Coronet/MTI Film and Video
108 Wilmot Road
Deerfield, IL 60015
(800) 777-2400

Father-daughter incest is thought to be one of the most common types of childhood sexual abuse. These young girls may repress memories of this abuse in order to survive their childhood. This video presents an edition of ABC's *20/20*, in which reporter Bob Brown investigates a case of incest between a father and four of his daughters. The daughters accuse their father, an FBI agent and a nationally recognized expert in the field of child abuse, of sexually molesting them when they were young children. The father refused to help the daughters pay for the therapy and other services necessary to help them heal from the experiences, and two daughters filed suit against him. Reporter Brown reviews the case and discusses the implications of trying to pursue legal action against the offender after the statute of limitations has expired.

Double Jeopardy
Type: VHS
Length: 40 min.
Date: 1979
Cost: 16 mm: $99; video: $99; rental: $80
Source: Coronet/MTI Film and Video
108 Wilmot Road
Deerfield, IL 60015
(800) 777-2400

Children who have to appear in court in cases of child sexual abuse are often frightened and have a difficult time convincing participants that they are credible witnesses. This award-winning documentary helps explain to the viewer the issues involved in having children appear in judicial hearings. Using case histories to help illustrate the benefits of using a multidisciplinary approach in dealing with the many problems that may arise during this process, this video demonstrates the advantages of close cooperation among all involved agencies and the benefits of specialized training in helping children survive a judicial hearing. This video can help law enforcement personnel and prosecutors understand the problems involved and expand their abilities to help children through this process. *Double Jeopardy* is accompanied by a leader's manual that was developed by the Sexual Assault Center staff at the University of Washington.

Every Parent's Nightmare
Type: 16mm, VHS
Length: 16 min.
Date: 1983
Cost: 16mm: $290; video: $99; rental: $50
Source: Coronet/MTI Film and Video
108 Wilmot Road
Deerfield, IL 60015
(800) 777-2400

Having a child abducted and molested by a stranger is the worst thing many parents can imagine. But, according to this video, even if a molester is caught, there is little chance that he or she will be sent to prison; fewer than 10 percent of all convicted child molesters are sent to prison. Produced by ABC's *20/20* program, this compelling video examines several well-known cases of child molestation as well as many of the lobbying groups that have been formed to help reduce the incidence of child molestation and to tighten laws to protect children from these offenders. Ways that parents can help protect their children from molesters are also suggested.

Four Men Speak Out on Surviving Child Sexual Abuse
Type: VHS
Length: 28 min.
Date: 1991
Cost: $99.95
Source: Varied Directions International
69 Elm St.
Camden, ME 04843
(207) 236-8506
Fax: (207) 236-4512

The effects of sexual abuse perpetrated against boys are less well known than the effects on girls; most research has been conducted on girls. This video, produced by the Planned Parenthood Association of Cincinnati in Ohio, presents four male survivors of sexual abuse telling their own story about the abuse, how it has affected their lives, and what steps they are taking to recover from their abusive experiences. By sharing their emotional, compelling stories, these men hope to encourage acceptance and understanding of the problems unique to boys who have been sexually abused. The experiences of these four men as children vary from isolated and violent assaults to long-term sexual abuse perpetrated by fathers, other trusted adults in their lives, and other adolescents. The men talk about their fears of being or becoming homosexual, the effects of being viewed a victim on their psychological development as men, the embarrassment they feel, the difficulty they had in trusting adults, and the fear of later becoming perpetrators themselves. They describe their own recovery process and the feelings of confusion, pain, and relief they have experienced along the way. This video dispels the myth that boys rarely are victims of sexual abuse, identifies the many reasons why males usually do not disclose their abuse or in some cases do not realize that they have been sexually abused, examines the short-term and long-term effects of sexual abuse, and discusses the various strategies for recovering from this experience. The video can be used in training professionals, course work, and public awareness efforts.

Healing the Trauma of Sibling Abuse
Type: Audio cassette
Length: Not available
Date: 1994
Cost: $12.95
Source: VOICES in Action, Inc.
             P.O. Box 148309
             Chicago, IL 60614
             (312) 327-1500

Being sexually abused by a brother or sister can be terrifying for a child. This workshop addressed the issue of sibling incest by reviewing the factors that make sibling abuse more traumatic than many other types of sexual abuse. Many of these factors differ from the factors involved in parent-child incest. Other topics addressed include the difficulty that many survivors have in establishing and maintaining healthy, intimate relationships and in dealing with their own sexuality. A model is presented to help survivors and their families develop healthy relationships.

**The Hope of Recovery: A Message of Hope
and Encouragement for Multiple Personality
Clients and Those Who Treat Them**
Type: VHS
Length: 59 min.

Date: 1992
Cost: $59.95
Source: Varied Directions International
69 Elm St.
Camden, ME 04843
(207) 236-8506
Fax: (207) 236-4512

Multiple personality disorder may be found in some people, usually women, who have been sexually abused as children and who have repressed the memories of this abuse. In this compelling video, three women who have multiple personality disorder describe the difficult issues they face while in treatment. Each woman shares her own personal feelings and process of healing. Psychotherapists and other professionals who may work with clients who have multiple personalities will find this video helpful and insightful in treating these clients. Some clients who have multiple personalities and other dissociative disorders may also find this video helpful as they progress in their recovery.

How To Tell If a Child Is Being Abused
Type: VHS
Length: 15 min.
Date: 1988
Cost: $149.95
Source: Bureau for At-Risk Youth
645 New York Avenue
Huntington, NY 11743
(800) 999-6884
Fax: (516) 673-4544

This video offers valuable information on all major forms of child abuse, including physical abuse, emotional abuse, sexual abuse, and neglect. Photographs are used to help the viewer identify children who have been abused or neglected; this video is a good training tool for teachers, medical professionals, legal professionals, law enforcement personnel, and human resources personnel. An instructor's guidebook is included.

Identifying, Reporting and Handling Disclosure of the Sexually Abused Child
Type: VHS
Length: 25 min.
Date: 1987

Cost: $125
Source: Committee for Children
172 20th Ave.
Seattle, WA 98122-5862
(800) 634-4449

Dealing with allegations of childhood sexual abuse is particularly difficult for many helping professionals. Many indicators of childhood sexual abuse are subtle, and allegations of such abuse may often be difficult to prove. This video offers information on the most common behavioral indicators of childhood sexual abuse. It gives the viewer clear and understandable guidelines on the responsibilities of mandated professionals for reporting cases. Viewers are also provided with examples of appropriate responses to a child who has just revealed that he or she has been sexually abused.

Incest: The Victim Nobody Believes
Type: VHS
Length: 23 min.
Date: 1990
Cost: $99; rental: $70
Source: Coronet/MTI Film and Video
108 Wilmot Road
Deerfield, IL 60015
(800) 777-2400

Girls who are sexually abused by their fathers or other close relatives have a particularly difficult time dealing with all the emotions they experience throughout the ordeal and even after the abuse has stopped; these emotions may include fear, guilt over being a victim and allowing the abuse to occur, confusion, and an inability to trust other adults. In this poignant video, three young women tell their stories about what it was like to be abused as a child. This is an excellent video for use in training educators and other children's services workers; it can also be used in college counseling groups and support groups for victims of incest.

An Invaluable Tool
Type: VHS
Length: 25 min.
Date: 1994
Cost: $85

Source: One Voice
P.O. Box 27958
Washington, DC 20038-7958
(202) 667-1160
Fax: (202) 462-4689

Produced by Marilyn Van Derbur, Sharon H. Lions, and Sandy Cummins, this video focuses on presenting information on childhood sexual abuse to health care professionals. Helping health care professionals understand the trauma that children endure when they are sexually abused, diagnosing sexual abuse in adult patients, improving health care, learning how to talk with patients about the abuse they suffered as children, avoiding additional trauma, offering referrals, and helping therapists help their clients to get in touch with their emotions and their physical problems are all topics presented in this video. Similar to *The Missing Link*, it is a guide for women searching for better health care. Also provided is a training manual, which includes a guide for presenting the video, handouts, case studies, suggestions for additional resources and referrals, and recommended reading.

**Kids Have Rights Too: A Program
about Child Sexual Abuse**
Type: VHS
Length: 18 min.
Date: 1991
Cost: $350
Source: Coronet/MTI Film & Video
108 Wilmot Road
Deerfield, IL 60015
(800) 777-2400

Many children have a difficult time revealing the fact that they have been sexually abused. This video, based on the puppet program *Kids on the Block* created by Barbara Aiello, emphasizes the importance of telling someone about being sexually abused. This story involves Joanne, who has been sexually abused, and her friends Nam and Jason. Joanne tells them about the abuse she has experienced, and Nam and Jason start working on a class project that lets other children know that it is not all right if someone touches a child in ways that cause embarrassment or other bad feelings. The children learn, based on Joanne's experience, that anyone can be abused and that children should always tell an adult if they are being sexually abused.

The Last Taboo

Type:	16mm, VHS
Length:	28 min.
Date:	1990
Cost:	16mm: $500; video: $99; rental: 75
Source:	Coronet/MTI Film and Video
	108 Wilmot Road
	Deerfield, IL 60015
	(800) 777-2400

For a long time, childhood sexual abuse was a topic that no one wanted to talk about; many people thought it was too horrifying to discuss or that it rarely happened to children and did not need to be discussed. In this compelling video, six childhood sexual abuse victims tell their stories, allowing the viewer to see and understand how frightening and traumatizing the experience can be to a child. This video demonstrates the need for counseling and other strong programs that support the victims of childhood sexual abuse.

A Medical View

Type:	$\frac{1}{2}$" and $\frac{3}{4}$" video
Length:	30 min.
Date:	1985
Cost:	$\frac{1}{2}$" video: $195; $\frac{3}{4}$" video: $210
Source:	Coronet/MTI Film and Video
	108 Wilmot Road
	Deerfield, IL 60015
	(800) 777-2400

Physicians and other experts in the field of childhood sexual abuse are beginning to understand the need for complete and detailed examinations of children who have been sexually abused. While there often is little, if any, actual medical evidence of sexual abuse in children, observant doctors may be able to determine physical signs of abuse. In this educational program presented by Dr. Astrid Heger, a well-known medical authority on childhood sexual abuse, viewers learn the steps that need to be taken in evaluating cases of suspected sexual abuse. Heger also describes ways to make the child comfortable and to reassure the child that no harm will come to him or her during the examination. Procedures for following up on these cases and the legal obligations of reporting suspected cases of child sexual abuse to the proper authorities are also discussed. This video is part of the Response: Child Sexual Abuse Series, along with *The Clinical Interview* and *When Children Are Witnesses.*

Memory and Reality: Emerging Crisis
Type: VHS
Length: 100 min.
Date: 1993
Cost: $69.50
Source: Gemini Productions, Inc.
18630 Detroit Ave.
Lakewood, OH 44107
(216) 228-9440
Fax: (216) 228-8024

This video brings together 14 prominent memory researchers and mental health professionals (Elizabeth Loftus, Richard Gardner, Steven Garver, Harold Lief, Campbell Perry, Martin Seligman, Paul McHugh, Lisa Richette, Michael Yapko, David Dinges, Richard Ofshe, George Ganaway, Margaret Singer, and Melody Gavigan, whose therapist persuaded her that she had been sexually abused as a child even though she denied it). Topics discussed include what memory is and what it is not, false memory syndrome and how it is therapeutically induced, recovered memory therapists, memory repression, recovered memory patients, the consequences of recovered memory, and the effects of recovered memory therapy. The mental health profession is deeply divided over the issue of repressed memories, with many experts believing that these repressed memories are valid and must be dealt with in order for the patient to recover, while others believe therapists are unethically suggesting to the patients that sexual abuse is the cause of all their problems. This video helps the viewer sort out all the information and understand the bitter divisions in the mental health profession.

The Missing Link
Type: VHS
Length: 24 min.
Date: 1994
Cost: $85
Source: One Voice
P.O. Box 27958
Washington, DC 20038-7958
(202) 667-1160
Fax: (202) 462-4689

Produced by Marilyn Van Derbur, Sharon H. Lions, and Sandy Cummins, this video presents information on childhood sexual abuse to health care professionals. Helping these professionals understand the trauma that children endure when they are sexually abused, diagnosing sexual abuse in adult patients, improving health care, learning how to talk with patients about the abuse they suffered as children, avoiding additional trauma, offering referrals, and helping therapists help their clients to get in touch with their emotions and their physical problems are all topics presented in this video. Also provided is a training manual, which includes a guide for presenting the video, handouts, case studies, suggestions for additional resources and referrals, and recommended reading.

The Non-Gay Therapist of
Gay/Lesbian Survivors
Type: Audio cassette
Length: Not available
Date: 1994
Cost: $12.95
Source: VOICES in Action, Inc.
            P.O. Box 148309
            Chicago, IL 60614
            (312) 327-1500

Therapists must understand the special issues that lesbian and gay clients bring to therapy for childhood sexual abuse, including those of growing up in American society as a gay man or lesbian. This workshop, from VOICES 1994 international conference, explores the many issues involved in being a gay or lesbian survivor of childhood sexual abuse.

Now I Can Tell You My Secret
Type: VHS
Length: 15 min.
Date: 1985
Cost: $295
Source: Coronet/MTI Film & Video
            108 Wilmot Road
            Deerfield, IL 60015
            (800) 777-8100

Revealing sexual abuse is frightening to many children. Many of them have already lost their ability to trust other adults, and some find that when they tell an adult, the adult doesn't believe them. In the gentle style of this video, which tells the story of a young boy who has been sexually abused by a neighbor but has not revealed the abuse to anyone, children are told that sexual advances are wrong and that they have a right to protect themselves from being sexually abused. The video emphasizes the basic ways to prevent childhood sexual abuse, including an explanation of the differences between "good touches" and "bad touches," how to say "no" in situations that are uncomfortable or threatening, how to get away and find a safe place, and the importance of revealing the abuse or the attempted abuse to an adult. This is an excellent video to stimulate classroom discussions of childhood sexual abuse.

Offender-Victim Communication
Type: VHS
Length: 57 min.
Date: 1994
Cost: $100
Source: The Safer Society Program and Press
            P.O. Box 340
            Brandon, VT 05733-0340
            (802) 247-3132

Treating people who have abused children sexually and bringing them face to face with their victims are difficult things to do. Working with perpetrators of sexual abuse may help sex offenders break down their denial and accept responsibility for their actions, help families stop blaming the victim, help the families of the abusers understand the reasons why the offenders think and behave in these unacceptable ways, and help the victims of sexual abuse stop blaming themselves. In this unique video, seven sex offenders, who are in various stages of treatment, describe themselves, their offenses, and their victims. They are asked questions by a woman who was sexually abused as a child, among others, why they did what they did, why they lied about the abuse, how they separated their abusive lives from their "normal" lives, and whether or not the victim could have done anything to stop them from abusing him or her. Many of their answers are brutally honest, sometimes self-centered, and always enlightening to the viewer.

Once Can Hurt a Lifetime
Type: VHS
Length: 22 min.
Date: 1994
Cost: $54
Source: One Voice
P.O. Box 27958
Washington, DC 20038-7958
(202) 667-1160
Fax: (202) 462-4689

Produced by Marilyn Van Derbur, Sharon H. Lions, and Sandy Cummins, this video helps to educate the general public about the sexual abuse of children. Addressing sexual violence, exploitation, and abuse of children, it focuses on the prevention of childhood sexual abuse through education, compassion, and hope. Using the poignant stories of survivors, information is presented on the consequences of abusive sexual behaviors. It encourages young people to find help and stop the abuse before they continue the abusive cycle by abusing others. This video is an excellent resource for all groups interested in learning more about sexual abuse of children, including schools, church groups, youth groups, and therapy groups.

Prevention and First Aid for Therapists
Coping with Backlash
Type: Audio cassette
Length: Not available
Date: 1994
Cost: $12.95
Source: VOICES in Action, Inc.
P.O. Box 148309
Chicago, IL 60614
(312) 327-1500

Many therapists working with survivors of childhood sexual abuse find themselves in the middle of a controversy over repressed memories. Some people believe that repressed memories do not exist, that clients respond to suggestions made by their therapists about possible sexual abuse and finally come to believe that they were sexually abused as children. Others believe that repressed memories do exist, that therapists do not suggest them to clients, but rather the clients discover them through the therapeutic process. Therapists caught in this controversy often experience outrage, then fear because they are being attacked for their efforts to help clients find the source of their problems. This tape, from the 1994 international conference, discusses the effects of this backlash on therapists and what steps therapists can take to help themselves survive.

Professional Occult Response Team:
A Multidisciplinary Approach
for Responding to Ritual Abuse
Type: Audio cassette
Length: Not available
Date: 1994
Cost: $12.95
Source: VOICES in Action, Inc.
            P.O. Box 148309
            Chicago, IL 60614
            (312) 327-1500

Cases of child abuse in situations of satanic ritual abuse are increasing, although many people still believe that few instances of such abuse actually exist. This workshop examines satanic ritual abuse and why a multidisciplinary response increases successful treatment of these cases. How to organize this type of response, what to expect in the process of organizing it, and guidelines for operating a multidisciplinarygroup are presented in this workshop conducted at VOICES' 1994 international conference. Reasons for developing a multidisciplinary approach and the strengths and weaknesses of such groups are also presented.

Projection and Projective Identification:
Tracking and Healing in MPD
Type: Audio cassette
Length: Not available
Date: 1994
Cost: $12.95
Source: VOICES in Action, Inc.
            P.O. Box 148309
            Chicago, IL 60614
            (312) 327-1500

When therapists have a good, solid understanding of dysfunctional families and dysfunctional patterns in families, including projection and projective identification, they are better able to diagnose and treat people with multiple personality disorders and other dissociative disorders. Conducted by Dr. Jeanne Fleming, this workshop helps therapists understand their clients' and other people's motives for behaving in the ways they do, prevent some types of problems before they arise, and either approach their clients or distance themselves from their clients with more ease.

Recovery Issues When the Perpetrator Is Female
Type: Audio cassette
Length: Not available
Date: 1994
Cost: $12.95
Source: VOICES in Action, Inc.
P.O. Box 148309
Chicago, IL 60614
(312) 327-1500

Because the majority of studies and research conducted on childhood sexual abuse have focused on male perpetrators, therapists working with clients who have been sexually abused by a female may have a difficult time finding information related to female perpetrators and the effects that this may have had on their clients as children. This workshop presents a discussion of the issues involved in cases of sexual abuse perpetrated by a female, including lack of a nurturing female role model, the shame many children feel when their mother has sexually abused them, feelings of alienation experienced by survivors in group therapy settings, and the common belief that incest perpetrated by females is less severe and less traumatizing to the child involved.

Renee Has a Secret
Type: VHS
Length: 25 min.
Date: 1993
Cost: $29.95
Source: RISK
P.O. Box 756
Brentwood, CA 94513
(510) 634-4902

Jodi Lang Santry is a respected educator, consultant, and lecturer on the process of healing from childhood sexual abuse. She tells her own story of being sexually abused as a child in order to help the viewer understand the various issues surrounding childhood sexual abuse. She presents information on the physical, emotional, mental, psychological, and spiritual effects of sexual abuse; the behavioral indicators of sexual abuse; and the profile of a perpetrator. She helps viewers to understand how to identify when an abusive situation may be occurring, how to reduce the chances that it will happen to your child or his or her friends, and how to facilitate the healing process.

Stories No One Wants To Hear
Type: VHS
Length: 27 min.
Date: 1993
Cost: $79.95
Source: Varied Directions International
69 Elm St.
Camden, ME 04843
(207) 236-8506
Fax: (207) 236-4512

Retrieving memories of childhood sexual abuse that have been buried or repressed for many years is often difficult and traumatizing to the individuals involved. Many people are unable to believe that they were sexually abused as children when they have no conscious memory of such abuse. This video documents the process of retrieving these memories, telling the stories of four women who discover that they had been sexually abused as children, in three cases by their mothers and in the fourth by a brother. This video is interesting not only because it discusses the controversial subject of retrieval of repressed memories, but also because it talks about mother-daughter incest, a type of incest not often talked about. The four women candidly discuss their experiences with past abuse. Using vivid images and compelling music, the video presents the subconscious and the repression of memories of traumatic experiences as extremely powerful. This video can be used in treatment programs with survivors and in training professionals in the fields of social work, psychology, and psychiatry.

A Story of Hope
Type: VHS
Length: 15 min.
Date: 1991
Cost: $24

Source: Marilyn Van Derbur Institute, Inc.
P.O. Box 61099
Denver, CO 80206
Fax: (303) 322-9374

This video presents the powerful and poignant story of Marilyn Van Derbur, former Miss America and incest survivor. She tells about her journey from incest victim, as a child and teenager, to an empowered survivor. She helps survivors realize that there is hope, that they can overcome the burdens they feel because they were sexually abused as children, and that they can become survivors rather than victims.

Strong Kids, Safe Kids
Type: VHS
Length: 43 min.
Date: 1984
Cost: $24.95
Source: Paramount Pictures Corporation
5555 Melrose Ave.
Hollywood, CA 90038
(213) 956-5000

This video can help parents protect their children from sexual abuse by offering tips on how to keep their children from being abducted by strangers, providing the major warning signs of sexual abuse, and suggesting parenting skills that may lessen the chances that their children will be abducted. Some of these parenting skills include never leaving a child alone where someone could pick them up; getting involved in activities that are important to the child; and observing their children and becoming aware of any behavioral or emotional changes. A parent's guide is included with the video.

Survivors
Type: VHS
Length: 32 min.
Date: 1989
Cost: 16mm: $595; video: $495; rental: $75
Source: Coronet/MTI Film and Video
108 Wilmot Road
Deerfield, IL 60015
(800) 777-2400

While most research has indicated that a cyclical pattern exists in cases of physical and emotional abuse, that is, that children who are physically or emotionally abused as children will often grow up to physically or emotionally abuse their own children, little research has been conducted on cyclical patterns of sexual abuse. This compelling documentary examines the cyclical nature of physical and sexual abuse. Laws enacted to help break the cycle by incarcerating or treating the offenders and various methods of treatment of offenders are discussed. Stories of adults who were victims of abuse as children help explain the experiences of people who have been physically or sexually abused and the effects of that abuse. This video is recommended for high school and college classes, public libraries, therapists, and victim support groups.

A Time to Tell: Teen Sexual Abuse
Type: VHS
Length: 20 min.
Date: 1990
Cost: $295; rental: $75
Source: Coronet/MTI Film and Video
           108 Wilmot Road
           Deerfield, IL 60015
           (800) 777-2400

Encouraging children to talk about sexual abuse, to reveal to someone the fact that they have been or are being abused, is often a difficult task. This sensitive video, which dramatizes the experiences of students in a peer support group, helps by showing students the value of communicating their experiences of sexual abuse. Some of the adolescents have been sexually molested; a case of date rape and one of incest are discussed. Teenagers in the video learn to talk about their feelings and fears concerning their own sexuality and about the importance of sharing information about being sexually molested with people who can help them recover from their experiences.

What Tadoo with Secrets
Type: VHS
Length: 19 min.
Date: 1989
Cost: $395
Source: Coronet/MTI Film & Video
           108 Wilmot Road
           Deerfield, IL 60015
           (800) 777-8100

Encouraging a child to keep his or her sexual abuse a secret, that "this is our own little secret," is one way that many abusers are able to continue abusing a child for years without the child telling anyone about the abuse. This video uses an entertaining combination of live action, puppets, and animation to tell the story of seven-year-old Juliette, who learns that keeping bad secrets is not good, these bad secrets should be told to an adult who cares about the child. Characters such as Professor Sir Hillary Von Carp and his frog friends, What and Tadoo, work together to teach children about making choices, telling the difference between "good secrets" and "bad secrets," and learning how to get help in scary situations.

When Children Are Witnesses
Type: ½″ and ¾″ video
Length: 48 min.
Date: 1990
Cost: ½″ video: $195; ¾″ video: $210
Source: Coronet/MTI Film and Video
            108 Wilmot Rd.
            Deerfield, IL 60015
            (800) 777-2400

Helping children to testify in a courtroom in cases of child sexual abuse is often a daunting and difficult task. This video dramatizes the important parts of a criminal trial in such a case. Made primarily to help legal professionals make the court a less intimidating place for children, the video explores the issues involved in having children testify in court. Not many years ago, it was commonly believed that children were not credible witnesses, that they were not able to reliably report what had happened to them, and that they could be influenced by people wanting them to say specific things about the abuse or the abuser. Recent research has indicated that children can be credible witnesses and that, given the appropriate support, they can survive the courtroom without any significant emotional trauma. This video emphasizes that excluding children from the courtroom, in essence avoiding a trial if there are no other witnesses to the abuse, is morally wrong as well as legally suspect. When judges, attorneys, and mental health professionals understand children's special needs and abilities, they can offer the child a safe environment in which to testify. This video is part of the Response: Child Sexual Abuse Series, along with *A Medical View* and *The Clinical Interview*.

When Should You Tell?
Type: VHS
Length: 16 min.
Date: 1995
Cost: $95
Source: Sunburst Communications
            39 Washington Ave.
            P.O. Box 40
            Pleasantville, NY 10570-0040
            (800) 431-1934
            Fax: (914) 769-2109

Convincing young children of the importance of telling someone if they are being sexually abused is often difficult, but can be a major step in preventing additional abuse. This video, for children in grades two through four, tells the story of Karen, who is being abused by Tommy but is afraid to tell anyone. She worries about being abused and wonders why her mother does not figure out that something is wrong; she keeps hoping her mother will realize what is happening to her. Through her story, the importance of confiding in an adult is emphasized, and children are taught that they should not keep scary secrets, that being abused is not normal no matter what anyone tells him or her, and that they will feel better if they tell. A teacher's guide and eight student worksheets are included with the video.

Why, God—Why Me?
Type: VHS or BETA
Length: 24 min.
Date: 1988
Cost: $99.95
Source: Varied Directions International
            69 Elm St.
            Camden, ME 04843
            (207) 236-8506
            Fax: (207) 236-4512

Dramatizing the effects of childhood sexual abuse on a single woman, this video provides valuable insights into the trauma, fear, and confusion felt by many adults who were sexually abused as children. Emotional and poignant, this story helps viewers understand many of the feelings that sexual abuse victims have about themselves and their abuse, including the reasons they may view traditional family life as threatening.

Researched, edited, and produced by students, the video is a sensitive portrayal of the realities of childhood sexual abuse. It demonstrates how victims can turn their lives around and establish healthy, loving relationships with others. This video is produced for general audiences, including mature high school students, college students, and community groups, and for professional groups, including counselors, nurses, social workers, mental health workers, criminal justice personnel, treatment providers, child protection services workers, and rehabilitative medicine personnel. It can be a valuable resource for classes in health, sociology, psychology, home economics, and human rights courses. The video is accompanied by a facilitator's guide.

Why Me? Incest Prevention
Type: VHS
Length: 16 min.
Date: 1988
Cost: $335
Source: Coronet/MTI Film & Video
108 Wilmot Road
Deerfield, IL 60015
(800) 777-2400

This video focuses on the experiences that children have when they are abused by members of their own families. Why incest is such a serious problem in society today and what to do if it happens to the viewer are topics considered in this sensitive video focusing on young children, who are taught the importance of distinguishing between good touches and bad touches. Dramatizing a case of incest, this video helps children understand that they are not the only ones being abused, that they must tell an adult if they are being abused, and that it is all right to tell someone about the abuse even if their abuser says that it is not all right.

Yes You Can Say No
Type: VHS
Length: 19 min.
Date: 1986
Cost: $145
Source: Committee for Children
172 20th Ave.
Seattle, WA 98122-5862
(800) 634-4449

In this poignant video, a young boy, David, is being sexually exploited by an adult whom he once trusted. Using his own survival skills and with the help of his friends, David learns how to assert himself, resist the abuse, and report it to the proper authorities. Children viewing this video will learn the importance of reporting sexual abuse to adults and ways they can be strong and resist any abusive situation. A teacher's guide accompanies the video.

Index